SAVE
MY SON

"*Save My Son* is a powerfully written and deeply felt critique of the way we now deal with addiction in America. Best of all, the authors give us compelling descriptions of real-world programs that offer an alternative to the punitive warehousing of people with drug problems that now passes for a national drug policy."

—Elliott Currie
Author, *Crime and Punishment in America: Why the Solutions to America's Most Stubborn Social Crisis Have Not Worked— and What Will*

"This heartfelt book compelled us to take action and look to new models of treatment. Mike Carona and Maralys Wills convinced us the old ways do not work anymore, that it is time to save taxpayers' money and, more important, save people's lives."

—John Mike Flynn, Sheriff, Worcester County, Massachusetts
Mary Jane Saksa, Director of Substance Abuse,
Worcester County House of Corrections

"Drug addiction straddles the fence between psychological disorder and criminal behavior. It is often necessary to bring everything to bear on those afflicted to enable them to recover. . . . *Save My Son* touches all the bases. It is essential reading for anyone concerned in any way with addiction."

—Abraham J. Twerski, M.D.
Author, *Addictive Thinking: Understanding Self-Deception*
Founder and Medical Director Emeritus, Gateway Rehabilitation Center

"Like millions of Americans, Maralys Wills and Mike Carona have personally experienced the ravages of a loved one's substance addiction. In *Save My Son* they build upon those personal experiences to ask one of the most important public policy questions of our time: Are there better, smarter ways to combat the drug problem in America than attempting to incarcerate our way out of it? Public policy makers across the country should take serious note of *Save My Son*."

—Bill Ritter
Denver District Attorney

"In my twenty-six years of dealing with addiction in the court system, I have seen what doesn't work. I believe this book finally offers hope for a better solution."

—Nancy Clark
Alternative Sentencing Expert, Newport Beach, California

"The familial tragedy of substance abuse is recounted by Maralys Wills, an addict's mother, and Mike Carona, an alcoholic's son and an elected sheriff. Together they give us new insights into substance abuse and promising approaches to treatment. Such collaborations are the necessary innovative partnerships that can assist our understanding of addiction and related criminal activity, as well as our ability to control both."

—William G. Meyer
District Court Judge, Denver, Colorado

"*Save My Son* identifies the true victims of the crimes of addiction—society, the families of the addicts, and the addicts themselves—and charts the desperate need to develop programs to help them all."

—James B. Bruce Jr.
Superintendent, Chesterfield, Virginia, Men's Diversion Center

SAVE MY SON

A Mother and a Sheriff Unite to Reclaim the Lives of Addicted Offenders

Maralys Wills and Mike Carona

◪ HAZELDEN®

INFORMATION & EDUCATIONAL SERVICES

Hazelden
Center City, Minnesota 55012-0176

1-800-328-0094
1-651-213-4590 (Fax)
www.hazelden.org

Library of Congress Cataloging-in-Publication Data

Wills, Maralys.
   Save my son : a mother and a sheriff unite to reclaim the lives of addicted
offenders / Maralys Wills and Michael S. Carona.
      p. cm.
   Includes bibliographical references and index.
   ISBN 1-56838-554-4 (paperback)
      1. Criminals—Drug use. 2. Drug abuse—Treatment. 3. Narcotic
addicts—Rehabilitation. 4. Recidivism—Prevention. I. Carona, Michael S.,
1955– II. Title.

HV8836.5 .W55 2000
362.29'18'086927—dc21

                                                            00-058193

Editor's note
The Twelve Steps are reprinted with permission of Alcoholics Anonymous
World Services, Inc. (AAWS). Permission to reprint the Twelve Steps does
not mean that AAWS has reviewed or approved the contents of this publication, or that AAWS necessarily agrees with the views expressed herein. AA is
a program of recovery from alcoholism *only*—use of the Twelve Steps in connection with programs and activities which are patterned after AA, but
which address other problems, or in any other non-AA context, does not
imply otherwise.

04 03 02 01 00   6 5 4 3 2 1

Cover design by Steve Clement
Interior design by Donna Burch
Typesetting by Stanton Publication Services, Inc.

*Dedicated to all the caring people who are trying
to make a difference in addicts' lives.*

Contents

Acknowledgments

Mike Carona

My deepest gratitude goes to my wife, Debbie, and my son, Matthew, for giving up our family time so I could work on this book.

I also wish to thank Assistant Sheriff John "Rocky" Hewett, Captain Tom McCarthy, Captain Dave Milewski, Captain Kim Markuson, Lieutenant Jo Ann Galisky, Sergeant Dave Wilson, Sergeant Jerry Alvis, Sue Alvis, Captain Cathy Zurn, Deputy Brad Olsen, Deputy Derek Rivas, Elaine Vasquez, and Susan Belanzi, all of the Orange County sheriff's department, and Frank Madrigal, Kevin Smith, and Alexandra "Sandy" Rogers, Ph.D., of the Orange County Health Care Agency for their belief in stopping the cycle of addiction and their willingness to join with me in creating a therapeutic community within the Orange County jail system.

And finally, I offer this book in memory of my mother, who was an unknowing inspiration for my contributions to it, and who I am sure watches over me to this day.

Maralys Wills

A big thanks to Nancy Clark, for wise insights into how addicts think, and for her insistence that I meet Sheriff Mike Carona. Warmest thanks to Mike himself, for doing something about entrenched addicts—and also agreeing to write a book with me. Without these two, this project would never have started. Additional thanks to Mike for being the perfect co-author.

Thanks to my agent, Barbara Braun, who was enthusiastic from the beginning and devoted to finding the right publisher.

Special thanks to our editor, Steve Lehman, whose insights and guidance kept the book on track. But more than that, for being a gem to work with—the ideal mentor from start to finish.

Heartfelt thanks go to people around the country who stopped what they were doing to give us time, enthusiasm, insights, and unlimited ideas . . . a special group of people, indeed. Our list is organized by area.

Nationwide. Thanks to Rick Faulkner, National Institute of Corrections, Washington, D.C., Ray Barneman, Counselor, and Director Sandy Buell, of the Key-Crest Program, Delaware.

Virginia. Deepest personal gratitude to the Honorable Lydia C. Taylor, who paved my way in the state of Virginia. From then on, the rest was easy.

Our thanks to: the dedicated people at Chesterfield Men's Diversion Center, Director James Bruce, Dr. Carole Hannigan, and Carl Smith; Supervisor Larry Hales, Virginia Correctional Center for Women; Director Patty Bass, Women's Diversion Center, Southhampton; Director John C. Loving and Russell C. Schools, Jr., of the Southhampton Men's Detention Center; Director Irene Green of the Tidewater Detention Center for Women; the enthusiastic staff at Indian Creek Correctional Center, Director Maxine Porcher, Warden Pat Terrangi, Laura Corner, John Garman, Major Calvin Brown, Jackie White, Susan Troyanos, Julius Franklin; Dr. Donna L. Boone, Drug Court Coordinator for the state of Virginia; Coordinator B. J. Hice and Counselor Diana Keegan of the Richmond Day Reporting Center; Reverend Jake Manley, Byron Joyce, Evelyn Cherry, and all the dedicated staff at Bethany Church; Norfolk's Probation/Parole staff, Chief Probation and Parole Officer Christopher F. Pate, Deputy Chief Thomas L. Chafin, Senior Probation/Parole Officer Joseph J. Hutton, Senior Probation/Parole Officer Jonathon G. Creede; Judge Junius P. Fulton III of Norfolk Drug Court; the Norfolk Community Services Board, consisting of Director George Pratt, Anthony Crisp, Dawn Mejstrik, Rosetta Smith, Martha Raiss, Otelia Ponton-Reid, LaVerne Jordan, Honorable Charles Griffith.

Deepest thanks to Ken and Melanie Wills for all their help during the Virginia research trip.

Denver, Colorado. Special thanks to Verna and Brian Goral, whose help was invaluable; special thanks, also, to Adam Brickner, Denver Drug Court Coordinator, who directed me to everyone else. Thanks to: Visionary Judge William G. Meyer; Chief Probation Officer Ed Mansfield; Judge Leonard Plank; Drug Court Judge Joseph Meyer; Drug Court Supervisor David Gill; District Attorney Bill Ritter; Director Cenikor Foundation, Eugene Strauber, Counselor Tiffany Benedict, Cenikor; Executive Director Mile-High Council, Flavia Henderson; Peer One counselor Paul Thompson; Haven Counselor, Penny; Continuum Care Center Manager for Denver Drug Court, Le Anna L. Day.

Phoenix, Arizona. Deepest gratitude to Clinical Supervisor, Adult Probation Department Kim O'Connor, who was my sole arranger and guide for two days. Thanks also to: Communications Officer of Supreme Court, John MacDonald; Community Punishment Program Supervisor Steve Davis; Drug Court Judge Susan Bolton; Deputy Chief of Adult Probation, Zachary Al Pra; Program Manager Randy Rice.

Southern California: Special thanks to Anne-Margaret Bellavoine, Administrative Assistant to Forensic Mental Health Association of California, for finding all the contacts anyone would need. Thanks also to: Dr. Jeffrey Fortuna, Prof. Cal State Fullerton; Ralph G. Rodgers, Assistant Director Criminal Administration of Superior Court; Director Bell Coll, Jane Sylva, Supervisor, Corcoran Prison Substance Abuse facility; Drug Court Judge Ronald Kreber, Teresa A. Risi, Administrative Services Assistant, Sheriff Deputy Bill Beam, Deputy Probation Officer Maureen O'Brien, all of South Court, Orange County; Terry Thornton, Information Officer, California Department of Corrections; Jay Adams, Ph.D.; Judith Titkinsky, LCSW; Attorney Rich Pfeiffer; Community Resources Manager Pete Flores, R. J. Donovan Prison; Walden House Clinical Specialist, John Stallone; Assistant Sheriff "Rocky" Hewett, Sergeant Jerry Alvis, Elaine Vasquez, all of Mike Carona's office; Brian Greenberg, Ph.D.; Columnist Jerry Hicks.

Warm thanks to my critique group for weekly help with the manuscript: Dorsey Adams, Win Smith, June O'Connell, and Pat Kubis.

Last but certainly not least, my love and thanks go to my husband, Rob, who gave me dinners, editing, newspaper clippings, time, and enthusiastic support throughout the entire project.

Introduction

What This Book Is About—And What It Isn't

Maralys Wills, Santa Ana, California

This isn't a book I ever planned to write.

When the whole community knows you have a successful family—your daughter is mayor of a city, your son is chief of orthopedics in the area's largest hospital, another son is a trial lawyer in the East, and you and your husband are both professionals—you tend not to mention that you also have a son who is in state prison.

Throughout our years of dismay over this youngest son, I saw no point in lamenting in book form a problem that seemed to have no solution.

And then something changed. I was led, by chance, to a meeting with Orange County, California, Sheriff Mike Carona.

After all those years of dealing, unsuccessfully, with our son's alcohol and drug addictions—and with the blunt words of an older child echoing in my head: "Mom, you've got to stop coming to Kirk's rescue. He'll never give up his drugs until you and Dad die," Mike made me believe that *something* can be done to help even the most intractable cases of addiction.

If this were just my son's problem and nobody else's, this book wouldn't be worth writing. One man who returns to jail for the tenth time because he couldn't conquer his addictions is not a trend and would not merit the attention of intelligent leaders.

But look at the statistics: **One in every thirty-four adult Americans is incarcerated or on probation or parole.[1] Eighty percent of all convicted criminals, nationwide, have a drug component in their crimes. Twenty-one percent of the inmates in California jails are there for drug offenses alone.**

So what's the solution? Build more jails? Mandate longer sentences? Or attack the problem at its root?

It was a suggestion from a friend who is an expert in alternative sentencing that led me to Mike Carona. A rarity among law enforcement officials, he believes that California's rush to build more and more jails and prisons is a waste of taxpayer money, and that there are cheaper and more effective ways of dealing with the overlarge population of addicted inmates—namely, lock-up drug facilities.

With Mike's enlightened ideas offering hope that great numbers of addicted felons can be returned to useful lives if the public is willing to try different approaches, I decided if we worked together we could bring his vision to a larger audience—hoping that the pen is indeed mightier than the sword.

Mike Carona, Sheriff, Orange County, California

Now, toward the end of our project, I suddenly realize this is not a book I ever intended to write, either. As sheriff of a huge metropolitan county, I did not necessarily want to lead my constituency back through my earliest years, to a childhood that held little glory but a great deal of personal sadness and, with the needless death of my alcoholic mother, the ultimate defeat.

Even as the thought struck me, I realized the irony of what propelled Maralys and me on this mission: our personal problems mirror each other. One of us is a mother desperately trying to save her son. The other is a son who was never able to save his mother.

Maybe these past sorrows helped make us who we are. Whether they did or not, they certainly gave us something to say.

∼

This book is driven by a wealth of published statistics that prove jails and prisons are largely ineffective in rehabilitating criminals, especially those whose crimes originate in drug abuse or mental illness; by hope that an enlightened American public will recognize the truth in these pages and vote for better ways of handling its huge addiction and mental health problems; and by our fervent belief that something can be done to rescue even the most difficult cases of addiction—like those in our two families.

~

In these chapters we make no attempt to address the very serious problems of violent crime and its origins, nor do we deal with the sociological and economic problems of inner cities that so often end up feeding their youth to the lions—to lives of drugs and drug dealing.

Nowhere do we suggest that violent criminals be turned loose on society. Some people simply have to be removed from the larger world and physically prevented from doing harm.

Rather, the purpose of the book is to start from where we are: among all the people who now clog our jails and prisons, a vast majority are nonviolent substance abusers who can be rehabilitated.

What are we going to do about it?

Shall we make an effort to save them, or just let them keep returning to our jails and prisons—until they rot away behind bars?

~

For simplicity and smoother reading, we have chosen to use the male pronoun when referring to addicts of either sex.

CHAPTER ONE

Pathway to Ruin:
How a Good Son Can Get Away from You

Maralys Wills

I'm not sure when we began to lose our youngest son.

I hear him as he is now when he calls home from state prison—at thirty-seven, flat, depressed, cynical, and suspicious—and the thought comes to me, as it has so often, that we *can't* let him fade away on us; we have to find a way to rescue him. We can't, we simply can't lose another son.

Yet Kirk is slipping away. And we don't know how to stop him.

With all our supposed brains, with all the solutions we've managed to find to other problems, we've so far had none for this one.

My husband, Rob, is a lawyer, and I'm an author and writing teacher. We live in an upper-middle-class suburb in Orange County, an hour south of Los Angeles. We weren't thinking "class" when we bought the lot, however, we were thinking "country living" and "space." Here was a generous half-acre nestled among orange groves, and we bought it cheap and built a house and had six kids, and we all more or less grew up together. Our children still think there was nothing more exhilarating, more sporting, than waging war in the groves and pelting each other with oranges.

In the last years I've written eight books, five fiction, three non-fiction, most accomplished after our children were into their teens or older. You can't really write, living with five rambunctious boys and a girl.

For years our house reverberated with energy, with a sense of adventure. And sadly, it was this yen for adventure that brought us

1

tragedies we couldn't foresee. Our third son, and then our oldest, both died pursuing a passion for hang gliding.

And now we are losing our youngest to drugs.

I remember the last time I saw Kirk in civilian clothes, one of those all-too-fleeting intervals between incarcerations, but on that occasion the briefest of all, only forty-eight hours.

That blink of time began as his days of freedom so often did, with Kirk arriving at our front door one morning at dawn, fresh out of jail—but not with a look of joy or relief or bright anticipation that life would now get better. Far from it. He stood on our front porch eyeing me as I opened the door, gray-hued and sullen, with a two-day growth of beard shadowing his face and hostility burning from his eyes.

"Oh, Kirk!" I said, "I wasn't expecting you." I sized him up quickly, the defeated posture, the probing stare of resentment, the lack of anything resembling a smile, all evidence of inner turmoil, none of it concealed very well.

"I walked all night," he said without preamble. "I can't stand here. I need to get to bed."

I stood back to let him in—this tall, aging stranger with the tight curly hair, this grown man who'd once been a cherished child.

"I'm sorry, Kirk," I said, an ineffectual response; my "sorrys" meant nothing to him. "They did it to you again, I see." With that, my own inner war began. How could I not ache for what he'd been through? Yet I was afraid, too, wondering how we'd cope.

Studying him, I tried to find some glimmer of the young man I'd raised and loved. A fleeting expression of gentleness, perhaps? The hint of a smile? "We weren't expecting you until next week. What time did they let you out, anyway?" However much I wanted to comfort him, to reach out and hug him, I couldn't, because he wasn't huggable. The prickly look of him kept me at bay.

"I got out at one-thirty in the morning," he said. "I tried to call you. Dialed the number three times, but all I got was the answering machine."

Oh guilt. A niggling sense that his ordeal was somehow my fault. "We could have left the phone plugged in," I said, "if we'd just known." And then, "They wouldn't let you stay until morning?" A useless question. I already knew the answer.

"I asked," he said. His eyes blazed with renewed fire. "They said get out. Leave. Said I'd better not hang around if I know what's good for me. So I left. It's a long walk."

There was no good response, so I just nodded.

"I didn't have enough money for a taxi. There was nothing else to do. Except walk." He came farther into the room, looking around as if our place was new to him. "It's dangerous out there in Santa Ana in the middle of the night."

"I know," I said. Suddenly I was furious. The inhumanity. The degradation. Whoever "they" were had treated him like an animal, and not for the first time. I knew what they did in jails, how they dumped prisoners just after midnight because that's when jails begin to get overcrowded and exceed their allowed capacity—but always without warning, so the dumpee has no chance to arrange a ride. "You walked seven miles, at least."

"Farther than that. The buses weren't running." He brushed past me. "I have to get to bed."

As he came closer, I thought I smelled alcohol on his breath, but I wasn't sure. I'm a lousy detective—part of the reason he managed, in the old days, to fool me for so long. "Get some sleep," I said. "We'll talk later. Cheer up, Kirk. Dad's going to give you a few days of R & R somewhere, maybe down by the beach." I knew my husband, Rob, felt as sorry for him as I did.

"Okay," he said. "I could use some beach time. After that I'll look for a job." He went into our guest bedroom and closed the door. I could hear the fan whirring, the fan he'd slept with as a young boy.

As I recall, that brief, early morning visit was as good as it got.

The next day, ensconced in a motel near the Huntington Beach pier with his bicycle—his only transportation—parked in his room, he used Rob's food money to buy liquor. Like a wick, the alcohol carried his deepest rages right to the surface. With hostility pouring out of every vein, he made angry phone calls, demanding that we give him enough money so he could break away and be on his own. "Give me two hundred dollars and I won't bother you anymore." He arrived by taxi and we paid him off. We were angry too.

With our money he went straight to the inner city to buy cocaine. He never went to the beach.

The cops picked him up in South Santa Ana, demanded to know what he was doing in that part of town, arrested him, and took him back to jail. He hadn't made even a stab at civilian life.

This time he went to state prison.

~

This wasn't how Kirk began. Not at all. When I stop to study the pictures of him hung here and there along our hall galleries, I see a winsome, curly haired baby gripping a rubber ball . . . in the next, a smiling, contented youth, secure in himself and happy with his lot . . . later still a young man in a gray tux standing with a beautiful girl, ready to leave for prom night. I find it inconceivable that a young boy who started out as he did, in our kind of family, could ever end up in state prison.

As the youngest of six children, Kirk was not so much spoiled as adored. With that many kids, Rob and I couldn't spoil any of them; there wasn't enough time. There wasn't quite enough room in our car, either, so Kirk often rode on my lap and I teased him about being my "lap baby."

In those days, Rob and I thought he was pretty terrific. He came to us, alone among the children—who are mostly brown-haired and hazel-eyed—with blond, curly hair and bright blue eyes, a fetching youngster who grinned easily and demanded little from life except a ball and the freedom to toss it around.

From the moment he could walk, we kept him supplied with balls, all of us, noting that he seemed to have unusual skills. At ages two and three he bounced rubber balls off the shingles and caught them, dribbled beach balls across the patio, spiraled footballs across the back lawn, even managed, somehow, to elevate basketballs high enough to reach our regulation hoop. His older brothers thought him so remarkable that they suggested we get a reporter out to document what he could do. So we did.

The Orange County Register photo shows a curly-haired three-year-old poised like John Elway, pulling back to throw a football, with his knee poking through a hole in his well-used cords. Another depicts a basketball arcing toward the hoop, with Kirk's hands still up as he watches its progress.

Our memories are spotty. Basketballs and baseballs evolved into tennis balls and tennis lessons, and eventually, into a Southern California tennis ranking of number twelve in his age group. As we did for all the children whatever their sport, Rob and I took him everywhere, cheering him on. I recall how my heart pounded and pride took my breath away when Kirk came from behind to beat somebody who was trouncing him. And how he always did it quietly, with unfailing good sportsmanship. You had to be proud of a kid whose line calls were so generous they drove you crazy. The determination was there, but you could only see it by the swing of his racket. Now we note sadly that those same young men are all on the international tennis tours.

In his freshman year at Foothill High School, Kirk was number one on the varsity tennis team, and we, the tennis parents, did what we could to help the team and tried to keep our pride under wraps. By then he'd garnered so many trophies they filled a huge bookcase, and his sister, headed for college in Pomona, California, remarked, "Kirk can get a tennis scholarship there. Easily."

But first he had to finish high school—which wasn't happening as expected. Kirk's grades were slipping and so was his ambition— hardly noticeable at first, and very subtle. There was the day the school secretary called to report that Kirk was caught off campus drinking beer with a friend. We were surprised, but not seriously worried. Schools didn't have zero tolerance policies back then, and a beer offense seemed pretty minor.

Then Kirk began losing tennis matches he should have won. And getting D's in courses he should have passed easily. We pushed harder, tried to make him study, but somehow never suspected the problem might be drugs. We were blindsided, caught off guard. In those days nobody from the better neighborhoods "did drugs." Or so we thought. We'd heard rumors that his high school harbored a few "druggos," but they certainly weren't anybody known to us.

Sadly, during that period the family's attention was diverted else-where. When Kirk was thirteen—just after his best friend was struck and killed in an intersection—we lost the first of two sons to hang gliding. Later, when he was sixteen, our oldest son was killed in the same sport. How little awareness we had, right then, that we were also losing him in a more sinister way.

With the other tragedies on center stage, we numbly boosted Kirk through his high school classes, helped him secure a diploma, and sent him off on scholarship to Cal Poly–Pomona.

It took his sister to alert us to trouble. "He showed up for intra-mural volleyball last week," she reported back, "and Mom, he was so stoned he could hardly see." We didn't absorb the information fully; it didn't hit us in the gut the way it should have. Now, in hindsight, this looms as a turning point, a moment when we should have stopped him dead in his tracks, made his world come crashing down.

We didn't. We were frozen by ignorance.

For Kirk, Cal Poly was over almost before it began. Without gar-nering even one college credit, he was home mid-semester, with big money needs—his skis, his radio, his surfboard, had somehow dis-appeared—and he'd acquired a web of strange new behaviors. Where once he'd been open, affable, and a pleasure to have around, he was now secretive. Occasionally belligerent. Mysterious.

But not always—so we still didn't get it. The changes had sneaked up on us, come so gradually we failed to make the connection. Of course it is all obvious now, condensed and summarized on paper, but it wasn't then. We never *saw* him stoned, never *witnessed* him using anything, never *heard, saw, or spoke to* any shady friends. In fact nothing ever happened where we could see it; the evidence was all circumstantial.

We thought we had an IQ problem and had him tested. Average. Rob offered Kirk a job as legal courier, and for a while he picked up and delivered documents around town—though he made so many errors he was almost useless.

Finally, finally, we began to believe the worst about him. Our youngest boy was one of the "druggos." But since I'd never seen him dazed, or even slurred, my logical mind demanded evidence.

One day I cornered him in his bedroom and began quizzing him. "Okay, Kirk, what have you been up to? Where's the money going?" When he denied being up to anything, I spoke louder. When he still stonewalled me, I gathered every ounce of energy and yelled at him. Looming over him where he sat on the bed, I shouted into his face: "Tell me, Kirk! Damn it, you'd better tell me, because I already know." I was bluffing. "I've seen how you've changed. I've seen your money disappear. I know you vanish for hours on end, I *know* you're doing *something!* Is it drugs, Kirk? Is that what you've been doing? Drugs?" In desperation, I swore. "GODDAMIT, YOU'RE NOT LEAV- ING THIS ROOM UNTIL YOU TELL ME EVERYTHING!" By sheer force of will I overpowered him until he was helpless and cowering.

I was so hoarse I was nearly incapable of speech, yet still I kept shouting.

Finally he broke down and told the truth. For the last five years he'd been using not only marijuana, but also cocaine. And he'd been getting it right here on our street, from all the "nice" kids. Our per- fect neighborhood was as bad as any ghetto.

Instead of diminishing, Kirk's addictions escalated. We took him to a counselor, who told us we had to cut him loose, make him hit bottom by turning him out of the house with no money and nowhere to go.

Rob and I shook our heads. We couldn't do it; we didn't have it in us.

"He'll do something desperate," I argued. "He'll end up in jail."

"Better now than later. The sooner he hits bottom, the better."

Instead, we staged an intervention, and with all the family pre- sent, confronted him with his problem. He agreed reluctantly to go to a hospital for thirty days of drug rehabilitation, but when the in- terventionist showed up the next day to drive him away, she had to chase a drunk and bleary-eyed Kirk across the house and into his bed- room. It was the first time we'd ever seen him in such a condition. Sullen and crazed, he arrived at the hospital in a wild state, fighting everyone. Only after three days of detox was he willing to speak to us.

The organizers of the program knew what they were doing; drawn into family counseling sessions, Rob, Kirk, and I seemed to grow closer. We were so confident he'd come home changed that during his stay my husband gave him a few dollars for candy at the canteen. A mistake.

Somehow Kirk found a way to escape and buy beer.

~

Later years became a blur . . . jobs held briefly . . . questionable friends drifting in and out. But certain memories stand out like blood stains. Kirk's first arrest for a D.U.I., his first night in jail. We hired a lawyer and bailed him out. When he was offered a halfway house instead of jail, his choice was easy. But now he couldn't find a job. As his zest for job hunting diminished, his willingness to fill empty days with liquor increased, and his stay at the halfway house ended.

More trouble with liquor and the law, events I no longer remember.

A longer stay in jail. And now he was there long enough for visitors. I thought, This is my son I'm going to see in this dismal place, and I gaped at him in his orange jumpsuit and felt like a criminal myself, staring at him through a wall of glass and picking up a phone so we could talk. I said, "This is humiliating," and he said bitterly, "You think it's humiliating for *you*."

Sometimes they wouldn't let us see him for hours, and I had the feeling that relatives of criminals were scarcely more respected than the criminals themselves. All the rules we had to follow. The sense that Cop is God, and you'd better not make a false move. Fill out this paper, follow those lines, no visiting between such and such, wait for the gates to open, wait for them to clank shut. No purses. Wait till we call you, which is when we're damn good and ready, but leave exactly when you're told to leave.

As I sat in the waiting room with other grim-faced relatives—surely they were desperate too, but you could never be sure—I began to feel schizophrenic. One day peering through glass at my jailed son, the next day hearing another son respectfully paged over a hospital loudspeaker. Dr. Wills. Dr. Chris Wills.

Who was the *real* son? Who were we?

It seemed impossible that Kirk's problems could grow worse, but they did. Another D.U.I., this time on a friend's motorcycle. A suspended driver's license. Days spent job hunting, and nights spent . . . where?

We told him to move, and he found a squalid room in a run-down house. One night he appeared back at our home limping. Though he said little, still dazed from his latest bout with whatever, it was obvious he was in pain.

"What happened?" I asked.

A quick answer—very strange. "I took my bike upstairs to a friend's apartment and fell down the stairs." The truth came out later; he was hit by a car in South Santa Ana—no doubt while buying cocaine.

We took him to see Chris, and I felt I'd entered a strange biblical world of Cain and Abel, where the good brother tends the bad one. Chris gave Kirk two Vicodin for his pain, and then two more, and even then he was hardly affected. X rays were followed by surgery and then by a steel rod in his ankle.

Kirk became a prisoner in his squalid room. No job. No way to get out because he couldn't ride his bicycle. I stopped by to bring him groceries and looked around in revulsion. He wasn't quite homeless, but it felt like it. A dirty room. A hot plate. A decrepit refrigerator. And unending boredom. Surely this was some kind of bottom—wasn't it?

How deep did he have to go?

Even with his ankle healed, job hunting became impossible. Nobody wanted to hire someone who arrived on a bicycle, red-faced and dripping with sweat, mumbling with low self-esteem. We decided Kirk needed to start over in a new town, someplace where the police wouldn't know he had a target painted on his back.

~

We found him a condo six hours away, in San Luis Obispo—a college town you could conquer on a bicycle. Rob and I bought him some furniture, enough to get by, and he promised he'd soon have a job.

He didn't.

The college kids got the jobs and Kirk got drunk. And he brought his target with him. In a blacked-out state he entered a stranger's parked car and ended up in jail, only this time he was too far away to visit.

After jail, we bought him a little moped, not knowing you can get a D.U.I. as easily on a moped as anything else.

~

After San Luis Obispo, Kirk came home and stayed briefly in his old bedroom. One day when Rob was out of town, he came home mid-afternoon looking dazed, and I stared at him and finally did what I'd never had the courage to do earlier. I ordered him out of the house.

Kirk couldn't believe I meant it.

"I do mean it," I said. "Just leave, Kirk. Take your bicycle and go."

"Go where?" He was utterly baffled.

"I don't care where. Find someplace. Go to the Salvation Army. Sleep under a bridge. I don't care. I've had it with you."

"But I was up all night, Mom. I'm exhausted. Just let me sleep it off."

"Sleep it off somewhere else, then. But not here. You're leaving this house. And I mean now. This minute. I don't care where you go, just get out. Go. Out! Out!"

When he still stared at me—first bewildered, then defiant—I said, "If you don't leave, I'm calling the cops." I almost choked on the words.

I watched as he took a backpack and stuffed in a few clothes. Then I followed him out to the front door and watched him get on his bicycle. I stood on the porch until he was out of view, and in my mind's eye I can still see him riding slowly away, his back curved by the unnatural hump of the backpack, his legs pedaling slowly. Headed for nowhere. He rounded the corner and disappeared.

I should have been relieved.

I wasn't. I'd never felt more miserable.

That night I took a sleeping pill and managed to drop off. But in the middle of the night, as though jarred into consciousness by an earthquake, I woke up. Suddenly I was crying. No, worse, sobbing uncontrollably. The image of Kirk was right there; I could see him pedaling away into a void, this son I'd loved, and it seemed more terrible than anything I'd ever witnessed. I couldn't shake it, couldn't stop feeling that I'd somehow murdered my own child.

I called Chris, waking him up at two in the morning.

He said, "You've done the right thing, Mom. Trust me, you did what was best. It's the only way you'll save him. Now he'll hit bottom and start to recover."

"But what about me?"

"You'll just have to endure it. You'll be okay. And Kirk will start to get better. You'll see."

"Chris, you don't understand. It's tearing me up. I'm not sure I can stand this. Seeing him go off like that, all alone. With no place to sleep."

"You can stand it, Mom. You will. Trust yourself. You have to believe you've done the right thing."

For half an hour Chris spoke soothing words, trying to still the raging tempest in my heart. I believed him. Or tried to. Maybe I slept a little, I don't know. But the pain didn't go away.

The next day, before noon, Kirk was back.

I looked at his drooping face, saw the utter exhaustion on his features, the despair, the hopelessness. If he'd stayed away, I might have survived. But I couldn't summon the will to throw him out twice.

We all have limits, I thought. We can only be so cruel, we can only hurt one of our children so much.

Okay, so it might have been for the best. Banishment might have succeeded where nothing else would. But I wasn't capable. I simply wasn't. As I looked at him, love and compassion came rushing in and there was no room left for punishment. If you love, you love. It can't be explained any other way.

Most parents would understand. The limits are there, they come with having the baby in the first place. And I say without shame, what Chris expected of me was impossible. There is just a barrier beyond which no parent can go, even if it's for the child's ultimate good. Somebody else would have to banish him, because I couldn't. And neither could Rob.

$\sim$

The world has gone on hurting Kirk. Or rather, he has continued hurting himself. We tried other remedies, all without success. With his cooperation, we enrolled him in a month's treatment at St. Joseph Hospital. The month seemed productive, but the benefits didn't last.

He needed skills. Translation: he needed a job. Twice he tried enrolling in government-sponsored job training courses—ROP—but the first time, five hundred people took numbers for forty openings, and his wasn't a winning number. The second time, at a different location, he sat up all night outside the ROP office—from six at night until eight the next morning. He was third in line, in a group that swelled eventually to more than a hundred applicants. But when the doors finally opened, a lady came out and said, "All the classes are filled by prior enrollees."

One night we got a call from Western Med Hospital. Kirk had stolen back his moped, and he'd collided with a car in Santa Ana. At a cost of eleven thousand dollars, he had one night's hospital housing, with a few stitches thrown in.

New plan. We gave him a week to heal, and then together we found him an apartment near the beach and he enrolled in Orange Coast College—luckily, within range of his bicycle. The classes he wanted, fundamentals of restaurant cooking, were filled, but he seemed willing to start with English and math. We felt a surge of hope; maybe Kirk was finally on track.

One day he called home and said matter-of-factly, "If you don't get me out of here, Mom, I'm going to die."

"What do you mean?" If he intended to shock me, he'd succeeded. From a standing start, my heart had gone from normal to racing in three seconds.

"Jim Tucker [his slickest, most oft-lying friend] comes around all the time, talking me into cocaine. I've gotta get out of here."

"And go where?"

"I don't know. Somewhere. As far away as possible. If I don't leave, I won't be alive next month."

"What do you want me to do? I can't just drop everything and start driving."

"You don't need to, Mom. I'll take the train."

That was the fastest I'd ever moved. The train. The train. Where do trains go? Not south, that would only take him closer to the Mexican border and more drugs. I thought of all the big cities north of us . . . Seattle, Portland. How well could a bicycle get around in those places? Not well, I imagined; he needed someplace smaller. A town. A small, manageable town. I took a flying leap.

By noon that August I had him on a train to . . . somewhere. Klamath Falls, Oregon. Two duffel bags. A couple of hundred dollars in his pocket. A one-way train ticket. And gone.

The next two months were probably the happiest of Kirk's adult life. He'd landed in Klamath Falls with nothing, but he had a mission, albeit limited—to create a nest for himself in a new town. From an expensive by-the-night motel, he moved to a cheaper, by-the-week motel. Then to an even more reasonable by-the-month apartment. He went out each day to secondhand stores and found cheap pots and pans, used bedding, bargain clothes. Eventually he found a giveaway house—so reasonable, by California standards, it seemed almost a joke. We talked long-distance to a Realtor, who admitted it was old—early thirties—and small, but, like Kirk, he raved about the view.

We obviously didn't ask enough questions.

The Realtor said nothing about the near-vertical street. He didn't tell us that the kitchen was filthy, the carpeting even filthier, the bathroom doorless and hidden behind a dingy curtain, the front bedroom propped up by rotting timbers and ready to topple into the ravine. And he didn't think to mention that in winter Klamath Falls gets several feet of snow. What he knew, but we didn't, was that this lovely hilltop often got so icy it was almost inaccessible, even by car.

Nobody was thinking bicycle. Including us.

So we bought the tiny house, and a month later, Rob and I went up to visit and saw the place for the first time. We were horrified. First, by the house, then by Kirk. From our first dinner together, the visit was a disaster. That night, out of our view, Kirk drank an excess of red wine, and the next morning, when we tried to arrange for new carpeting, we couldn't find him. He finally showed up, so belligerent that conversation was impossible. I remember his getting out of our rental car in the middle of downtown Klamath Falls and slamming the door so hard I was afraid it would fly off the hinges.

Rob and I were furious; he was an animal. After futile attempts to locate him—and almost glad we couldn't—we gave up and went home, relieved to escape from all that tension.

After that, his deterioration was rapid and breathtaking. For whatever reason, probably because he hadn't found a job and was lonely, Kirk made another disastrous decision. He imported his old "friend," Jim Tucker. The results were predictable. He and Tucker went back to their usual pursuits, and before long the loyal import persuaded him to try Klamath Falls's drug of choice—methamphetamine.

Kirk's brain went into an immediate tailspin, and he became a monster. He tore up his house, sold his possessions, thought he saw people with guns outside his home holding him hostage. He imagined he was being stalked. Once more he called home. "You've gotta get me out of here, Mom. They're gonna kill me."

I was past getting excited. "Who's going to kill you?"

"I don't know. But I've seen them outside my door. They're trying to get in. I'll die, Mom. They're going to murder me."

I had no answers. Stay put, I said, and sober up. I'd helped him escape too many times. I was through making hair-brained arrangements. He had a house. He'd survive.

His agitation increased. They—whoever "they" were—engaged him in a brutal fistfight. Kirk called the police, but he'd called them a dozen times too often about his manic visions. The police knew a crazy when they saw one, so he was given no help and no sympathy.

Yet he *was* injured, it turned out. By taxi, Kirk got himself to the hospital. He was nuts, all right, but nuts with a broken jaw.

The hospital called us, and now we were forced to act. Long distance, we arranged for repair by an oral surgeon, but getting Kirk to the doctor's hospital in nearby Medford proved nearly impossible. It took three false starts, Visa cards over the phone, and a long taxi ride before he showed up for surgery. One day later, the doctor said, and the jaw would have been inoperable, beyond fixing.

More Visa cards. A motel room near the doctor's office. Arrangements with a nearby pharmacy for liquid food. No liquor, we said, but Kirk found a way to get it anyway. He drank his beer through a straw.

The brain's response to methamphetamine, it seems, does not disappear right away. In some cases never. Still agitated, with his jaw wired shut, Kirk went on wild rampages. He threw a rock through a bicycle shop window. He stole a truck and parked it near his motel.

He ended up in prison. He was now a genuine criminal, and we were no longer willing to find him a lawyer or do anything else to help.

This time Kirk's sentence was relatively long, nine months. When he got out—what? Rob and I couldn't look that far ahead.

Long distance, we had a tiny, mostly destroyed house to fix up and sell. But no furniture and no possessions to worry about or move. Kirk's destructive rampages had made all that unnecessary.

Nine months later, genuine sobriety at last. With arrangements made at a sober-living house in our area, Rob and I forced ourselves to fly to Oregon to bring him home, and Kirk talked the probation officer into releasing him back to California.

Oregon knew what it was doing.

After twenty-four hours of frantic activity, gathering his few possessions, shipping two bicycles, tying up all the frayed strings that bound him to Oregon, Rob and I were ready to board the plane. Except suddenly Kirk wouldn't go.

"Why not?" we asked.

"I've still got some stuff to do."

"Like what, Kirk? We've handled everything."

"Just arrangements," he said stubbornly. "I'll come tomorrow."

"Your plane ticket is for today."

"I'll change it."

"They won't let you."

"Don't worry. They will."

We were sure they wouldn't, but you can't physically force a grown man onto a plane. Rob and I left, knowing quite well Kirk wouldn't come the next day.

He didn't. But he did arrive three days later, once more showing the anger and belligerence of drugs. What he got, or from whom, we never knew, but we were glad they'd sent a man from the sober-living house to meet him at the airport. Slouching there in the terminal, Kirk stared at us as if we were the most loathsome people he'd ever known. He wouldn't have gone anywhere with us.

The rest happened with incredible speed; Kirk seemed to whirl away from normalcy like a tornado. One week in the sober-living house, a drunken binge, a rescue by an adept counselor. A few more weeks of sobriety. Then Kirk showing up at our house full of loud talk and raging-bull behavior, hearing nothing we said, but stealing all the money out of my purse. For our own protection, we called the cops. With police officers watching, he took a taxi back to the sober-living house. But he didn't stay long.

Once more he left his sanctuary, and once more he attracted the law by getting belligerent in a bar and snatching someone's beer right off the table. This time he was put back in jail. He knew that jail well; he'd been there before.

Kirk's last period out was the briefest yet. By now I'd located a six-month inpatient treatment facility that handles hard-core addicts, and when he got in trouble again, I pleaded with the judge to sentence him to that facility, at our expense. "It'll save the state money," I reasoned. "And it stands a chance of saving him too." I tried to be logical. "Jail has never helped, it's never made him anything but worse."

The judge studied Kirk's rap sheet regretfully, and then he looked at me. "You're very eloquent, Mrs. Wills. I hear exactly what you're saying." He shook his head. "I'm sorry. I'd like to do this, but I can't." Later, Kirk's court-appointed lawyer explained the judge's decision. "When the rap sheet hits the floor, the judge has no choice. He'd lose his job if he did that."

So Kirk is finally in state prison, once again wasting months of his life. Sentenced to sixteen months this time, he'll be out in eight.

Getting angrier. More hostile and bitter. Less inclined to ever go straight.

One day my idealistic brother said to me, "Why don't you take a year out of your life, Maralys, and concentrate on Kirk? Give him all your time. Isn't it worth a year of your life?"

I almost laughed. Of course it's worth a year of my life, but my brother doesn't understand the problem. I can't be in the same room with Kirk anymore; I can't even drive him anywhere in my car. The last time I had him as a passenger, we hadn't traveled a mile before we started arguing. He got so hostile, so threatening, I no longer dared say a word. I was seriously afraid of what he might do.

I knew then my influence with him was over. Finished. His anger had transferred to me, and there was nothing I could say to him any longer, nothing I could do that would reach him. Every move I made, he hated me more. No words of mine would ever help; they'd only make us enemies.

For years, people who are supposed to know have told us Kirk needs to "hit bottom." Oh sure, I think, please tell us where we can find a bottom he hasn't already hit. How many more are available? He's already been to jail and prison. He's had accidents, beatings, hospitalizations, public humiliation, rejection by his family, nights on the street, loss of everything he's owned, his bed set afire in jail.

Of course, he hasn't yet hit the ultimate bottom. Death.

CHAPTER TWO

A Mother Who Couldn't Stop Drinking

Sheriff Mike Carona

Drug abuse is not a new problem. It's not a curse recently visited on our generation and ours alone.

Chemical dependency has been a thorn in society's side for centuries. Whether it was the "Scourge of the Fermented Grapes" during the era of the Roman Empire, or the addictive powers of opium that swept through China during the Opium Wars in the mid-1800s, or the devastating "Soldiers' Disease"—the morphine addiction that enslaved thousands during the Civil War (heroin ironically was developed as the "heroic" drug that would eradicate addiction to morphine)—alcohol and drugs have been a societal problem for hundreds, if not thousands, of years.

My age group, the baby boomer generation, was not much different from preceding generations in that we, too, were plagued with alcohol and drug abuse issues. While my peers didn't invent chemical dependency, we did have several unique features that set us apart from earlier generations.

Since 1946, when the first baby boomers were born, medical technology has provided newer, more effective, more powerful pharmaceuticals. That is both good news and bad. Drug traffickers quickly learned how to replicate these new drugs cheaply and get them on the street for sale. They also experimented with derivations of traditional addictive drugs, such as heroin, cocaine, stimulants, and depressants, all of which flooded the market from the late 1950s through the 1980s. Hardly surprising that drug use peaked in the seventies and eighties.

19

Our second and most significant baby boomer characteristic was size. The baby boomer generation was, and still is, the largest mass of humanity to ever hit American soil. No generation before us or after us matches us in sheer numbers. So when we, like previous generations, began experimenting with and becoming addicted to alcohol and the various drugs of our time, we produced more than our share of addicted individuals.

The final contributing factor of my generation was the casual acceptance of "turning on." Baby boomers didn't hide their drug use like prior generations; they flaunted it like a badge of honor. It was "cool" to do drugs, and even the sports and entertainment industries gave more than tacit approval to getting high.

The combined effect of all these attributes allowed my generation to do what we've done in other areas—set new, all-time records. In retrospect, this is one record we could have done without.

Thus I've seen societal changes in chemical dependency from two vantage points. First, as a child born in 1955 and growing up through the sixties and seventies, when recreational drug use was at its zenith. The other was as a peace officer through the seventies, eighties, and nineties, when both law enforcement and society as a whole began to deal with the destruction caused by chemical abuse.

It would be nearly twenty years before I'd learn how to do trend-event analysis as part of my graduate studies on futures forecasting. But even as a rookie deputy, I knew intuitively that drug abuse was going to be a big problem for our country.

As a young deputy working in a court detention facility, I watched the growing number of "custodies" coming into our facility who were repeat offenders for "under the influence" or "drug possession" charges. A number of regulars cycled through, and I remember watching the slow deterioration of their bodies and their minds. I remember thinking, If the public could see what I see, they wouldn't think drugs were so great. But it was the mid-seventies, and drugs were "cool" and cops weren't, so I just kept my comments to myself.

While I watched hundreds of "regulars" destroy themselves over those years, to this day one sticks in my mind. She was a beautiful young girl, brown hair, brown eyes—a surfer girl who spent most of her youth hanging out in the various beach communities that make up Orange County. When she wasn't surfing with her friends, she was partying with them.

The first couple of times she came through the system, she'd been arrested for minor violations—drunk in public, possession of marijuana. She cycled in and out of custody for more than a year, and I watched both her beauty and self-esteem degrade markedly.

One of the last times I saw this young woman, she had been arrested for being under the influence of heroin. By itself that wasn't remarkable, but she was now some five months pregnant. That combination, and my having watched her deteriorate so much over such a short period, caught my attention. I remember feeling sorry for her, but more important, feeling sorry for her baby, who wasn't even born yet.

It was just after I had handed out the sack lunches to the prisoners in the facility. Jails are generally noisy places, but during meals things become relatively quiet. I remember hearing yelling from the female tank and then running over to see what was the matter. When I arrived at the main holding cell, this same young lady was on the floor in convulsions. The paramedics were called, and I went into the cell to administer basic first aid. I cradled her head to check for injuries, and as I lifted one of her eyelids to examine her pupils, she threw up her lunch and, yes, most of it landed on me. The paramedics arrived and she was transported to the hospital—another druggie going through withdrawal.

I showered and changed my uniform, thinking to myself, This scene is happening way too often. I wondered if it was just a problem in Orange County, or if other parts of the country were seeing what I was seeing. Twenty years later I know the answer.

The next day the young woman was back in the detention facility. What happened next left an indelible impression on me. I asked her how she was doing. With a well-rehearsed laugh, she said, "Fine. Just kickin' and when I'm kickin', I get sick to my stomach. But this is the last time. I am done being a junkie. You will never see me again."

I told her that I had heard that a hundred times.

"No, I'm serious," she said. "I am sick and tired of being sick and tired. Besides, I am going to be a mom. I've got responsibilities now; I have to get my shit together. I'm clean now. I'll do my time, have my kid, get a job, maybe even move away from here. But I'm done with dope."

There was a part of me that wanted to believe her. Maybe because I wanted her to succeed, or maybe because I wanted her child to have its mom around. Or then again it might have been the wishful thinking of a rookie deputy who hadn't heard enough lies yet to turn him into an eternal skeptic.

Whatever the reason, I really believed this woman was going to make it. But if she was going to succeed, she'd have to do it on her own. Back then there were no programs, no internal or external support groups. All addicts did it the way she'd have to. You kicked the habit in jail, stayed clean for your thirty-, sixty-, or ninety-day sentence, and then fought like hell to stay clean once you were released to the streets. Alcoholics Anonymous (AA) and Narcotics Anonymous (NA) weren't cool yet either.

The very last time I saw her, the young woman had been arrested for—you guessed it—being under the influence of heroin. She had had her baby while serving her time on the prior arrest. It had only been six months since I'd last seen her, but her face had aged far more than six months' worth.

I remember walking over to her cell to talk with her. "What happened?" I asked. "I thought you were going to stay clean."

The fake laugh popped out. "Yeah, I was clean," she said. "I was just partying with some friends, and with my luck got caught chipping for the first time. I mean, I'm not really using, just chipping to be social."

I asked where her baby was, and once again she had a good story: "Hey, I had a baby boy, a real cutie, big brown eyes just like me. The cops took him to some children's home until I do my time. When I get out this time, I'm never coming back. I am gonna get a job and I'll be a great mom to him—you'll see."

I was transferred to a different assignment, so I don't know the final chapter on the girl with the brown hair and big brown eyes—or her son. For years I told her story, about how you can never trust a hype, how they'll always lie to you.

When I began writing this book, I recalled all those old experiences. Now I am not so sure she was lying to me. Maybe she really did want a different life for herself and her son. But nobody was there to give her the tools.

~

As a deputy, I saw this same scenario over and over with different offenders. All of it—the repeated appearances in court, the lack of headway in conquering addiction, the escalation of legal problems—seemed like a dismal pattern, and our part in it an exercise in futility.

Whatever we in the criminal justice system were doing with these addicts, we weren't making noticeable progress. They kept coming back and coming back, which was bad enough, except new cases were constantly added. The tide of addicted offenders had long since outstripped our courtroom capacity and overwhelmed the jails.

I knew when I ran for sheriff I would inherit what seemed like an unsolvable problem. Our jails were bulging to 145 percent of their intended capacity, and the experts were concerned that shorter sentences and early releases would only produce more crime and decreased public safety. It was obvious to me, if not to everyone else, that innovation and change were called for. With these problems in mind, I began researching answers long before I was elected Orange County sheriff. I ran my campaign based on a promise to try some unique solutions.

It was only after I met Maralys and we agreed to write a book together that I realized my motivation for solving the jail and public safety problems might be broader than I'd originally imagined. After reading her chapter about her son, I began remembering the problems I'd had as a child—and I recalled the pain of living with an alcoholic mother.

Somehow in the intervening years I'd managed to leave this behind—way behind.

I had forgotten about the many times I'd found my mother passed out at the kitchen table or in her bed or in front of the TV. I had forgotten about her alcohol-induced convulsions in the middle of the night. I had forgotten about the fights she and my father had about her drinking. I had forgotten about finding the bottles of scotch hidden around the house. I had forgotten about making excuses to my friends about why they couldn't come to my house to play.

It had been thirty-three years, and I had forgotten all those memories. My life didn't give me the luxury of looking back—or perhaps I kept myself so busy I never let myself look back—until Maralys came along . . . until the book came along.

After we started writing, all my own memories came back, and I knew that hers was not the only up-close-and-personal look at addiction. I, too, had a story to tell—a story that must have shaped me more than I ever knew.

～

It was a typical summer morning in July 1966. I did everything the way it seemed I had done things a thousand times before. Woke up. Gave a halfhearted shot at making my bed. Made an even less noble stab at washing my face and brushing my teeth, but all in all, not too bad a start for an eleven-year-old on a school-free day.

I remember vividly the sequence of events that morning, not because my daily routine was so programmed, but rather because of a single wrenching event that started me down a path of self-inquiry, of trying to figure out what I could have done differently . . . of wondering how I might have changed what happened.

I could smell coffee brewing in the kitchen, so I knew my dad was awake, but the smell of eggs cooking or bread toasting wasn't in the air, meaning my mom was still asleep. On my way to the kitchen, I stopped by her room to wake her up. I knocked on Mom's door but there was no answer. I opened the door and walked into her room and laughingly called her name—and still she didn't respond.

None of this was unusual; this scenario, too, had become a normal start to my days. But then I did something I hadn't done before. I ran across her room, jumped on her bed, and yelled, "Get up!"

Now I didn't do this with the normal laughter and joking with which my own son often jumps on my bed. I did it out of anger and resentment; my mom was behaving the way she had all too many mornings of my life. I was angry, and it was that emotion that made me feel guilty for years afterward.

You see, that day, unlike all the others, my mom wasn't sleeping off a hangover or languishing through the tail end of an alcoholic stupor that she'd come to mistake for sleep. That morning my mother didn't stir groggily and come to and try to arouse herself.

Sometime during the early hours of July 9, 1966, after yet another day of a fifth of scotch and a six-pack of beer, my mother had died in her sleep.

The fear that my mother's alcoholism was going to kill her had finally become reality. And fate made it me, her eleven-year-old son, who discovered her body.

No son should ever have to find his mother this way.

I remember shaking my mom, trying to wake her up and realizing, even at that age, that she was gone. As traumatic as it was, I wasn't surprised. I'd known this day would come and somehow, in my own way, I'd even prepared for it.

I left her room and walked down the hall to the kitchen, walked over to my dad, who was sitting at the kitchen table with a cup of coffee and a cigarette. I said almost coldly, "Mom's dead."

The rest of that day was, and still is, a kind of surrealistic blur. The fire trucks arriving with their sirens blaring, firemen working on my mom to no avail, neighbors in and out of the house, the medical examiner taking my mother's body away. I remember being embarrassed by all the attention that was being focused on me. And yet there was still the anger. I recall how mad I was that she was dead, that she drank herself to death—that she chose her love of alcohol over her love for me.

∽

On January 4, 1999, I took the oath of office to become the sheriff of Orange County.

I can't say what first motivated me, exactly, to look for different approaches to the addicted prisoner problem. Until this book project came along, my focus for developing programs to treat addiction came from extensive study and analysis as a law enforcement professional. I realized that the strategy of simply warehousing addicts was not working.

As a politically conservative sheriff, I believe strongly that criminals should be off our streets and in jail. I oppose the wholesale legalization of drugs. But I am also a pragmatist who believes in identifying a problem and then looking for solutions.

Before I became sheriff, I did some research and marveled that a few jails and prisons were actually treating addicted prisoners inside the walls and were able to dramatically reduce recidivism rates.

I would like to believe that was, and is, my sole motivation for creating programs to deal with the addicted jail population in Orange County.

But today I am not so sure.

CHAPTER THREE

Why Jails and Prisons Make Addiction Worse

Like everyone else in America, the city council of Tustin, California, saw the horrifying 1997 TV footage of two would-be bank robbers sprinting through the streets of North Hollywood like movie extras, spraying machine gun bullets in every direction—for all the world like a scene from *Bonnie and Clyde.*

Trouble is, the scene was real—and a lot of ordinary, noninvolved citizens were at risk of losing their lives.

Within a week, the policeman who happened to be on Tustin's City Council asked his fellow council members to vote on arming Tustin's police with the ultimate in swat-team weaponry—high-powered assault weapons and associated ammunition in every patrol car. With such firepower they could presumably bring down a helicopter.

Critics spoke up on both sides. Nobody wanted to see the Tustin police at a firepower disadvantage if such a situation should ever occur in Tustin. And the citizens of the town certainly deserved to feel as safe as possible.

Yet others wondered if it was in the public's best interest to arm ordinary policemen with weaponry that required specialized training and know-how. Experts argued that a stray bullet from one of those police guns could conceivably penetrate the walls of a home blocks away and kill a resident who was innocently eating dinner.

Over the protests of Mayor Tracy Worley, and despite strong reservations expressed by the city's Police Chief, the City Council listened to its policeman and implemented the proposal.

The council's reaction was understandable; fear of crime drives much of Southern California's current legislation—even though, in the long run, North Hollywood's terrifying scenario may prove to be a rare occurrence.

When it comes to battling crime and coping with addicted citizens, America is definitely on the offensive.

~

In today's crime-spooked society, the average citizen who reads the newspapers has learned that overall crime rates throughout the United States have recently fallen and that some large cities, such as New York and Boston, are enjoying significant reductions in violent crime—rape, burglaries, and particularly homicides. Aware as well that prisons are being built at greater rates than ever before in the country's history—and with no further information as to whether these two facts are related—the informed citizen assumes that the two are inexorably linked. Therefore, he concludes, prisons and jails are good, and the more the better.

It is this mind-set that savvy politicians play into, declaring themselves "tough on crime," and promising an apprehensive public that the prison explosion will continue in only one direction: up. Any knowledgeable candidate brave enough to speak out and sound a warning that our country's prison-building mania comes at horrific cost, and may actually make America's crime problems worse, finds himself labeled "soft on crime" and stands to be defeated at the voting booths.

The statistics are truly alarming, but not in the way politicians will admit. Although we have now built the world's largest prison system—with 1 in every 150 U.S. residents currently incarcerated—we still remain the most violent advanced industrial society in the world.

In the last decade alone, the United States has spent $30 billion to build more prisons and, as of the last twenty-five years, the prison population has sextupled. Yet over this longer span, violent crime has risen markedly, and the more recent declines reflect only a lessening of the *rate of rise.* Furthermore, the leveling off of crime has not been consistent throughout the country. While cities like New York and, to a lesser degree, San Francisco have experienced a decrease in violence, others—Los Angeles and New Orleans—have seen homicide rates rise. In the case of New Orleans, the rise in homicides has been horrific—between 1970 and 1995 they rose 329 percent.[1]

If increased incarceration were the main reason that crime has abated in some parts of the country and not others, the states that imprison their citizens at the highest rates should be able to demonstrate the lowest per capita incidents of violent crime. But, curiously, this correlation doesn't hold. New York State, basking in a significant decrease in crime, is considered by criminologists to be generally underpunitive; whereas Louisiana, a hard-boiled state known for incarcerating its population at a rate second only to Texas, suffers the highest number of homicides per capita in the country.

In California there seems to be no consistency among its cities at all. Between 1970 and 1995, with two successive tough-on-crime governors and an electorate asked to approve bonds for new jails and prisons in almost every election, San Francisco experienced a 13 percent decline in its homicide rate, whereas Los Angeles found its murder rate had increased by about 70 percent.[2] Same state, different results. The answer is obviously more complicated than everyone thinks.

The response of citizens and politicians alike to the dubious benefits of building ever more prisons has been strangely illogical, perhaps best illustrated by two analogies.

First, consider the indoor plant whose leaves are turning an unhealthy yellow, and the homeowner who supposes that the plant's malaise is due to lack of water. The owner gives the plant a big drink, and when this doesn't work and the leaves yellow even more, he floods the greenery until it dies—realizing too late that the original problem had not been too little water, but too much.

Or a second illustration: picture the small boy who, from an early age, is soundly spanked for every minor infraction. When stepped-up spankings don't bring a cooperative attitude and greater compliance, the punishing parent redoubles her efforts, convinced that if lesser paddlings don't work, all-out beatings surely will—until the force and frequency of corporal punishment turn the child from a cowering youngster into a hostile, antisocial teenager, if not an outright delinquent.

While common sense would tell most people that the behaviors illustrated above are self-defeating—when something doesn't work, why do more of it?—somehow when it comes to criminals and meting out punishment, logic is not a determining factor.

In the *UCLA Law Review,* Australian Law Professor John Braithwaite offers a tart comment on society's view of punishment: "Pandering to punitive emotions does not satiate them: it accelerates a lust for vengeance. Promise to deliver tougher prison terms and you engender outrage that the devils are not being hung. Hang them and the political criticism will be that not enough are being hung. Hang them all and there will be political condemnation that they are not being boiled in oil or drawn and quartered."[3]

The punishment issue gets even less logical when applied to addicted, nonviolent offenders. Here, our policymakers' lack of information and insight has proved disastrous. Few have recognized that harsh punishment of addicts simply doesn't work. Fewer still seem overly concerned that the country is spending horrendous sums of money locking up addicts and getting a negative return. And none, it appears, read the statistics that prove our criminal justice policy as applied to addicts is mostly a failed strategy—that untreated addicts continue to cycle in and out of jails and prisons with a regularity you could set your watch by.

Instead, public stereotypes prevail. To most nonaddicted citizens, all drug addicts are *dangerous.* They do what they do *on purpose.* And the best solution is *punishment.* If mild forms of punishment don't cure their addictions, surely harsher and more punitive forms of reprisal will do the trick.

While no one denies that most violent criminals—especially those who are demonstrably sociopathic and apt to be repeaters—need to be removed from society and given as little opportunity as possible to inflict further harm, the same principles do not hold for the nonviolent offender.

In his well-documented and cogent book *Crime and Punishment in America*, Elliott Currie writes: "The experience of going to jail reduces recidivism among some offenders. But it is equally undeniable that it *increases* recidivism among others. Indeed, the tendency for incarceration to make some criminals worse is one of the best-established findings in criminology."[4] And in another passage he adds, "No matter how the numbers are manipulated, the results confirm that prison makes sense for some offenders but not for others. It makes a great deal of sense for truly violent people, but its utility dwindles to the vanishing point for minor property offenders, not to mention minor drug offenders."[5]

And indeed, perceptive and honest leaders in law enforcement will admit that for all too many prisoners, jail becomes Criminal Justice 101—that what inmates are most apt to learn behind bars is how to be good criminals.

~

We believe that few people give much thought to the deleterious effects of jails and prisons. To the extent that law-abiding citizens think about criminals at all, they have a Gertrude Stein attitude: a criminal is a criminal is a criminal. Anyone who's convicted of anything probably deserves what he gets from the penal system. Punishment is not supposed to be pleasant. Most offenders are basically evil, so tough treatment is called for. Criminals are like mules—you have to knock them on the head just to get their attention.

With scant protest from citizens on the outside, the late eighties and most of the nineties have seen a changed emphasis in incarceration—away from rehabilitation and toward the realities of coping with a burgeoning prison population. Sheer numbers have forced many of the changes. There simply aren't enough facilities, enough beds, enough manpower to cope with so many criminals. A great mass of angry humanity all cooped up in a too-small area becomes difficult to manage. And prisoners show remarkable ingenuity about taking advantage of the situation.

When prisoners use forks and other table implements as weapons, you have to take them away and substitute plastic. When offenders arrive with head lice, which can spread to others, it's necessary to shave their heads. When relatives persist in sending packages with hidden stashes of illegal drugs, you have to eliminate packages from the outside. When exercise weights are used as weapons, prisoner against prisoner, weights have to be confiscated.

Unfortunately, good programs and helpful measures have also fallen or been scaled back because wardens find it impossible to offer what some outsiders consider "luxuries" on such a large scale. Educational classes, frequent and regular exercise, job training, all have taken a back seat to the basic necessity of maintaining order and preventing mayhem in an explosive situation. Our country's criminal justice system is dealing with more felons than it can gracefully handle. First things must come first: food, clothing, shelter, and public safety.

The diminution or loss of in-prison programs that might actually bring about change or improvement in individual inmates is not mourned by ordinary citizens. In fact, an indignant public reacts vehemently to what it perceives as the "coddling" of prisoners. *I have to PAY for my kid's college education. Why should a prisoner get it for free?* Or, *Air conditioning is expensive. Why give it to all those felons who don't deserve it?* Or, *I don't have time to play baseball and handball, why should they?*

The public, by and large, does not find the loss of such privileges alarming or inhumane, since inmates are generally regarded as undeserving creatures that rank somewhere below "human."

To the punitive extremist who argues that, God forbid, amenities like job training, education, books, and sports might make prison tolerable—or worse, give inmates the impression they're doing time in a country club—let this be said: there is no danger that prisoners who must sleep on narrow bunks inches from other men, with no freedom, no privacy (even in the bathroom), limited access to showers and medical care, a bare minimum of food, degrading clothes, and a continuous sense that they're little more than a number, will imagine for one second that they are confined in a country club.

In fact, it is often the prison wardens themselves who inveigh against removing such "perks" as books, classes, and out-of-doors exercise—having learned all too well that inmate anger and pent-up hostility can be dissipated through physical activity, and that minds focused on books and classes are less inclined to dwell on ways of "getting even" with jailors.

There was a time in the late nineties when the California Department of Corrections was considering, among other measures, the removal of all weight lifting equipment and many of the law books from the California prisons. The *Los Angeles Times,* in an article on February 9, 1998, called those get-tough moves "extraordinary" and warned that such measures came at a time when California's thirty-three prisons were increasingly overcrowded, and tension behind the walls was at an all-time high.

The *Times* pointed out that the push toward a harsher prison environment coincided with the Governor's (then-Governor Wilson) renewed efforts to get the State Legislature to approve $1.4 billion in bonds to help finance four new prisons.

The article, which covered numerous proposed restrictions, concluded with a statement by John Irwin, a retired sociology professor at San Francisco State University, who, in the 1950s, spent five years at Soledad Prison for armed robbery. In an era when rehabilitation was a goal of California prisons, Irwin helped write the Inmates Bill of Rights. He says now, "We're going back decades and decades in terms of punishment." Predicting that such changes would ensure that parolees have a much harder time reentering society than he did, he adds, "Along with losing their mobility, they are losing what little choices they had inside prison. . . . Imagine spending years having everything determined for you. It's maddening. Convicts come out and they're enraged."

∼

It's a rare prisoner, indeed, who doesn't undergo profound psychic changes as he adapts to the prison environment . . . and an equally rare parent who can accept these changes without a great sense of loss.

∼

As his drug-induced misdeeds accumulated, Kirk Wills was given ever-longer prison sentences. His calls home from Corcoran State Prison had a changed quality, a new hardness of tone, a tension, an underlying anger that sounded near-explosive. "How do you think I'm doing?" he asked sarcastically. "You should try spending time in this place. You wouldn't ask such dumb questions."

"Isn't there anyone you can talk to?"

"In here? Like who? The less you talk about yourself in prison, the better. If they ever find out you're sending me money . . ." His voice trailed off and he changed the subject. "I nearly got in a fight yesterday. A guy set me up, tried to get me mad."

"But you didn't fight?"

"No. I didn't. But that's what the guards want—they're looking for excuses to beat us up. They hope we'll do something like that. They're just waiting."

Kirk's letters reveal the same dullness of spirit. Once a positive and upbeat man during his periods of sobriety, he now writes letters that reflect his meager attempts to find something to be glad about.

~

Letter from Kirk Wills, Wasco State Prison (interim prison before Corcoran):

"Hi, today is Tue, Sept 23. This is the only paper I have 2 write on. . . . My other letter probably didn't go out till yesterday. Anyway I'm gonna be here 30–90 days w no phone. Also, this is my last envelope. Could u please mail me some stamped envelopes? I use them to buy food. I won't be able to buy anything (at the canteen) for 4 weeks. I'm abbreviating 2 save paper. We get some sunshine every day which is nice."

And a month later:

"Hi, just got your package w envelopes. I will probably be here about 60 days. Most people are. When I get where I'm going, there will be phones and I will call. At this place we get to sit on an outside patio 3 or so X's a day which is nice. We also get yard 3 X's a week to play ball or walk a track. Besides that, the only thing to do is watch TV. Long boring days. I guess it will be next summer before I'm out. I know I didn't deserve the *last sentence nor do I deserve this, even though you feel I deserve punish-ment. The only hope 4 this country is to legalize drugs and educate young people about the dangers. I know you disagree and that's o.k. Alcohol is definitely one of the most dangerous, and it is legal. I'll write later. Kirk."*

~

It becomes apparent then, if it's the criminal justice system's intent to return its drug-addicted (approximately 80 percent of inmates), nonviolent (some 53 percent of all inmates) prisoners to their com-munities as contrite, better-adjusted human beings who are less likely than before to get into trouble, the system is making dubious choices. Certainly no one who's locked up in a typical jail or prison perceives such a goal.

All the added layers of punishment and humiliation that ordinary citizens support, and overcrowded jails and prisons have no option (at times) but to carry out, only push the goal further out of reach. To the average prisoner, incarceration's aim is punishment, pure and simple. Revenge. A stripping away of pride and self-esteem. Incessant humbling. A removal of any ability to make decisions or think for oneself. Conformity. Absolute, mouth-closed, lie-low, make-no-waves conformity.

Prison trains men and women for one thing—to be prisoners. For certainly none of the qualities listed above are of much use in the outside world.

~

The problem is, prisoners get out.

Though few throw-away-the-key advocates give this part much thought, most of the nonviolent offenders will eventually be back, dumped on society with all their beaten-dog conformity, combined with bucketsful of anger, some suppressed, some not.

In spite of their need to cope with a new, flammable mix of passiv-ity and hostility, most released inmates hope to find jobs. Contrary to public perception, the number one priority for freed prisoners is work—both to earn money and to enjoy normal respect. (Most would rather work inside jail, too, but this is a luxury few ever get.)

Yet what prospects do most ex-prisoners have?

What are the chances of normal employment for a newly released inmate who possesses less-than-normal maturity, a paranoid fear of making a misstep, great hostility toward authority, a lack of salable skills, a prison record that looks terrible on job applications, and an overwhelming need to feel happy again for the first time in months?

What would one expect from a man or woman who has long since demonstrated a lack of discipline and self-control, but who is now suffering as well from psychic pain and fear and insecurity and a hangdog self-image, an addicted person who knows only one way to get immediate relief from all these terrible feelings?

The answer is obvious. And this is the direction in which all too many released addicts head. A few dispiriting attempts to find work. And then back to the behavior that got them in trouble in the first place. Back to immediate gratification and release from pain—in drugs and alcohol.

~

A last letter from Kirk Wills reflects his vanished optimism and his own assessment about his chances of leading a normal life.

"Hi again. Just got your letter—as usual nothing new in jail but the date—a person can go crazy in jail cuz there's nothing 2 do every day all day. No books to read & very little on TV. They put cartoons on most of the time. I'm writing this letter with a puny pencil cuz that's all they give you. I have nothing but problems as soon as I get out, so I guess it really doesn't matter when I get out. I'm on a top bunk, which I hate. My back and neck are giving me lots of pain. They won't let me have a doctor's appointment. I've put in 4 slips.*

"Nothing positive to say. It all boils down to life is not fair, but I've known that for a long time. Millions of people have been cheated out of happiness from wars, crime, earthquakes, floods, etc., and they didn't break the law or anything like me, so I do take some responsibility for my

---

* Kirk had back surgery years ago, but could never convince anyone in the prison setting he wasn't goldbricking.

situation. It just seems never-ending b-cuz I think I've been locked up about 1000 out of the last 1200 days.

"I don't know if I can live in society. It doesn't appear that I can. I don't have much hope. I am more like the people in here than the people on the street. Most of the people in here are not aggressive. Just drug charges and stuff. 80% don't need to be locked up, in my opinion. The system is broken. Kirk. "

~

In the early nineties, a group of American citizens, concerned about the unprecedented and costly expansion of the prison system since 1980—coupled with ever-higher public fear of crime—formed a commission to study criminal justice in America and make recommendations. The National Criminal Justice Commission, comprised of thirty-four people from all walks of life, including an Olympic champion, completed an exhaustive study of crime in America and published their findings in a book called *The Real War on Crime.*[6] At the end of a well-written treatise, the commission made eleven recommendations—not surprisingly, along the same track as those offered by author Elliott Currie.

The commission's first recommendation would come as an eye-opener to tough-on-crime advocates. "Recommendation 1. Adopt a three-year moratorium on new prison construction until a systematic assessment of prison needs can be completed. Replace some prison sanctions with alternative programs that are less expensive and often more effective at reducing crime."[7]

The commission listed thirteen alternatives to prisons and jails, among them halfway houses and drug treatment.

Now hear what the commission had to say about addiction as it relates to the criminal justice system: "Recommendation 2. Replace the war on drugs with a policy of harm reduction where the police work with public health and other professionals to stem substance use. Substance abuse should be treated as a public health challenge rather than a criminal justice problem."[8]

Under this recommendation the commission added several incisive pages, arguing that America's recent approach to criminal addiction—the war on drugs—has not only cost taxpayers an astonishing $100 billion, but has had "few tangible results [and] devastating collateral consequences." Furthermore, even after five years, the group found, the war on drugs has been so ineffective that the illegal use of drugs continues at the same high levels, and street drugs are as potent as ever.

The commission stated: "The purpose of harm reduction is to minimize the harmful effects of drug use rather than to wage a war against drug users." They urge that arrested addicts be coaxed into drug programs as an alternative to jail, and that those who must be incarcerated be offered drug treatment within prison walls.

In an excerpt from a later passage the authors write:

> Harm reduction is necessary because drug abuse does not respond well to punishment. *Drug cravings are irrational.* . . . *Most drug users do not care if the punishment is one year or five years in prison* [our italics].

> . . . A statewide study in California found that every dollar spent on substance abuse treatment saved taxpayers seven dollars in lowered crime and health care costs.

> . . . Three out of four men in California prisons have a history of drug use, but only 10 percent are involved in a drug treatment program. Only 1 percent receive comprehensive full-term treatment as defined by the National Institutes of Health. . . . Most cities have long lines of people who *want* drug treatment and cannot get it. While we are willing to spend millions of dollars on prisons, we are unwilling to spend a few thousand dollars on treatment programs.[9]

Echoing this theme, an article in the February 24, 1998, issue of the *Los Angeles Times* describes the changed views of an ex-inmate of a federal penitentiary—a lawyer who was once a member of the California assembly. Titled "Paroled Lawmaker to Push Prison Reform," the article describes the metamorphosis of Pat Nolan—once a conservative assemblyman who led the state assembly's efforts to get tough on crime and lengthen prison sentences.[10]

But Nolan's two years of imprisonment for political corruption brought a much-changed perspective. He now views sentencing through "whole new lenses" and believes that drug abusers and nonviolent prisoners may be spending an excess of time behind bars.

Nolan now argues, "We should reserve prison space for people we are afraid of, not just that we are angry at," and urges that prisons serve not only to incarcerate criminals, but also to rehabilitate them into useful citizens. In the end, Nolan makes a startling admission about his former views. "I didn't think of inmates as humans."

~

For every parent of an addicted son or daughter, the word addict *stops being a generic term and takes on the face of a lost child. Just such a daughter was Nancy Halloway, who lived with her parents and an older sister in Bellflower, California. Her father was in the newspaper business, and her mother was a homemaker. The parents divorced when Nancy was only six, and the two girls went to live with their father in La Palma, later joined by a new stepmother.*

For Nancy, the trauma of her parents' divorce was made worse by emotional battering from her stepmother. At age fourteen, she ran away and was taken to live with her mother in Huntington Beach. Still feeling the diminishing effects on her ego, Nancy escaped into marijuana and LSD. She was soon caught selling Kanibinal, a horse tranquilizer, by her best friend's mother, an English teacher in her high school. The teacher chose to tell Nancy's mother instead of having the girl dismissed from school.

It was a heart-to-heart talk with her mother that temporarily rescued Nancy for a few years. The mother suggested her daughter simply drink at home, an offer the mother now regrets. After high school, Nancy held a good job—until she had problems with her mother and moved out. At age twenty-nine, after holding two respectable jobs and one not-so-good (as a cocktail waitress), a friend introduced Nancy to methamphetamine. What happened next was like the progress of a plane that rises too steeply, goes into a stall and drops, spinning toward ultimate destruction.

For a while all seemed well with Nancy. At age thirty-two she was making a handsome living selling methamphetamine, but more than that, she felt important and needed by her vast clientele.

From the top of the climb, her personal disintegration brought the stall that started the fatal dive. "People on drugs don't remember to pay their rent," she says, and soon she was evicted and selling drugs from a motel. She furnished her new quarters from nearby Dumpsters.

Eventually her car was stopped by police, who found guns and drug paraphernalia, but even this momentary scare didn't slow her selling and using. Nancy's habit was now becoming costly, made a thousand percent worse when she began absorbing her drugs in a new way. "Smoking speed takes you right down the chute," she says. "It destroys your mind." Soon her behavior became so abrasive, so scary, she was abandoned by friends and began living in a trailer—doomed, apparently, to permanent destruction. Even when she was clubbed by a naked man in a public shower, she lacked the will to change her life.

There was a new apartment, yelling and screaming, more cops, an arrest, and then jail.

Out of jail, she was rearrested on a bicycle and this time earned four felony counts for possession. By now she looked terrible. Scraggly brown hair, sunken cheeks, a haunted expression. "You start looking like what you're doing," she says.

Sixty days in jail and a suspended sentence of five and a half years still didn't make the kind of impression she needed. Her next two arrests brought her longer sentences, and she was now serving time for felonies in two different cities. In spite of rescue attempts by her father, who put up his house to make bail, Nancy could not stay clean. After twelve "dirty" urines, her probation officer returned her to jail. And there she would have stayed for a full year, except for the intervention of Nancy Clark, an expert in alternative sentencing, who convinced the judge her client would do better in a halfway house.

By now, both parents had lost hope. Nancy was forty-one. She'd been using drugs, on and off, for twenty-seven years. She seemed hopeless, doomed to die from a habit she couldn't break—though all along a single refrain ran through her mind: "I can quit any time I want."

~

In another part of the country, a young man was growing up on a farm. Tim, the oldest of three boys, was handsome, musically gifted, and lazy, always looking for the easy way out.

When Tim was eight, his parents divorced and his mother took her boys three thousand miles away, crossing the country to live near her parents. When the mother remarried a year later, Tim began a new and wholly different life as a farm boy, making an easy adjustment because he was loved and respected by his stepfather.

Still, this new man wasn't his real father.

In his rebellious teens, Tim yearned for his dad, believing, as the immature often do, that a REAL father would meet his every need and let him do what he wanted.

At eighteen, Tim gassed up his old, red Volkswagon bug, threw in his few belongings, and headed back to his father in California.

The reunion he envisioned was not the reality he encountered. A new stepmother considered Tim a nuisance and wanted him gone, but the dad—out of both obligation and guilt—offered him a job at his nightclub waiting tables. Tim's only joy came from playing drums with a small ethnic band after the patrons had eaten. And it was there he fell in love.

At first his chosen lady wanted no part of him, but Tim persisted—one of the few goals he'd ever pursued and stuck to—and a few years later they married. Money came easily to them; the wife owned a successful business, and Tim was now the restaurant manager. They had a strong mutual interest—cocaine.

Life was one big high until Tim was bent double with a kidney stone. With a prescription for Vicodin, a codeine derivative that was supposedly nonaddictive, Tim entered a new addictive phase. For a while he was able to fool his doctor into giving him refills, and soon he was consuming a month's worth of pills in less than a week. Needing a second supplier, Tim made friends with a dentist and the flow of pills continued.

For the next several years, Tim was a reclusive addict—until a pharmacist discovered his secret, alerted both Vicodin providers, and eliminated his supply on the spot.

No one offered to help him over the hump, so Tim took the easy way out. A street dealer talked him into the ultimate thrill, a speedball—cocaine to get high, heroin to extend the high into a velvety peace.

One unbelievable trip hooked him immediately. And, most important, as long as he had the money, the supply would be there.

Eventually he no longer had the money. His habit cost him his car, his home, and his business. He and his wife resorted to living behind a Dumpster. Homeless and in and out of jail, he was, at last, sentenced to sixteen months in state prison.

There, thanks to a fellow inmate, he was guided to a Twelve Step program offered by Narcotics Anonymous.

~

We have seen, then, that a number of thoughtful people recognize that the exploding prison system has failed to accomplish what Americans had hoped for—a significant lessening of violent crime. Instead, at great expense, it has swept unthinkable numbers of offenders into one massive net, making scant distinction between those who physically hurt others and those who hurt mainly themselves. In this great lumping together, little effort is being made to segregate and treat the nonviolent addicts, whose lives might be reclaimed—if only we had the will to do it.

In the criminal justice system's zest for inflicting harsh punishment on *all* offenders, there has been an ironic by-product: dangerously violent criminals with indeterminate sentences have been released from prison early to make room for drug addicts and nonviolent offenders with minor crimes against property.

As both Elliott Currie and the Criminal Justice Commission authors point out, jails for hardened criminals are expensive overkill for nonviolent addicts. Drug abusers would do far better serving their sentences in less-secure facilities run by less-costly rehabilitation professionals.

As we noted earlier, the net effect of successive incarcerations on nonviolent addicts is mostly negative and invariably dehumanizing. The prison environment gradually erodes the very qualities an individual needs to succeed on the outside: confidence, boldness, ability to think creatively, courage, leadership, willingness to take necessary chances, good psychic energy.

Then why isn't something being done?

Currie makes the point that in the fifties and sixties the public supported rehabilitation for prisoners, at least in theory. But after a time, when rehabilitation didn't seem to accomplish much, attitudes changed. The problem was, many such efforts were halfhearted and didn't last long enough to demonstrate their effectiveness. But also, far less was known then about what works and what doesn't.

Unfortunately, public perception has not caught up with today's reality. Too many people believe all efforts at rehabilitation are a waste of time, so why bother?

$\sim$

Yet today, quietly, and almost out of view of public awareness, a few bold and effective options are being offered to addicted offenders.

In states like Virginia, Colorado, Arizona, Minnesota, and yes, even California, small knots of activists are beginning to recognize the problems created by great numbers of addicts cycling uselessly through jails and prisons. These frontline problem solvers recognize that better solutions are needed if we hope to stop our insane squandering of public funds and human lives.

Some alternative solutions, like diversion centers and detention centers (described in later chapters), now being tried in the state of Virginia, came about almost by accident—ironically, when penitentiaries became overcrowded as a result of the state's recent "get tough on crime" legislation.

Drug courts were created by Attorney General Janet Reno and others—like Judge William Meyer of Denver—when they became weary of seeing the same addicts return to court over and over, having made zero progress in conquering their addictions.

Therapeutic communities (TCs), which have existed since the 1960s, are at last finding new advocates, both inside and outside of jails and prisons, mainly because small groups of addicts can testify that they were able to modify their behaviors in such a setting.

While all of this may sound like significant progress, the solutions mentioned above are a few puffs of warm air in a blizzard—like trying to pay off the national debt with piggybanks.

As of 1996, only 1 percent of the men in California prisons who need comprehensive, full-term treatment were getting it. Even if that number were multiplied by five to account for the intervening years, California would still be treating effectively only 5 percent of its addicted male inmates.[11]

When it comes to percentages of people helped versus those who need it, these few alternatives to incarceration are just a start. A brave beginning. And a trend that may falter and die unless our nonaddicted population becomes educated.

Unfortunately, the public at large is mostly unaware of the problem—or, if aware, they do not have the knowledge or the will to demand better solutions. There is such a muted, polite, nonconfrontational public discussion about the need for change that few politicians have heard it. Except in the state of Arizona, where the voting public demanded alternatives to prison, too few mothers are storming Congress crying to be heard; too few judges are thundering from the bench; too few criminal justice experts are making waves.

Are we, then, willing to look the other way and let our huge addicted population cycle endlessly in and out of prisons . . . or just rot there?

If the answer is yes, would we feel the same if one of these people was a son, a daughter, a brother, a sister?

If the answer is still yes, then perhaps we simply don't understand the nature of addiction. We don't know how subtly, how smoothly, how gracefully, addiction overtakes its victims. We don't perceive that addiction invariably arrives as a good-natured friend. We don't know how lucky we are that this addicted person isn't *us*.

CHAPTER FOUR

The Nature of Addiction

When it comes to addiction, there are no surprises.

To those who understand the disease best, anything is possible. There is no one group of humans for whom the threat of addiction does not exist. Addiction makes no distinctions between affluent and penniless, doctor and high school dropout, teenager and senior citizen, the confident and the cowering, the athletic and the indolent. Drugs and alcohol are equal opportunity providers. Anyone can get hooked, and anyone can find a way to be rescued—even the saddest, the most depraved needle-pushing derelict.

The story of a champion illustrates this very well.

~

The young man was once a famous hang glider pilot. Before that, he'd been a competition skydiver, and before that, a Navy Seal. At the peak of his hang gliding career, Rich Pfeiffer won more competitions than anyone else who was out there running off the edges of cliffs. For seven years he dominated the sport and was photographed endlessly as he soared in space. To some he was a legend. And perhaps it was the very legendary nature of his life that pointed to his downfall.

Did Pfeiffer, perhaps, have the sense that he was impervious and could survive anything?

He thinks not.

In any case, toward the end of his hang gliding days in 1985, his girl-friend smuggled cocaine into the tubes of his hang glider. Pfeiffer tried the drug—casually at first. He was always celebrating one win or another, and cocaine was a spirited addition to parties.

For a while he got away with it.

But sometime in 1987 he smoked the stuff, and that marked a disastrous change. "Smoking cocaine is nothing like sniffing it," he says. "Once I used it that way, I was addicted immediately." From that day the downward spiral began, and he did things he once would have considered unthinkable.

Out of control, he rampaged through a short, hellish period that included armed robbery. All the crimes he ever committed in his life occurred during a two-and-a-half-week time frame. But no one took them lightly, and he was brought before an unsympathetic judge. Pfeiffer knew he'd undergone a basic physiological change and pleaded with the sentencing judge to send him to rehabilitation instead of prison. The judge was adamant; he wouldn't consider it. Pfeiffer was taken away to begin serving six years in prison.

No one who knew him could imagine how he'd plummeted from such heights—literally—to this. To all appearances, Rich Pfeiffer's useful life was over.

∽

For the purposes of this book, we intend to separate addictions to substances (chemicals that can be sniffed, swallowed, inhaled, or injected) from addictions to process (to activities that *may* be harmful, but aren't necessarily so, like exercise, eating, shopping, gambling, or sex).

It's safe to make the distinction here that, unlike the processes listed above, which most people engage in without incident, the use of addictive chemicals is, with sufficient repetition, always harmful.

Anyone researching this subject, however, will discover a number of authors who write about addictions as though all are essentially alike. Whether the addiction is to heroin or shopping, these authors find an underlying vein of similar personality traits. From this they conclude that the same treatment methods apply to all equally.

We do not believe such generalizations are valid. Whatever one concludes about the common threads that run through addictive personalities, even the common flood of endorphins released into the system by both chemicals and certain addictive behaviors, we maintain that only chemicals can produce profound, measurable changes in the human brain. Thus, for our purposes, we will focus on the problems caused by drugs and alcohol. Here, the word *addict* will be reserved for people who abuse chemicals.

The only reason for further discussion of process addiction versus addiction to substances is that some experts believe there is no physiological basis whatever to any addiction. They argue that all dependencies, even those to chemicals, are essentially psychological. They refuse, therefore, to call addiction a disease.

In a controversial book called *The Truth about Addiction and Recovery*, Stanton Peele, Ph.D., and Archie Bro[dsky] to put three provocative bullets on the cover: "Why alcoho[l] [a]buse, smoking, over-eating, and other addictions are n[ot] Why Twelve Step programs are *not* the only answer. How [re]cover *without* treatment." Inside, they make this stateme[nt: W]e] do not regard addiction of any kind as a disease. Th[ey do n]ot recommend that you see a doctor or join a twelve-ste[p] ganized for one disease or another as a way of dealing with addiction."[1]

Peele and Brodsky go further, disputing the very nature of addictive drugs and chemicals: "In reality, no drug is addictive in and of itself. Rather, drugs have characteristics that make them addictive for some individuals and groups at particular places and times. Their addictiveness depends on how they are perceived and how and why they are used and by whom."[2]

Even nicotine gets an undeserved whitewash: "Nothing about tobacco's reliably stimulating effects is inherently addictive; the reliance on these effects must be acquired over time."[3]

∼

Hence we begin this topic by wading into a messy swamp of controversy. Experts don't agree on whether addiction is physical or psychological. They don't agree on whether it's one problem or many. They don't agree on the nature of addictive substances. They certainly don't agree on how to fix it.

Fortunately for the layperson seeking to educate himself on the nature of addiction, the dissenting opinions mentioned above are in a minority. The great weight of anatomical research and medical opinion is in agreement that addiction *is* a disease and that the following facts apply:

1. All addictions, whether chemical or process, include strong psychological elements.
2. A rush of endorphins and other "feel good" neurotransmitters can accompany compulsive behaviors that don't involve outside chemicals.
3. Some addictive chemicals alter the user's ability to think rationally; others don't.
4. Certain chemical addictions—to alcohol, for instance—occur because of the individual's own genetic predisposition. On the other hand, some people have genetic aberrations that actually protect them from chemicals like nicotine.
5. Most addictive chemicals alter the body's basic physiology in some significant way.
6. Addiction to most chemicals is not instantaneous. It takes repeated use—always uncertain how much—to bring about full-blown addiction.
7. Even addictions that alter the individual's capacity for rational thought can be treated successfully with psychological and other methods.

All these points will be discussed in detail later in the chapter.

~

But first, let's stop for a quick discussion of nicotine. Since smoking is not an inciting activity—smokers don't become abusive, or steal to support their habit, or kill people with their cars—smokers don't end up in jail or prison. Consequently, we are not making cigarettes or smoking a focus of this book. Society has no serious desire to punish smokers, although there is increasing legislation aimed at limiting their activities. (The same tolerance does not exist for tobacco companies.)

However, the topic needs to be discussed, because both therapists and laypeople frequently compare nicotine addiction to all other chemical addictions. They draw unwarranted conclusions that all can be treated alike—labeling smoking as just another form of chemical addiction.

Well, it is, and it isn't.

In the first place, smoking is one of the most dangerous of all addictions, ultimately killing more people than all the illegal forms of substance abuse combined. Statistically, cigarettes have proved so lethal it would make sense to ban them above all other substances. Yet because smoking is mainly a private affair—until the smoke or the medical bills start to mount—the smoker endures only slight social stigma. Until the last decade, smokers enjoyed a fairly high level of public tolerance.

Adding to the health menace of cigarettes, nicotine is conceded to be among the most addictive of all chemical substances. Anyone who intends to smoke and keeps at it will get hooked. It's not by accident that a number of tobacco moguls once cynically endeavored to increase the nicotine content of their cigarettes, knowing that the more nicotine per puff, the greater the addiction, and the fewer smokers who would escape.

We maintain that tobacco *is* inherently addictive. No scientific evidence could be stronger than this cold-blooded, profit-motivated conspiracy to use the addictive power of nicotine to enslave the consumers of the product.

Yet, alone among addicts, a majority of smokers who manage to escape the grip of nicotine do so without support groups, counseling, or AA. It was newspaper columnist Russell Baker who said, "To give up smoking, you quit smoking."

It's seldom easy and generally requires great willpower, but somehow millions of Americans have given up cigarettes with little or no outside help. Their success at quitting seems to be related to the strength of their resolve and their belief that stopping is necessary.

So why can they quit without outside help while other addicts can't?

Let's analyze it. Unlike other addicts (assuming for the moment these are separate groups), smokers don't suffer altered perceptions from nicotine. No matter how many packs they consume a day, smokers are able to work and function—and *think*. Their reasoning isn't disrupted, nor their ability to think logically. Since smoking doesn't turn people into antisocial misfits (or out-and-out monsters), they don't lose their friends, their marital partners, their social networks. Few wives have ever said, "I'm leaving him because he smokes."

When he finally decides to quit, the smoker has an arsenal of weapons to call on—his friends, his spouse, his willpower, his maturity, and the unimpaired use of his brain.

A last characteristic that makes nicotine addiction unique is the ex-smoker's gradual distancing from any desire to resume his habit. Given enough years, the compulsion disappears, and it's often said there's no one more turned off by the unattractive aspects of smoking than an ex-smoker.

∼

As a final interesting note on the role of genetics in nicotine addiction, the National Institute on Drug Abuse (NIDA) has found that some people carry genes that actually protect them from such addiction. An enzyme called CYP2A6 is responsible for metabolizing nicotine in the body. For those people who have defects in the genes that produce CYP2A6, smoking never becomes a pleasant experience. Nicotine is so poorly metabolized that they continue to experience the beginner's nausea and dizziness. Dr. Edward Sellers and co-investigator Dr. Rachel Tyndale of the University of Toronto conclude, "Three different gene types, or alleles, for CYP2A6 have been identified by previous research. . . . We've calculated that the frequency of defective alleles that we've found would be protecting about 7 million North Americans from becoming smokers."[4]

∼

Alcohol. Cocaine. Heroin. Opium. Methamphetamine. These are the drugs that disrupt individuals—and the rest of society—so severely that law enforcement officials, the courts, and disturbed neighbors and acquaintances demand that the user be punished.

Alcohol and other mind-altering substances are not at all like nicotine—beyond the fact that all are addictive. Yet it is important to stop here and analyze alcohol separately, for among all the mind-altering chemicals, alcohol is unique in that it is immensely harmful to some people, somewhat harmful to others, and no problem at all to the great majority of users. In the book *Under the Influence* by Dr. James R. Milam and Katherine Ketcham, alcohol is called a *selectively addicting drug*.[5]

Here is where the "disease" issue arises. In the case of alcoholism, at least, 10 percent of the population carry genes which guarantee that, if they consume alcohol, they will eventually become full-blown alcoholics.

Scientists expect that gene-mapping of susceptible newborns will someday become routine, and individuals will know whether they are carrying genes that put them at risk for various diseases. But for now, prediction of a child's susceptibility to diseases like alcoholism is generally done only by looking at the child's biological family. If a mother and father are both confirmed alcoholics, their offspring will probably have the same problem—just as we can expect two blond, blue-eyed parents to produce blond, blue-eyed children.

That some people have genetically different reactions to alcohol is no longer open to debate. Though popular counselors like Dr. Laura Schlesinger insist alcoholism isn't an addiction but "a matter of character," scientific studies have confirmed otherwise. Not only has statistical data been collected from observations of identical twins raised in different households, but more elemental studies have been made of laboratory rats—and even probes into the genetic material itself.

Biologists who have studied the disease at the molecular level are able to describe what happens to the cells of the alcoholic-prone person. Unlike most people, the alcoholic has a liver enzyme abnormality that forces other cells to adapt and accommodate to alcohol in ways that are unique. This very accommodation becomes, at first, a positive attribute for the drinker. Unlike his friends, the potential alcoholic seems able to consume great quantities of the stuff with little outward effect.

In the beginning stages of their disease, alcoholic mothers like Mike Carona's, for instance, can consume large daily doses and still get up with their children each day, make them breakfast, and greet them after school. Families can be aware that a certain member is consuming more alcohol than seems reasonable but fail to observe any outward changes, such as slurring of speech, staggering, or other signs of drunkenness. It's drinkers like these who traditionally boast, "Don't worry about me. I can hold my liquor," and who can go on drinking, seemingly unaffected, when anyone else would be staggering, fall-down drunk.

Experts in the field know enough to be wary of the man who brags about his enormous capacity for alcohol, because they understand all too well there will come a day—maybe months, maybe years away—when his every move will be dictated by the drug.

In chapters 4, 5, and 6 of *Under the Influence*, Milam and Ketcham describe in great detail what happens in the liver and cells of the true alcoholic. The process is too complicated and detailed to include here, except to confirm that the genetic alcoholic's unique cellular accommodation to alcohol is the *cause* of his becoming an alcoholic, not the result of too much drinking.

Studies have shown that most children of alcoholic parents inherit their parents' liver cell malfunction and are unable to process alcohol normally. This deficiency is observed in children who have previously never drunk alcohol—which seems to confirm the authors' thesis that abnormal cell functioning causes at least some instances of alcoholism, rather than the other way around.

As the alcoholic's disease progresses, he soon loses his ability to function without the drug. Thus, the true alcoholic manages better on a high blood alcohol level (BAL) than he does when his BAL starts coming down. By the time his disease is advanced, the alcoholic has learned that if he intends to drive home, for instance, he'd better have a last "drink for the road," because all the normal signs of drunkenness will appear *after* his BAL starts to drop. Only then will he become dizzy, slurred, irrational, and uncoordinated.

Eventually the genetic alcoholic will drink more and more—because he absolutely must in order to feel normal. Without liquor he will shake, sweat, and feel sick to his stomach. But the more he drinks to overcome these unpleasant symptoms, the worse he feels when he stops. And so the problem escalates. For all these increasingly un-comfortable feelings, the only "cure" is more alcohol.

An alcoholic's impact on his family is nearly always devastating. Added to the physical damage caused by the drug are the psychological by-products within the family: anger, suspicion, feelings of help-lessness, fear, and finally estrangement.

⌒

Unlike Kirk, my mom never went to jail, nor did she go to a rehabilitation facility. It wasn't fashionable back then. In fact, it wasn't customary in the late 1950s and early 1960s to even talk about your family problems, especially outside the home. Most of us were still programmed to believe in Ozzie and Harriet, Leave It to Beaver, *and* Father Knows Best. *But in the Carona household we did have our problems.*

My dad was a hardworking mechanic who eventually became a garage foreman. Pop always held two or three jobs, and the combination of those incomes allowed us to have a small home, a car, and food on the table—but not a great deal of what we now call discretionary income or what Pop called "walking around money." There certainly wasn't the extra cash to pay for Mom's increasing alcohol habit.

And so my mom and dad fought constantly about her drinking. From as early as I can remember, they fought. Looking back on it, my dad hated my mother's drinking for two reasons. First, he was watching a woman he truly loved destroy herself with alcohol, and he was a blue-collar guy who had no idea how to help her—and being helpless didn't sit well with him.

So he did what he did in the garage when his mechanics slacked off—he yelled. Pop raised yelling to a whole new art form. He always seemed able to snap people into shape with the power of his voice. Mechanics. Me. But not my mom. Pop could scare the hell out of just about anyone. But no matter how loud or long he hollered, he couldn't change my mother's addiction.

The second reason my father hated my mother's alcoholism was what it was costing our family financially. With all his extra jobs, we weren't getting ahead. As my mother's drinking grew worse, she began impacting the family budget. When Pop wouldn't give her money for booze, she found creative ways to finance it—like not paying the electric or gas bill for a couple of months, or skipping a house payment.

My dad was a proud man and didn't like being embarrassed. He was mortified by my mother's drinking and humiliated when he got notices that the gas or electricity was going to be turned off.

How often did I watch my dad search the house for my mother's hidden bottles of scotch and then unceremoniously pour them down the drain or break them in the trash can. Pop yelling, my mom crying; it was quite the impressive ritual. Every three or four months it started over. My dad would get pushed to his limits and the ritual would begin. But no matter how he fought to save her, no matter how many bottles he discovered and destroyed, no matter how many times my mom promised to stop, nothing worked. M.C.

⁓

Extreme selfishness is a hallmark of addiction. Nowhere do we see this trait more graphically displayed than in the alcoholic, who all too often preys on family members by exploiting their sympathy. It is one of the sad truisms that the more his relatives hover nearby, ready to fly to his side, the more selfish the alcoholic becomes. The following story illustrates a typical drunken episode, self-centered from start to finish.

⁓

For my son Kirk, his most recent binge served as a shock—and a stronger wake-up call than any I could have delivered. With money we'd given him for a motel, he chose instead to buy pitcher after pitcher of beer and ignore his need to sleep. "I wanted to stop drinking," he says, "but I just couldn't."

He has no idea when or how he finally stopped. He just remembers he blacked out, and sometime in the middle of the night he came to and found himself sitting in an unfamiliar car. He hadn't an inkling about how he got there or what he might have done in the interval between the last beer and his entry into a stranger's car. His ID and backpack were gone, both hopelessly beyond reach of his memory. Since three days earlier he'd left a mandated stay at a halfway house and was now wanted by the police, we could only imagine how fast he must have scrambled out of that unfamiliar car.

The blackout was over by the time he reached our house, at 3:30 in the morning. But he was good and scared—about as scared as we were, wakened by the doorbell at such an ungodly hour.

I opened the door cautiously and there he was, bleary-eyed and disheveled. And not for the first time. We'd had all too many of these sloshed, middle-of-the-night appearances. Like a lost child, Kirk always struggled to get home. But he was hardly a child anymore; he was almost thirty-nine!

Kirk was aware that he was waking us before dawn, but as usual he didn't mind.

"Kirk!" I cried, "I thought we gave you money for a motel."

He looked sheepish, admitting he never got there. When I asked what he'd used the money for he said, "Uh—beer. But not all of it. I still have twenty dollars left."

He asked for food and a place to sleep. I looked him over and felt terrible; he was still my son. Yet I didn't want him and his unpredictable behavior at large in our house. Over the years we'd taken a beating, letting him in drunk. Once inside, he was a firecracker with a lit fuse; we never knew what would happen next. At times the fuse merely fizzled out. Other times he exploded, swearing savagely as he advanced on us with clenched fists. There was simply no way to gauge his behavior. Furthermore, he'd been known to help himself to our liquor and our money.

"I'll find you some bedding," I said. "You can sleep on the lawn."

As he settled onto the front stoop, I said, "Your timing couldn't be worse," and reminded him that in a few hours we'd be hosting our grandson's wedding reception in the backyard.

I doubt he even heard me. To him, our noon wedding was just an abstraction, nothing he could relate to. He was occupied with himself, with how he felt.

As I stood there talking with him, the sprinklers in the adjacent rose garden came on. I'd never seen them before; I was never up at that hour.

While he waited on the stoop, I brought him blankets and a pillow and a towel to spread on the grass. I warmed a can of soup and made a bag of *popcorn. He took it all and stood up, suddenly staring down at his pants. "I'm wet!" he cried. "Those sprinklers got me wet!"*

I thought, You sat right there with water spraying your pants, and you didn't notice?

He shuffled off the porch and I went back to bed and tried to sleep.

A joke. Sleep was now impossible.

Twenty minutes later I got up again and talked Kirk into letting me take him back to jail. By now, the police were almost certainly looking for him. "Better than being picked up with new charges," I said, and he agreed. But that was our last rational moment together.

Minutes later he changed his mind and I found myself chasing him down the street in my nightie, calling into the night, "Please, Kirk, come back! You promised." Then I was driving him to jail, blackmailed on the way into stopping for "one last beer." Without it, he said, he wouldn't go. Another change of mind and he'd jumped out of the car and I was pursuing him down the empty streets of Santa Ana, shouting entreaties out the window. "Kirk! Kirk! Get back in the car!" Eventually I left him near— but not in— the jail. I felt an utter fool.

Yet it wasn't over. As we arrived home from church shortly after noon, to my astonishment Kirk came staggering out of our house, sober from a seven-mile trek, but as disheveled as the worst-looking bum in a Western movie. He refused to stay and get cleaned up. "You can take a nap," I offered, but he drifted away and down our street.

Luckily, the wedding guests never knew about the day's underlying drama. My daughter, son, and brother— three humane people— left the festivities to go find him and drove slowly behind him as he wandered aimlessly down a nearby road. But instead of stopping to talk to him, they called the police. "For his own good," they said. I disagreed violently.

As it turned out, they were right and I was wrong.

Kirk's trip back to jail in the squad car of a decent police officer was a relief, which he admitted to us later. "I couldn't have gone back on my own—I know that now." M. W.

~

In the advanced stage of alcoholism, blackouts are common. The inebriate wakes up to find himself in a strange place doing something he has no memory of starting—like driving a hundred miles an hour down an unfamiliar freeway. It's bound to be a scary moment, waking up to find you've been operating a car virtually unconscious. Luckily or unluckily, blackouts are mostly reserved for the true alcoholic. At that level of alcohol consumption, the nonalcoholic with normal genes passes out, physically unable to do anything.

The following illustrates what happens when blackouts become an everyday occurrence.

~

As my mother's addiction to alcohol continued to worsen, it became a terrifying experience for me and for her. The blackouts were the first really noticeable change in her behavior. In the beginning I remember thinking she was joking around with me the way most "normal" parents play with their kids. She would wake up in the morning and begin cooking dinner instead of breakfast or would walk out to her car in her bathrobe and tell me she was going grocery shopping. The first couple of times it was funny, and even she laughed, no doubt to cover her embarrassment. But as these blackouts and other strange acts continued and became more frequent, it stopped being funny and became a child's nightmare.

Her behavior went from odd to downright bizarre. My mom would wake up at 1 or 2 A.M. and start making breakfast. She would come into my room at midnight and get me up for school. Before she died, I remember worrying each night as I went to bed about what she was going to do that night. It was literally a Dr. Jekyll and Mr. Hyde routine. I couldn't understand how this wonderful woman who could be so loving during the day could, as a result of her drinking, become this zombielike creature who didn't know whether it was morning or night, a weekday or a weekend, or, most devastating, didn't even know whether I was her son.

While the blackouts and aberrant behavior both disgusted and frightened me, what I remember most vividly just before my mother died were her seizures. Now, I am not a doctor and I can't be sure whether the alcohol abuse caused her seizures or whether the alcohol simply masked a different medical problem. What I do know is, during the last year of her life, as her drinking increased, the seizures began.

At first they happened late in the afternoon when she was well into her daily fifth of scotch and six-pack of beer. Then the seizures started happening late at night. My dad worked nights, and I remember being scared that I had to be alone in the house with her. I didn't know what she'd be like when the shaking ended, had no idea how she'd behave. I never knew whether she'd survive one more episode, or if this would be the one that would take her life. I remember being terrified that the alcohol was going to kill her and I would have to grow up without my mom.

It did and I did. M. C.

~

And so we see from the above illustrations what must be typical drunken scenarios: the bizarre waltz of the alcoholic and the enablers that deal with him.

As for the alcoholic who's in the blackout stage and getting worse, his blood pressure goes up alarmingly and he feels increasingly depressed. Forgetfulness, an increased risk of accidents, a vulnerability to heart problems, pneumonia, and liver damage all accompany the final stages of the disease. True alcoholics die, on average, ten to twelve years earlier than nonalcoholics.

These are the drinkers that AA targets with the message that abstinence is the only road back to health. Everyone in AA knows that a real alcoholic can never pull back and drink like everyone else; moderate drinking is simply not built into his or her genes. Thus when certain authors imply that a diagnosed alcoholic can, by altering his outlook, revert to a limited intake like everyone else, they overlook or deny the very real biological component to addiction. Such people are born different genetically, and their body's unique response to alcohol remains an anomaly they can never overcome. The brown-eyed alcoholic might just as well wish for blue eyes!

~

Authors Milam and Ketcham describe a category of heavy drinkers for whom moderation may be possible, a group known as the *problem drinkers*. This category would probably include most of the college students who get wildly drunk at parties and on weekends, but have no trouble staying sober when they need to study. Since their cells respond normally and don't accommodate well to above-average quantities of alcohol, these individuals are not doomed to an ever-escalating dance-macabre with liquor. Problem drinkers can benefit from AA meetings, but when they become focused on issues more important to them than drinking, their interest in alcohol fades.

For the great majority of people, drinking is of only passing interest, a take-it-or-leave-it activity reserved for social occasions. It has been our observation that nonalcoholics gradually lose interest in drinking as they get older.

~

The last group of addictive substances, which virtually no one handles well, would include cocaine, heroin, morphine, opium, and methamphetamine (or "speed"). Yet even among these highly addictive drugs, human reaction varies from one substance to the next. Heroin, for instance, is addictive for almost 100 percent of its users—morphine for 70 percent.

Cocaine—once considered nonaddictive, and even included in small amounts in original colas—produces an intense, hyperalert high. Cocaine leaves the user with an exaggerated sense of exhilaration and power and the illusion that he is invincible and can do anything—work for days on end and go without sleep or food or relaxation.

To illustrate how cocaine incites the brain, Dr. Jeffrey Fortuna, a professor of pharmacology at California State College, Fullerton, describes the effects of various stimuli on the brain's pleasure center. While at rest—awake but not stimulated—the pleasure center fires at 3 electrical impulses per minute. Stimulated by music, the rate rises to 15 impulses per second—a three-hundred-fold increase. With cocaine, the rate is 210 impulses a second! Even such exhilarating activities as downhill skiing, estimated to produce 30 impulses per second, and skydiving, at 45, cannot come close to duplicating the rush produced by cocaine.

Business executives and artists often use cocaine to sharpen their brains and increase their productivity. They get fooled into thinking such use is harmless, since they experience no withdrawal symptoms when they stop. Yet the human body cannot take such a high level of stimulation for long, and more doses are needed to sustain these exaggerated feelings. The "crash" inevitably comes.

Addicts less interested in being productive or creative combine cocaine with alcohol, claiming they need to "mellow out" from the fierce stimulation of coke. As the drug begins to wear off, the cocaine user becomes agitated and nervous and quick to take affront. With cocaine, anger is always right near the surface, ready to make the user explode.

Few of us will ever know which notorious crimes, exactly, were caused by cocaine rages. But when we hear rumors that a celebrity-turned-murderer was known to have used cocaine, it's reasonable to guess that cocaine entered the picture at just the wrong time.

After a several-day binge, the cocaine user finally collapses into a deep, numbing sleep that lasts far longer than seems reasonable. In the absence of other explanations, episodes of abnormally deep and uninterrupted sleep—sometimes for as long as two or three days—should alert others that the individual may be coming down from an intense cocaine high.

For addicts trying to escape dependence on this profound, artificial stimulus, Dr. Fortuna suggests filling the void with natural, athletic highs that can't do any harm.

～

Heroin and opium produce quite different responses in the human body. A large injection of heroin sends the user into an immediate comatose-like state, where he nods off as though in a trance. The owner of a business describes a female employee, later discovered to be a heroin addict: "Sometimes we'd see the girl just standing at the Xerox machine with her eyes closed, like a zombie. Or sitting at her desk strangely upright, yet with the appearance of nodding off. We had no idea what on earth was wrong with her. But something was. When we found out she'd been using heroin, we couldn't understand how she could be in such a trance—seemingly asleep—without falling over."

Opium, once smoked by nearly a third of the male population of China, produces lethargy and dull-wittedness. Both heroin and opium depress the breathing and heart rates, and an overdose shuts down the respiratory system and becomes lethal.

~

Of all the mind-altering substances available to the addictive-prone personality, many experts believe methamphetamine, or "speed," is the worst—the most damaging, long run, to the nervous system and brain.

Abusers on meth exhibit a number of easily identified symptoms. The drugs give them hot flashes, and they constantly complain about the heat. They sometimes vomit. Their skin is pale and they sniff frequently. Their noses change and become distorted, with one nostril turning noticeably larger. Unable to sit still, they fidget restlessly, jiggling their knees up and down.

Worse by far, though, are the effects on the nervous symptom. Meth has the power to alter pathways in the brain, sending aberrational messages to the user. An individual on meth sees people or animals that aren't there, and he has irrational fears that others are out to get him. He becomes paranoid in the extreme—and thus dangerous. If you believe you're under attack by malevolent forces, you feel justified in fighting back.

The scariest aspect of meth is that its effects wear off slowly and can last far beyond the last use, sometimes for years. The brain's altered perceptions and the user's paranoia become a semifixed part of the personality, so that every new human encounter is seen through the dark lens of fear and suspicion.

The stories of two young men from the same neighborhood in Southern California illustrate the capacity of meth to inflict permanent, devastating harm.

~

Long before the "drug scene" really hit California, a young teenager from a well-known Orange County family went to Hawaii and used some kind of meth-like drug and disappeared. For at least a year the devastated family searched for him, in vain. The father went to Hawaii and could find no trace. With no clues to the teen's whereabouts, the family could do nothing except sit at home and wait.

Several years later, the son showed up. Even as the community rushed to offer congratulations, the family retreated into glum silence. Their reclaimed son had changed into someone they didn't recognize. Once an outgoing young man with a wry, appealing personality, he was now withdrawn and strange. His eating habits were bizarre and he preferred to sleep on the floor. He wouldn't communicate. His few words were erratic and made no sense. He spooked easily. He was so altered, in fact, that the family soon realized he had scant hope of living a normal life.

Indeed, from then on, the son either lived in a state-run facility or escaped from time to time to wander the streets aimlessly. Some unknown form of speed had taken away his life.

Additional details about how methamphetamine affects human behavior serve to fill out a story begun in chapter 1.

Now, nearly four years later, my husband and I have been unable to convince our son that the gun-wielding people he saw on the rooftops near his little house in Oregon were not real. Kirk still believes there is an organized gang waiting in that town to kill him.

Under the influence of methamphetamine, Kirk was wilder, angrier, more irrational, and more fearful than at any other time in his life. His calls home were frequent and hysterical. Sometimes he was terrified, sometimes rabidly angry. But the calls served no useful purpose, because he was unable to process anything we said.

In a short three-week period he sold or destroyed all the furniture and appliances we'd bought him over a period of fifteen years—things he really cared about. He even damaged his own house, hacking at the supporting beams with a sledgehammer.

When at last we brought him home, he hadn't enough possessions left to fill the back of a station wagon.

Yet Kirk has not yet forgiven us for discounting his tales of being under siege. M. W.

~

People working in the field acknowledge that methamphetamine presents a unique problem. Bill Ritter, district attorney of Colorado, says, "The programs for successfully treating meth have to be longer than for cocaine or heroin, because of the time it takes to rewire. You need to get the circuits in place where they're functioning appropriately.

"There are people who take a dim view of meth addiction treatment. Others are more hopeful. Yet even these people say a different program is needed because of the short-term damage that it does to the function of the brain."

~

How does drug abuse begin?

Researchers believe that most addicts are introduced to drugs by a friend in a social context. It isn't the pusher on the street corner who makes the first approach, but the buddy who offers a joint, a drink, or a sniff. Nor does the naïve youth typically feel any menace in that first offer. Trying the drug seems like a harmless act, a titillating adventure shared between friends.

A sampling of addict autobiographies from a men's diversion center in Virginia clearly reveals such a pattern. Each of the youths started life in a home where he was cherished by one or more people. One young man writes, and these are his exact words:

"As I remember, my mother and father took very good care of us; we never wanted for anything. My father always taught us to work and always put some money away."

He describes his jobs, his marriage, the death of his wife, and being left with four children to raise.

"Then one day, I met a girl named Sheilda W. She introduced me to cocaine, and I was curious about how it made you feel. Now I regret it. None of my sisters and brothers used drugs and I wish today I'd never started."

Another young man describes his positive attitude toward school and then a high school job. His unusual spelling and unique "voice" have been left unedited:

"Everyone loved me. They call me little lover boy because I was a nice person and tried to help any and ever'body on my job. . . . . I use to jog every day until the day I was innerduce to getting high, then I started going out to house clubs and started hanging out in the street . . . letting myself be influence to do the wrong things, from selling to buying cocaine. . . . At the age of twenty-three I was in jail for the first time, didn't know what I was going to do. That's all I could think about, was how my mama felt and how she was going to be with me."

His autobiography ends with the statement "Friends didn't take me down; I took myself down by not listening and being disobedient."

~

All too many parents have learned, sadly and firsthand, that no neighborhood today, whatever its socioeconomic class, is immune from the scourge of drugs.

Kirk got his first marijuana from the boy next door, and his first cocaine across the street. This in an affluent neighborhood where most of the fathers are professionals and all their children are expected to go to college.

All the parents involved were caring people and over the years have remained close friends. No one is blaming anyone. For a few years the parents could only commiserate with each other, concerned and dismayed that within each family a son had managed to go astray. M. W.

In each of the above cases, the substance abuse began not because the teen had problems he was trying to escape, but because he became friendly with someone who was already using. In every case the addict was lucky enough to have one or more family members standing by—a mother, at least—who worried about what was happening.

~

However drug abuse begins, a user's reasons for continuing seem to be as diverse and complex as the people involved. For some, the first sniff of cocaine or the first encounter with heroin is so compelling, so exhilarating, that the newcomer is driven to repeat the experience over and over—ignorant of the fact that one's first highs can never be duplicated.

For many, psychological factors push the neophyte to continue using: the hurt child whose parents abused him physically or psychologically; the deeply bored teenager whose life is devoid of meaning; the insecure young person desperate to be as rich and important as the youths selling drugs in his neighborhood; the thrill-seeker; the inadequate adult who snorts coke because it's what the "in" people are doing. All these disturbed people have compelling reasons to continue.

Yet there are other, less-urgent syndromes: the relatively well-adjusted teen who sticks with drugs for no better reason than to be "cool" like his friends; the struggling student trying to escape the pressures of a high-achieving family and a blue-ribbon school system; the youth who simply finds it exhilarating to be "bad."

Sooner or later, a large percentage of the less-driven teens find their way back to normal, drug-free lives. Unfortunately, this doesn't happen for everybody.

Eventually the other two young men in our neighborhood overcame their addictions and are now leading normal, productive lives.

Sadly, only Kirk is not.

Parents like us are quick to send our kids to therapists and drug rehab centers. We talk to everyone in our desperate search for help—psychiatrists, counselors, defense attorneys, judges. . . . And then, after a while, we stop hiring lawyers and stop bailing the kid out of jail. We've heard too often that we're not helping—and we know for certain we're throwing away too much money.

Worst of all, we've lost our optimism. M. W.

What becomes of a drug abuser, once he's no longer a member of the family, but an outcast—an addict?

The answer is, he changes. He becomes part of an underworld of other users, taking on standards of behavior and codes of morality that once may have been utterly foreign to him. He becomes unrecognizable.

Seen through the eyes of traditional therapists, the confirmed drug user needs therapy that will root out all the sick, nasty things that have doubtless been going on for years in his psyche. The childhood traumas. The parent-child conflicts. The emotional deprivations.

But all too often there *is* no nasty thing—except the substance abuse itself. Drugs alone are enough to turn a relatively normal young person into a sick abuser.

Once an individual uses drugs for any length of time, once he spends repeated periods in jails and prisons, his morals, his value systems, his ethics, drop to a lowest common denominator. He becomes as compromised as the average criminal in jail. He steals, he lies, he cheats, he manipulates. He swears angrily over minor irritations. He scorns normal society and rails against unfair rules and the police and what he deems as a gestapo government. He is indistinguishable from all the other addicts in prison.

~

How do you know when your child is using drugs?

Often, you don't. The first signs are not what most people think. Parents aren't likely to see slurred speech or bizarre behavior or an altered personality—not in the beginning. These changes come later.

The first sign, from most young people, is a change in ethics. They sneak around. They lie. Their property disappears. They can't account for their money or time. They're always broke. They constantly need cash, and if the parents can't or won't supply it, the parents' money disappears.

Any parent should be suspicious when a child's grades inexplicably start to drop, when his enthusiasm for sports or his willingness to do homework takes a sudden dive, when his friends change and none of them want to be seen or known by anyone resembling a parent. Parents should start probing when they observe strange absences from home and even stranger explanations.

Families need to be aware that a child using drugs has a twenty-four-hour mission not to get caught. To stand a chance in the ongoing battle, parents must be willing to devote at least half as much energy and time to learning the truth.

~

However your loved one got into drugs, the end result after a number of years will always be the same, and it's one of the few generalizations that can be made about substance abuse: he will have profound psychological problems. Your drug-using son or daughter (or husband, wife, or parent) who uses for more than a short time will become altered and distorted, acquiring a host of undesirable personality traits. He will be hard to manage, immature, angry, deceitful, at times psychotic, and always teetering on the edge of a new disaster.

The point is, some people get into drugs because they have deep-rooted psychological problems, and others develop the problems *after* they begin using. But the end result is the same.

All longtime substance abusers have compromised values and ethics. All are in some ways sick. All are immature. It's inevitable. It goes with being an addict.

~

Immaturity. Some may wonder how it comes about and why childlike behavior is such an inevitable hallmark of serious drug abuse. Long recognized and understood by experts, the immaturity of the long-time drug abuser is a phenomenon only dimly grasped by the public.

The rule of thumb goes like this: at whatever age a young person begins abusing drugs, his maturation and psychological growth stop, and, like Peter Pan, he will remain that age indefinitely—until he's been clean and out in the world for a considerable period of time.

Any parent forced to deal with a long-addicted son or daughter has observed that the mere act of getting older does not bring maturity. The adult who began using as a teenager simply can't cope with adult chores. He's unable to maintain an orderly bank account; he has little sense of the importance or value of money and bounces checks without concern for the cost; he can't ration his time; he isn't sensitive to how he appears to others; he's unrealistic in his expectations of himself and those around him. Trying to solve the simplest problem frustrates him as it would a child.

This same immaturity is evident in addicted inmates all over the country.

~

A young woman in a women's diversion center at Capron, Virginia, spoke candidly about her life, including the fact that she'd supported her cocaine habit with prostitution and finally got caught when she sold cocaine to an informant. For that, she went to jail. She was actually relieved when the police came and kicked in her door. She greeted the officers with, "Here I am." She says now, "Not once did I get mad. I was finally tired of living that lifestyle. My chest started hurting. I could hardly breathe. It was really getting on my nerves."

She spent five months in the Roanoke city jail and didn't mind at all. "I needed the rest. I needed to gain weight and get myself together."

When queried about her family, she admitted she had four children, though she hardly looked twenty herself. The problem of her children didn't seem to weigh on her. Asked who was keeping them, she said vaguely, "My aunt. And my mother-in-law." Then she added, "I'm not sure I can handle the kids. I can't take stress. They're probably in a better place."

Although she acknowledged receiving drug treatment in several different places, none seemed to "take." "I wasn't focused then. I was thinking about my boyfriend—and trying to stay clean." Now she keeps track of former treatment centers by tying each to a different pregnancy. Still, she kept relapsing. "I didn't take any of them seriously. I thought I could do it on my own." Besides, she noted, there was always that recurring problem. "I just kept popping up pregnant."

~

In the Orange County jail, deputies are confronted daily with immature addicts who have scant awareness of what they've been doing. After a few days in jail, mothers sober up and become extremely remorseful when they realize they've sold their children's clothes for money to buy drugs.

~

According to Dawn Mejstrick, a supervisor in the drug court of Norfolk, Virginia, drug-induced immaturity is an expected phenomenon and can be likened to the automatic, unreasoned responses of a newborn baby. As drugs increasingly become the user's way of coping—his response to stress and his means of solving problems—he fails to learn other problem-solving strategies. He never wrestles with innovative solutions, doesn't figure out any of the coping skills that the rest of us take for granted.

Furthermore, his altered brain and nervous system compound the problem. In the addict's brain—as in everyone else's—reactions and responses to stimuli and stress become conditioned, and thus automatic. Habitual reactions are imprinted in the brain and the individual gives them no conscious thought. Thus, the addict's brain quickly accommodates to drugs as a means of resolving stress. At the first sign of anxiety, his brain demands relief. And the only relief it recognizes is oblivion, a blurring of the problem with some kind of feel-good substance.

Mejstrick points out that every stage of human development—whether it is learning to walk, talk, or face the first day of school—has its uncomfortable period when the individual feels insecure and ill at ease. I'm not good at this, he thinks. But the normal child quickly perceives that the new activity can be conquered with coping skills he's used before. He adjusts and gains a feeling of mastery. Then he moves on to the next phase.

In the case of the habitual abuser, all such learning ceases. Whatever new, adult problems the addict faces, he no longer goes through the usual steps of unease, problem solving, mastery, and success. He simply cannot tolerate uncertainty or the uncomfortable feelings that go with it. Instead, he falls back on substances that will make the discomfort go away.

Not only do new coping skills fail to develop but old ones are soon lost. For the addict, delayed gratification is no longer possible. He must solve his problem now. This minute. And thanks to a blurring of mental faculties, he forgets the downside of drug use and won't allow himself to look at the consequences—which is one reason why longer and longer jail sentences are so ineffective at deterring the longtime drug abuser. The man who's out there trying to buy relief on the streets is not weighing his options. He isn't thinking to himself, This time my prison sentence will be two years instead of one. He isn't looking ahead at all. Instead, his subconscious is telling him, "I will die if I have to stay one minute longer in this pain."

And that's another of the bizarre reactions caused by the drug-distorted brain. To the abuser deprived of his usual means of relief, the simplest of life's problems looms so large as to seem insurmountable: "I can't stand going out to look for a job—what if I get turned down? My bicycle has a flat tire—I can't handle this; I'll never be able to get around. Now that I've lost my ID, where will I get a new one? I'm afraid I'll never find a place to live and I'll be out on the street."

All these worries, and more, are regularly voiced by inmates who call home from jail. The sober abuser becomes a monumental worry-wart, expressing the same fears over and over, taking scant comfort from any reassurances.

What few people realize is the extent of the addicted inmate's discomfort—that his anxieties cause him enough distress to seem unbearable. Even life-threatening. Were he on the outside, he would almost certainly relieve his apprehension in the only way he knows how: by using or drinking.

As Mejstrick says, "Addiction works. It reinforces itself over and over. It becomes its own incentive for repeat behavior."

～

Among the behaviors seen over and over in addicts is denial. They deny that their use of drugs is extreme or even abnormal. They deny that the drug has control over their behavior. ("I can quit anytime I want.") Some deny that there is anything wrong with their lives at all. As California substance abuse expert Nancy Clark says, "How many times do you need to get arrested before you connect the dots and realize you have a problem?"

Often, the first task faced by substance abuse counselors is to get the user to accept that yes, his use of drugs or alcohol is out of control and he is, indeed, addicted. Without this kind of acknowledgement, it is hard to begin treatment. How do you help an abuser who honestly believes no problem exists?

~

Everyone who deals with addicts has noted the compulsiveness that accompanies chronic addiction, how the addict will continue to seek and abuse drugs even after it's clear he will suffer terrible consequences. Drug use is, by its very nature, irrational and not governed by normal constraints.

Recovering addicts, looking back on their former behavior, invariably label themselves crazy, out of control. "I had to have it," said one. "I didn't care what happened to me. I didn't worry about getting thrown in prison. I didn't think about who I was hurting. I just had to get that one last hit."

~

Above all, addiction is a relapsing disease. Even after the addict is thoroughly convinced that he must change his behavior, his intense desire for drugs persists.

Dr. Barry Everett, a psychology professor at Cambridge University, in England, speaks of the "amazing property" of drugs like cocaine and methamphetamine to stimulate powerful responses to cues that were associated with using the drug. Like Pavlov's dog, the recovering addict is abnormally responsive to all the details that bring back memories of former highs—a restaurant or house where he used; seeing someone he habitually drank or used with; glimpsing the paraphernalia involved in his getting-high ritual; revisiting an old bar where he once got drunk.[6]

Dr. Jonathon Pollack, a program officer at the National Institute on Drug Abuse, talks about emotional memories, noting that they are the ones that remain with you the longest. Just as people remember what they were doing when the *Challenger* exploded, they also remember the elements that make up such highly pleasurable events as a wedding, or the small, sad details that surround a death.

Because intense emotion is tied to the event, it leaves a vivid imprint on the brain, and all the surrounding details are recalled, too, becoming an emotional memory that seems to operate outside conscious control.[7]

In the same way, addicts have imprinted on their brains the intense feelings associated with their highest highs—memories that are apt to return in certain circumstances and cause a renewal of old, intense cravings.

When he revisits old haunts, the user can experience such intense cravings that his desire to use again soars out of control. His mouth becomes dry. His heart rate accelerates. He anticipates how the drug will make him feel. Only a quick call to a sponsor, or attendance at a Twelve Step meeting, can turn him away from another sampling of his drug of choice.

It is well known that veterans who became addicted in Vietnam have high success rates in treatment because, in part, all the situations, places, and people associated with their drug use are now behind them. The veteran has almost none of the cues that once turned him toward addictive behavior.

On the other hand, an addict who must return to living in the same area where he once got high faces the dire threat of numerous relapses. Successful therapists are forced to take setbacks into consideration as they work with addicts, and not give up on or dismiss the user who at first can't stay clean for more than a short period.

The act of relapsing itself brings additional trauma: guilt. A recovered addict in Denver—a now-successful woman—says, "Every time an addict tries to quit and fails, when he gets back into his addiction, it's always worse because he's got so much guilt. God, I almost made it, I could have made it, my family thought I was going to make it, but I didn't, so on top of the using it's like, Oh God, I failed everybody, and it is always so much worse when you relapse. It always was for me and I think that's pretty common."

~

We know that mind-altering chemicals produce observable psychological changes in the user. We also know that alcoholism has a measurable genetic component. But what about other addicting substances? What changes, if any, do they produce in the brains and neurological pathways of the user?

For the experts who insist that addiction is a purely psychological problem and not a disease, there is a "must" article in the October 1998 issue of the *National Institute of Justice Journal:* "Addiction Is a Brain Disease—And It Matters," by Alan I. Leshner, Ph.D, director of the National Institute on Drug Abuse (NIDA). The journal's cover shows a picture of two actual brains—the brain of a nonaddict and that of a drug addict, as revealed by positron emission tomography (PET scan). These two photos offer convincing proof that an addict's brain is severely altered by addicting substances. Nobody who sees these pictures could deny that the brain of the substance abuser undergoes significant biological change.[8]

The article points out that dramatic advances over the past two decades in both the neurosciences and the behavioral sciences have revolutionized our understanding of drug abuse and addiction. Leshner says: "Drugs hijack the mind by hijacking the brain. Scientists have identified neural circuits that are involved in the actions of every known drug of abuse, and they have specified common pathways that are affected by almost all such drugs."[9]

Not only do the brains of addicted and nonaddicted people differ from one another, but all addicted people share some common elements, regardless of which drug they use.

Scientists have identified a single pathway deep within the brain called the mesolimbic reward system. It is this pathway that is affected, directly or indirectly, by all the drugs of abuse. The mesolimbic reward system functions as its name implies: it is responsible for the sensations of euphoria and pleasure that keep addicts coming back to the drug over and over.[10]

Researchers have learned that significant changes in the brain are produced by both long-term and short-term use of chemicals. While a brief, intense episode modifies brain function in important ways, longer-term use brings changes that last long after the user gives up his drugs. Scientists have seen the effects of long-term, chronic drug use at all levels: molecular, cellular, structural, and functional.

Some of these changes are peculiar to certain, specific drugs, while others are common to a great variety of drugs.

With so much information already documented in scientific journals, our knowledge of the physiological basis for addiction increases daily. In the September 16, 1999, issue of *The Orange County Register*, a large daily newspaper in Southern California, a banner headline proclaims, "Protein Buildup May Be Key to Addiction." William McCall of the Associated Press writes that the highly addictive property of cocaine may be due to a buildup in the brain of the long-lived protein called Delta-FosB. Research at the Yale School of Medicine suggests that this protein stimulates genes that intensify craving for the drug.

The casual cocaine user who doesn't consider himself "hooked" is nevertheless living dangerously. In experiments with mice, the Yale researchers learned that the protein isn't produced immediately, but starts to accumulate after the addict has used a number of times. Once the buildup starts, however, the craving for cocaine becomes so intense as to be nearly irresistible.

~

Since changes in the substance-abuser's brain are so marked and so readily verified, investigators in the field are convinced that drug abuse must be considered a brain disease.

Researchers believe that since addiction is a result of fundamental changes in brain function, the goal of treatment must be to reverse or compensate for those changes. Alan Leshner suggests that two routes are possible: medication or behavioral treatments. He notes that behavioral treatment has effectively altered brain function in other psychobiological disorders.

Unfortunately, the brain-disease aspect of addiction is not widely known outside scientific circles. Historically, prosecutors and judges have focused only on the social or criminal justice aspects of chemical abuse, relying on jails or prisons to solve the problem. The results have been worse than dismal.

As Leshner notes in his conclusion, "If the brain is the core of the problem, attending to it needs to be a core part of the solution."

⌣

It's fortunate for the naïve beginner that full-blown brain disease doesn't develop immediately. Since using drugs is initially a voluntary behavior, the beginning user has a momentary choice in whether to continue—what amounts to a second chance. But after a certain period, when the brain becomes altered, perhaps because of the added protein, a kind of "metaphorical switch" is thrown and the abuser no longer exercises control over his habit.

The problem is, nobody knows exactly when this will happen. How many "free" episodes does the user get? Two? Three? A couple of dozen? When does the beginner reach the point of no return?

Unfortunately, we can't say; it's different with everybody. Only one thing is certain: the person who's experimenting with chemicals is playing Russian roulette with his brain. If he doesn't stop quickly, he will, without the slightest doubt, become hooked.

But which day?

The answer is—you'll know when you get there.

⌣

Anyone who has lived with an addict will recognize most of the signs and symptoms we've discussed. We offer these detailed explanations in the belief that it helps to know more about the *whys* of addictive behavior. We hope, as well, that in reading about these many faces of addiction, the suffering relatives will realize they're not alone.

⌣

To summarize: we now know that addictive substances are not all alike, either in the way they affect the abuser or in how difficult they are to overcome.

We've learned there is a leveling factor that occurs after longtime drug use, making all abusers in some ways alike: all addicts are—in the throes of their disease—immature, mentally sick, irrational, manipulative, angry, compulsive, full of denial, prone to relapse, and willing to compromise their ethics.

We know there are strong physiological aspects to addiction. Not only are some individuals genetically predisposed to becoming addicted to substances like alcohol, but nearly every consistent user of any addictive drug suffers significant, progressive changes in his brain.

It's as though we humans are given a short grace period to change our ways before an unseen switch is thrown. Yet there is always hope, even for the worst and most stubborn cases of addiction. As proof, we offer this ending to the story of Rich Pfeiffer, the hang gliding champion in the beginning of this chapter, whose addiction led him to armed robbery and a six-year prison sentence:

As it turned out, the championship qualities that had seen Rich Pfeiffer through other tests now came to the fore. In a prison setting nearly devoid of programs for rehabilitation, Pfeiffer sought out what little there was and attended all the AA and NA meetings he could find. He sent away for Bible-study courses and devoted himself to prayerful study.

Through all this, he endured the scorn of antagonistic prisoners— addicted peers who were resigned to the revolving door and thought him a fool. At one point, hearing that one of the guards was about to be murdered, he managed somehow to get the gun and turn it over to the authorities. For this, he suffered seven inmate attacks, some serious enough to send him to the prison hospital.

Meantime, his long sentence was being appealed. When his appeal was brought before the original judge, the man was disinclined even to hear it. But statements and evaluations from sympathetic guards and counselors who'd seen Pfeiffer's progress in jail persuaded the judge to change his mind.

It is ironic that the same judge now takes Rich Pfeiffer into local high schools to talk to teenagers about the dangers of drugs. He admits, "I was wrong in my initial assessment of you."

Pfeiffer's story has an incredible ending. Once out of prison, he returned to school, and though he began with only a high school diploma, he started junior college, and in three years he studied hard enough to complete the equivalent of seven years of school, finishing at Western State Law School with a law degree.

Yet his ordeal wasn't over. Although he passed the California Bar on his first attempt and immediately got a job, it took another two years of outstanding work in the public defender's office to convince the California Bar Association that he, an ex-felon, should be admitted.

Pfeiffer is now a panel attorney for the appellant defender's office and is married with a son. He is determined to give back to the society that allowed him a second chance, and so he volunteers with prison ministry groups to visit prison inmates. He also talks to first-time juvenile offenders in such Orange County programs as Short Stop.

Last year Pfeiffer won the Paul Bell Memorial Fellowship Award for Appellant Defenders, and he also won the Volunteers in Parole, Attorney of the Year award.

~

Rich Pfeiffer's story not only illustrates vividly what can be achieved when an addict makes an all-out effort to prevail over his drugs, but proves that help is available everywhere, even in the most dismal of prison settings. You just have to look for it.

In further chapters, as we explore a number of programs and facilities around the country that have had marked success in treating addicts, it will be evident that Rich Pfeiffer's remarkable story is only one of many.

CHAPTER FIVE

Resistant Addicts and Desperate Parents

Addicts come in two primary colors: those who want help and those who don't.

Those who don't were once considered hopeless. The conventional wisdom has always been that an addicted person who doesn't believe he's got a problem—or doesn't want to fix it—is a lost cause. Relatives of abusers have lived with this adage for years, hearing on every side that nothing could be done to help an addict who was unmotivated. Until the addict actively sought treatment, there was no point in worrying about him; you might just as well give up and get on with your life.

Experts now know the adage is false. Intense efforts currently being made in therapeutic communities, jails, prisons, and drug courts have proved that unmotivated people *can* be helped—probably as much as anyone else.

However, it's worth exploring some of the fallacies that have long governed the addiction problem, since all too many people are still living with them. Friends and relatives hear these myths from numerous sources, and their lives are being made miserable.

Along with the great surge of cocaine abuse that overwhelmed our country in the mid-1980s came a body of beliefs about the nature of addiction and what could and couldn't be done to reverse addiction's grip on the individual. The big phrase, the maxim that everyone threw around like the Golden Rule, was this: "An addict will never change until he hits bottom."

Nobody was ever able to say for certain what "bottom" really was, but everyone knew there was one—and that every addict had his own version of it. Apparently bottom meant an individual's limit on how much agony he could endure.

Along with the general belief that every addict has a point below which he won't go was the assumption that every user would eventually say to himself, I've had it. My life is hell. I can't take another second of this torture. From this moment on, I intend to change.

For many addicts, that's exactly what happens. Some get down on their knees and give themselves over to a higher power, and others simply admit their helplessness to themselves or others. In any event, when the moment comes, the tortured soul knows he's on the road to recovery and feels humbled enough to accept whatever outside help he can find.

Most recovering addicts are only too happy to share their stories of how they turned themselves around. They describe their former lives in lurid detail, bringing us to the moment when everything changed, when they did, indeed, hit bottom. Sometimes it involved waking up in a hospital bed, or hearing a loved one say good-bye forever, or being locked out of the house, or finding oneself in prison, or literally waking up in the gutter, with everything of value gone.

Unfortunately, these pivotal moments don't happen for everyone. Sometimes that day of awakening is unbearably slow in coming. And sometimes it never comes at all. Far too many addicts just go on using and abusing and suffering until there is nothing left of them. Until they die.

Anxious relatives of abusers can wait years to see the day of epiphany—all in vain. In the meantime they listen to endless well-meaning advice. They're told to be gutsy, to deny their natural instincts, to offer the victim "tough love." Translated, this means back away and let the addict learn from his mistakes. Give him nothing. No money. No shelter. No food . . . well, maybe a few coupons from the local hamburger joint. No legal help. And, from the extremists, no collect phone calls. At the end of all these negatives comes a final exhortation: let the addict know you love him.

The logic of this stance can be hard to fathom. How does an abuser find work when he has no address and no phone number? How does he get to the job with no transportation and no money for bus fare? How can he pass himself off as a hirable person when he has no change of clothes, no place to shower?

Let's play the scene the way it actually happens. "I'm ordering you out of the house, son. No, I won't give you any money. Not even for food. But here are a few chits for hamburgers. Don't ask me where you'll sleep—you'll have to figure that out. I can't help you get a job. It's not my problem. If you land in jail, don't call me. I want you out *now*. This minute. Oh. And by the way, I love you."

How much of this message does the addict actually hear? Well, certainly not the love part.

⁓

When we say the tough love message is everywhere, it is. From a recovering addict, now a successful businessman and one of my creative writing students, I heard the repeated theme that Kirk would never recover until he hit bottom.

I kept asking what kind of bottom he was talking about. I described all the bottoms Kirk had already hit: loss of family and friends; loss of all his possessions; a pin in his ankle from being hit by a car as he was buying drugs; a broken jaw, smashed by a methamphetamine freak; repeated jailings; long imprisonments. I suggested that the ultimate bottom still hadn't been reached. Death.

Could anything be done short of . . . that?

No, he said. Nothing could be done. Kirk had to reach the defining point by himself.

Even Kirk's well-meaning older brother said to me one day, "You know, Mom, you and Dad aren't helping Kirk. I hate to say this, but he will never get his life together until both of you are dead." M. W.

⁓

A few parents have actually been able to follow the harsh dictates of conventional wisdom, and we offer the following as an example of a mother's extraordinary vision of tough love.

The son of a well-to-do Orange County family was on drugs, so the mother threw him out of the house. He disappeared and she didn't hear from him. Months later she happened to be driving onto a freeway, and there was her son standing at the freeway on-ramp. She glanced at him and saw his arms waving madly in her direction, saw his lips moving and knew what he was saying. He was crying out to her, "Mom! Mom! Mom!"

She didn't stop the car or even acknowledge him. She just faced ahead and drove onto the freeway.

While the above represents an extreme, most parents find it nearly impossible to impose on their offspring the kind of harsh, unrelenting discipline that traditional addiction therapy demands. Few could hear this story without getting a lump in their throats.

Yet the proponents of tough love advise parents to do all this and more. They insist the child needs to suffer every consequence of his negative behavior—even if it includes going to jail.

I remember what a local friend and treatment counselor told us years ago: "Let Kirk land in jail, if that's what it takes. Let him stay there; don't bail him out. The sooner he learns these lessons, the sooner he'll get himself together. He needs to know there are consequences for what he does."

Well, he did go to jail. Then a few years later he went to state prison. Twice. By his own calculations, in recent years he's been incarcerated more than he's been out.

The shock value of being locked up has long since vanished. As far as we can tell, none of these sessions behind bars have accomplished a single positive thing. They've changed him profoundly—but in negative ways. He's angrier now. More apt to fly off the handle and swear, more inclined to use language heard only in army barracks. To our dismay, he's learned to accommodate to prison, has even become inured to it. He knows the ropes "inside." Like a gypsy child forced to exist on the streets, he's picked up the survival techniques that prison demands.

He's accommodated because he must, because those who remain soft, or God forbid, gentle, become the targets of those who don't. But now he is no longer civilized. M. W.

While long imprisonment is almost always damaging, there is something to be said for the shock value of a brief incarceration.

The emphasis here is on "brief." For the offender unaccustomed to harsh treatment and severe limitations of freedom, a few nights or a week in jail can be a dramatic wake-up call. A jail stay that's long enough to be frightening but not long enough to be hardening can be a positive experience, producing a lifelong impact. Many an inmate realizes clearly, after only a few days, that this is not an experience he wants to repeat, and he leaves determined to do what he must to stay out of jail.

Imprisoned for months or years, however, the inmate has no recourse but to accommodate and change until he becomes "one of them." Survival demands it. Thus do the Patty Hearsts metamorphose into armed robbers.

For the nonviolent offender who eventually gets out, none of the survival techniques acquired during long imprisonment are useful on the outside. None will help him be a better citizen. Alternately cowering and raging are not useful societal attitudes. Numbly acquiescing to authority, making no decisions whatever about your daily life, but always "watching your back," do not prepare anyone for holding a job. Pent-up hostility, constant suspicion, and a deep sense of personal worthlessness do not bode well for intimate relationships.

~

The resistant addict inevitably produces unhappy relatives. For many, there is a source of comfort available that has worked extraordinarily well: Al-Anon.

Here, in group meetings, friends and relatives of addicts learn how to cope. They learn that they are truly powerless over another's decisions and behaviors—and thus find ways to "let go." With help, they experience the serenity that comes from this knowledge—this acceptance. In Al-Anon, family members are given tools for the kind of tough love they can live with. They acquire attitudes and strategies that sustain them through repeated dealings—or non-dealings—with the sick member of their circle.

Many, many people who have needed Al-Anon and tried it, swear by it. Parents and spouses have said the group helped them extricate themselves from the addict's sick life. Thanks to Al-Anon, they were not only able to deal more effectively with the drug abuser, but were also helped to lead better lives of their own.

~

When it comes to treating resistant addicts, it's necessary to be realistic about what will work and what won't. In general, for this population programs need to be coercive. Noncoercive programs and voluntary halfway houses can't accomplish much with the abuser who doesn't think he's got a problem—or knows he does but isn't ready to change.

Few halfway houses are set up to be coercive. Except for court-ordered residents, attendance is voluntary. For a while the addict in such a setting may do fine, may even see the benefits of treatment. But all too often his commitment to stay is weaker than the pull of his drug of choice. Knowing he can leave at any time without punishment, the resistant addict is apt to snap and heed the siren call of chemicals.

Of necessity, most halfway houses have a zero tolerance for relapse. Halfway houses can't retain residents who fall back, even momentarily, into bad habits. For the sake of the other residents, the person who drinks or uses drugs must be evicted immediately. Thus, the relapsing aspect of the disease prevents the resistant addict from being there long.

An additional unworkable feature of many drug programs, whether voluntary or not, is the overloading of addicts with more treatment than their brains can handle. Even the best programs are apt to keep addicts sitting in a limited area for the better part of a day. We have observed some of these everlasting sessions and noticed the restlessness of the abusers. When they begin nodding off, it's safe to assume they're not getting much out of the leader's words.

It is our belief, both from personal observation and from comparing treatment centers to public schools, that few people can focus for hours on end without some kind of exercise. Certainly public schools learned long ago that students concentrate best if vigorous play—or exercise—is interspersed with study. This point will be discussed in more detail later.

Another questionable aspect of some programs is that they dispense the same message over and over, talking endlessly about the injurious aspects of drugs and alcohol, with few other messages. We hear this complaint constantly from addicts: "Discussing alcohol and drugs hour after hour just makes me want to drink and use."

For the resistant addict, programs are most effective if they address the broad range of problems that afflict him. By the time an abuser has lived his immature lifestyle for a number of years, he needs a wide spectrum of help—sessions that address his personal problems, his social adjustments, his job-getting skills, his anger, his criminal thinking, his guilt, his shattered ego, his abusive nature, his immaturity. He needs, among other things, life skills.

Such programs often fail the resistant addict at the front door. He is told to go out and get a job—as though that were a simple matter he could handle if only he "wanted to." Job searches are difficult for the best prepared among us. For the addict who has no skills, no resume, no maturity, no patience, and a shaky ego, landing a job can be nearly impossible. More than anything, the resistant addict needs handholding when it comes to his job search. He needs someone to help make calls, someone to pave the way and vouch for him.

And finally, the difficult addict needs continuing structure in his life, a strong aftercare program that follows him after he begins working.

Lucky for all of us, a number of workable programs are available for the addict who is ready to change.

Luckier still, an equal number of effective programs are out there for the substance abuser who has no intention whatever of changing.

CHAPTER SIX

Helping the Addict Who Wants Help

This chapter is about giving help to people who want it. The following story about a counselor named Smitty describes the kind of motivated candidate for whom AA and other Twelve Step programs and halfway houses were made.

The young blond man with the lazy eyes was working as a transition specialist in the Men's Diversion Center in Chesterfield, Virginia. During an interview, he admitted freely he was an ex-con. When asked what he'd done in his bad old days, he responded, "What didn't I do?"

It seemed that for years, from 1967 to 1990, Smitty was a confirmed heroin addict, in and out of penitentiaries. "I never just got jail," he says ruefully. "It was always the penitentiary." Finally, in the early 1980s, he was sentenced to an eighteen-month drug treatment program. The treatment was only partially successful. Two years out of the program and living clean, he fell into a classic trap. He decided he'd been good so long, he "deserved something." He started using heroin again, sporadically at first. When his monthly flirtations with drugs brought no immediate consequences, the pattern changed to weekly and then daily.

Typically, the world crashed in on him again, and he was caught and "violated" (a corrections term) and sentenced to another long stay in prison. Out once more, he decided that heroin was changing his body chemistry. "It wasn't taking me where I wanted to go." He thought to himself, Something's not working, and realized it was time to change his values and beliefs. From 1990 to 1992, he managed to stay clean.

Unfortunately, Smitty did not change his friends and it was they who became his final downfall. He says, "Old friends ridicule you when you try to succeed. The crew who is not doing well will accept anybody."

In early 1992, a young woman borrowed his car and used it to commit a crime. Though Smitty had no direct part in the offense, he was convicted again as an accomplice and sentenced to ten years in prison.

One day, in his prison cell, he had an epiphanous moment when he decided he'd had enough. He got down on his knees and prayed that his cravings would go away. Even now, years later, the look of amazement is still in his eyes when he adds, "And they did! You can't tell me prayer doesn't work."

For the rest of that prison sentence, five years and ten months, Smitty was offered drugs and easily refused them. But he never got used to the prison experience. Living behind bars gave him a feeling of worthlessness. He found the whole system degrading and dehumanizing, with no respect offered anywhere. "People treat you like objects. Like something on the shelf."

In the mid-nineties, still in prison, Smitty was given the opportunity to lecture clients at nearby diversion centers on transition life skills. He was very effective, a high-energy person with a strong message. When he was released, he was offered the job of full-time academic instructor at the Chesterfield Men's Diversion Center. He looks back on his old life as a horrendous learning experience, an example of change that he is committed to sharing with others. Among the courses he teaches, he offers a humorous analysis of addicts and the way they regard money, which he calls "The New Math." His essay on "The New Math" appears in a later chapter.

Smitty's new life as a treatment counselor still seems something of a miracle, even to him. Yet anyone meeting him would know he has put his old, addicted criminal life behind him—for as long as he attends to his recovery and stays clean.

~

As others have said in describing their willingness to change, Smitty was sick and tired of being sick and tired. He had hit his own personal bottom.

Other important reasons can motivate an addicted person to seek treatment. Among them is the threat of losing someone or something that is cherished: a spouse, children, a valued career, or even personal possessions. Generally, the more an addict has to lose, the more readily he will respond to treatment.

Another example of a counselor for whom trust in a higher power was essential can be found in a Virginia church.

At Bethany Church in Chesapeake, Virginia, counselor Byron Joyce works with addicts who come to the church program voluntarily or are mandated by local judges. An ex-felon himself, Joyce looks like a youthful Marlon Brando. Joyce has been clean since 1991, and he, too, credits his faith in a higher power for rescuing him. He says, "If we can change how we think, we can change how we behave."

He says of his early years, "I met the dragon when I was about thirteen," which was when his parents were separated and he joined a group of street boys with similar backgrounds, boys who called themselves The Airplanes. Progressing from minor theft to serious drug dealing, then to heavy drug use himself, Joyce's loyalty to the dragon brought him ever more serious trouble.

In and out of jail, he was finally convicted of felony cocaine possession. Joyce considers it divine intervention that a judge gave him supervised probation instead of prison, albeit with a number of strict provisions: frequent drug testing, NA and AA meetings, and living at home under his mother's curfew. When he began attending church, the dragon slowly lost ground.

Four years after his conviction, and now a dedicated Christian, Joyce began teaching children, hoping to save them from similar wasted lives. He says, "With all the powers that anointed men of God have to draw a congregation together, none have the power to put together a congregation like the lure of crack."

Joyce is currently writing a book about his life.

∽

In most treatment centers and drug programs throughout the country, core groups of recovering addicts become counselors and help others who are taking those first hesitant steps toward sobriety. Seeing these counselors function as wise, mature adults, it's hard to imagine any of them having once been desperate addicts themselves.

Among the most astonishing stories of recovery from hopeless addiction is that of Paul Thompson, a head counselor at Peer One, a therapeutic community in Denver. Thompson willingly passes around a picture of himself as a heroin addict, and judging by the way he looks now, one can only conclude that in his case time ran backward. As an addict ten years ago, Thompson looked a haggard fifty. His hair was long, stringy, and greasy; his face was deeply lined as though he'd spent a lifetime squinting into the sun; his dull expression was the very stereotype of a needle-user in a drug-infested tenement.

Now, as a clean and vigorous man with intense pride in his job, Thompson seems to be at least twenty years younger. He is handsome and full of energy and has the bright expression of a science teacher. He looks forty at most.

Paul Thompson's background is typical of addicts twenty years ago. He abused heroin and had the attitude "No one can tell me anything." At sixteen he found himself in adult court with a charge of armed robbery. Out on the street once again, Thompson continued misbehaving, both with and without drugs, sometimes getting caught, sometimes not. He was proud of how often he evaded the cops. But he didn't win every time. He landed in prison more times than he can remember.

Eventually he was lucky enough to come before a compassionate judge. "A little old lady judge sentenced me to Peer One," he says. "I remember what she said as she handed down the sentence: 'I once had a young man before me for sentencing that nobody had any faith in, and I sentenced him to a drug program and he's now a counselor there.'" She did the same for Thompson, giving him both five-year and two-year sentences at the therapeutic community where he now works.

At first Peer One's message didn't sink in, and Thompson tried to manipulate his way to the top position. But the residents saw through him.

It was Thompson's mother and sister who finally helped bring him to his senses; he knew he was in deep trouble when they gave up on him and refused to accept his phone calls.

Now Thompson runs Peer One with the zeal of a Baptist minister, becoming misty-eyed and choked up when he thinks of where he once was in life compared with where he is now. As a final affirmation of his changed

*life, he was chosen to go to Russia with an inspirational team that edu-
cated the Russians on addiction problems.*

~

For motivated addicts, like the three men just described, treatment facilities abound, all with different styles and approaches, but all capable of bringing about amazing changes in the addicted individual—in
both attitude and behavior.

For most of us, Alcoholics Anonymous is the best known of all
the substance addiction support groups, recognized worldwide for
its reach and effectiveness in helping alcoholics. Whatever treatment program an alcoholic or drug abuser is offered, AA is always
there somewhere. It is an adjunct to some programs and the center-
piece of others.

Few of us know, however, exactly when or how AA came about.
The story has been well documented in such books as *Not-God: A
History of Alcoholics Anonymous* by Ernest Kurtz, *Alcoholics Anonymous
Comes of Age: A Brief History of AA* by AA World Services, *Bill W.* by
Robert Thomsen, and the television movie *My Name Is Bill W.* It's in-
teresting to note that AA began exactly as one might expect: it was
the result of a chance meeting between two alcoholics who found
they could best stay sober by helping each other.

Bill Wilson, an alcoholic stockbroker, and Dr. Robert Smith, known
as Dr. Bob, first met in Akron, Ohio, in 1935. Both had been struggling
with alcoholism for years. At the time, Wilson was already enjoying a
six-month respite from his disease, thanks to a life-changing experience in a hospital as he recovered from delirium tremens. Desperate
about his condition, he remembered the advice of a recovered friend
and uttered a heartfelt prayer, which he later recounted in the AA
bible, *Alcoholics Anonymous*. "There I humbly offered myself to God, as
I then understood Him, to do with me as He would. I placed myself
unreservedly under His care and direction. I admitted for the first
time that of myself I was nothing; that without Him I was lost. I ruth-
lessly faced my sins and became willing to have my newfound Friend
take them away, root and branch. I have not had a drink since."[1]

Wilson soon discovered an unexpected benefit from sharing his story with other alcoholics. While it seemed to have little effect on them, it was helping him stay sober.

It was during a business trip to Akron that Wilson suffered a disappointment that threatened his sobriety. Afraid the failure would make him relapse, he sought another alcoholic to talk to. The local clergy directed him to Dr. Bob.

The meeting became legendary. Shortly after their initial encounter, Dr. Bob had the last drink of his life. From that moment, realizing that their sobriety depended on helping others, the two teamed up to spread their message to hopeless alcoholics in hospital wards. Thus began the partnership that would change the drinking world forever. Slowly their sphere of influence grew. They brought in a third recovering alcoholic, and then a few more. Eventually the group swelled to a hundred.

From their initial meetings in each other's homes, the alcoholics progressed to holding their sessions in church basements. By 1939 they'd developed enough theories about their successes to publish *Alcoholics Anonymous,* most often referred to as the Big Book.

The well-known Twelve Steps became the foundation of the AA program. Alcoholics and counselors talk a great deal about "working the Steps." Since few of us could recite them except in a general way, we're including them here:

Step One: We admitted we were powerless over alcohol—that our lives had become unmanageable.

Step Two: Came to believe that a Power greater than ourselves could restore us to sanity.

Step Three: Made a decision to turn our will and our lives over to the care of God *as we understood Him.*

Step Four: Made a searching and fearless moral inventory of ourselves.

Step Five: Admitted to God, to ourselves, and to another human being the exact nature of our wrongs.

Step Six: Were entirely ready to have God remove all these defects of character.

Step Seven: Humbly asked Him to remove our shortcomings.

Step Eight: Made a list of all persons we had harmed, and became willing to make amends to them all.

Step Nine: Made direct amends to such people wherever possible, except when to do so would injure them or others.

Step Ten: Continued to take personal inventory and when we were wrong promptly admitted it.

Step Eleven: Sought through prayer and meditation to improve our conscious contact with God *as we understood Him,* praying only for knowledge of His will for us and the power to carry that out.

Step Twelve: Having had a spiritual awakening as the result of these steps, we tried to carry this message to alcoholics, and to practice these principles in all our affairs.

~

In jails, prisons, halfway houses, and treatment centers across the United States, Twelve Steps programs are the foundation of addiction treatment. At AA meetings it is universal to stand up and introduce oneself in the following manner: "Hello, my name is John and I'm a recovering alcoholic." If the day marks an important anniversary in the alcoholic's sobriety, he will mention that as well.

The group's response is a chorus of, "Hello, John." Sometimes group members are so impressed by the stated sobriety that they break into spontaneous applause—especially for the newcomer whose clean and sober life may be less than thirty days old. As everyone knows, the hardest steps come at the beginning.

AA groups are not run by professional counselors; the leaders— considered "trusted servants" only, with no power to make any decision affecting the organization—are always recovering alcoholics themselves. Among the tenets that guide the meetings is the insistence that nobody is ever considered "cured," that all members are forever recovering.

Meetings consist of members telling personal stories about their wretched behavior as alcoholics or addicts, concluding with the events that triggered their staying clean. The stories are always mesmerizing. It is hard to conceive all the bizarre and destructive things that people do while under the influence. It is harder still to imagine that any of them could one day throw over that much antisocial, self-destructive behavior and manage to live a normal, substance-free life.

Perhaps the strongest feeling one gets in an AA meeting is acceptance of others—even love. The group seems to personify the biblical story of the prodigal son, always eager to embrace the fallen member—figuratively and literally. There's a lot of group cheering, a lot of hugging in AA.

The members sometimes speak of themselves in metaphorical terms: they are a group of people who have survived a shipwreck and thus enjoy a common bond. They share a feeling of camaraderie, of genuine empathy: you were on the boat, too, you remember how it was. You recall those sick, early days when we were all floundering and nearly drowned. You know how lucky we all are to be alive.

As a final ritual, AA meetings conclude with a circle in which members hold hands and recite the Serenity Prayer—or one like it—in unison. At the end they call out the urgent admonition, "Keep coming back!"

Indeed, for the majority of recovering alcoholics, regular attendance at AA meetings is a necessity—a reminder that sobriety always hangs by a fragile thread, that a return to full-blown alcoholism is only one drink away.

Since AA meetings—and those of its sister group, Narcotics Anonymous, run on the same principles—can be found in nearly every community in the United States, the recovering alcoholic cannot offer the excuse that he couldn't find a meeting. Attendance at AA or NA meetings is voluntary (unless ordered by a judge), and therein lies their failure for the deeply entrenched substance abuser. Nobody is forced to go.

Alcoholics Anonymous and Narcotics Anonymous offer significant help in *staying clean*. But they often fail in the early stages—the point where the abuser must make a commitment. For many addicts, something stronger is needed.

∼

For the semi-committed addict, treatment centers abound. But this was not always the case. In the years between the formation of AA in 1935 and the proliferation of halfway houses in the mid-1950s, inpatient treatment for alcoholics was usually provided in hospitals. Alcoholics were generally considered to be a weak and inferior bunch, and what little treatment they received occurred behind locked doors, where they were often warehoused with the chronic mentally ill. All too often the prevailing attitude of their caretakers was resignation or even disgust.

But in the late 1940s things began to change. Thanks to the interest and efforts of six humane people, two of whom were recovering alcoholics who had attained sobriety through AA, Willmar State Hospital in Minnesota began changing the way it dealt with inebriates.

With the two recovering alcoholics offering guidance based on their AA experience, the new superintendent at Willmar State Hospital, Nelson Bradley, and the larger Willmar staff began attending AA meetings and building relationships within the AA community. From these beginnings, the hospital staff instituted important changes in how they handled their charges. Until then, the treatment of choice had been psychoanalysis. As William L. White says in the book *Slaying the Dragon,* "There has rarely been a treatment method more poorly matched to a problem than that of the use of psychoanalysis in the treatment of addictions."[2]

Dan Anderson, one of the six who was brought to Willmar by Bradley, described what was happening:

> Bradley and I were getting tired of psychoanalysis. It wasn't working for our alcoholic patients, and none of these patients could afford five years of intense psychotherapy. We realized that the primary condition we were treating was alcoholism—that all that alcoholic personality stuff was secondary. . . . [W]e developed the idea that alcoholism was multiply determined—that it had physical, psychological, social, and spiritual dimensions. We decided we'd treat alcoholism by working on all these areas.[3]

Thanks to this group of dedicated people, alcoholism was recognized not as a symptom of underlying problems, but as a "primary, progressive disease." As Anderson said, "Our motto was: 'Where it doesn't itch, don't scratch.' We would deal directly with the addictive behavior. We would not look for other presumed underlying causes of the condition.[4]

The new staff at Willmar was determined to organize treatment around the principles of Alcoholics Anonymous and to form new AA groups within the hospital. Among the revolutionary ideas adopted at the Willmar hospital was the unlocking of doors in the inebriety units. As a consequence, the "escape rate" dropped from 22 percent to 6 percent!

To their surprise, the treatment staff discovered that motivation, or lack of it, was not a critical feature in the outcome of treatment. Unmotivated clients, brought in under duress and coercion, seemed to do as well as those who were screened for their degree of motivation. It seemed that some of the patients once thought to be highly motivated were simply "going along" with the program on a superficial level.

Because there was no other place to go, abusers of other substances began entering treatment at Willmar, joining the alcoholics. The staff began seeing people who had multiple addictions, and thus the term *chemical dependency* came into use.

In time, the new concepts being developed at Willmar were brought to another treatment facility, Hazelden, by staff who were persuaded to transfer over from Willmar. At Hazelden, the principles that had guided treatment at Willmar were further refined. Whereas some of the original Willmar staff believed treatment of clients should be "pure," and delivered only by recovering alcoholics, new directions at Hazelden included a broader approach, incorporating both professional and nonprofessional counselors.

The philosophy of treatment developed more or less jointly by Willmar, Hazelden, and another Minnesota treatment facility called Pioneer House became known as the Minnesota Model. Now recognized worldwide, the Minnesota Model includes the following tenets:[5]

1. Alcoholism is an involuntary, primary disease that is describable and diagnosable.

2. Alcoholism is a chronic and progressive disease, which, without treatment, grows worse with time.
3. Alcoholism is not curable, but the disease may be arrested.
4. Motivation, or lack of it, is not critical to treatment outcome.
5. The treatment of alcoholism includes physical, psychological, social, and spiritual dimensions.
6. The successful treatment of the alcoholic requires that he be handled with dignity and respect.
7. Alcoholics and addicts are vulnerable to a wide spectrum of mood-altering drugs—all treatable as chemical dependency.
8. Chemical dependency is best treated by a multidisciplinary team who develop close, less formal relationships with their clients— all integrated within an individualized treatment plan.
9. Treatment works best with a primary counselor who is the same sex and age group as the client—usually a recovering addict himself.
10. AA, Twelve Steps, groups that combine both support and confrontation, lectures, care of the body through proper nutrition and exercise, and individualized counseling are the focus of the treatment plan.
11. The best aftercare involves continuation with AA.

Of all the departures from conventional treatment that were embodied in the Minnesota Model, the addition of respect, communicated from counselor to alcoholic, was paramount. Not only was respect given to clients, but also accorded to counselors. As Anderson said of the earlier days of treatment, "No self-respecting professional in their right mind wanted to work with alcoholics."[6]

Taking a broad approach to the addict's corollary problems, the Hazelden program addresses such issues as anger management, shame, living skills, and self-esteem. Each client receives a daily therapeutic duty assignment, called TDAs, meaning he assists in chores like vacuuming and taking out the trash.

～

Like all good programs, Hazelden strongly recommends that its departing clients go to a halfway house for six months to a year, to further solidify newfound skills and beliefs.

And here we come to a discussion of halfway houses, which have sprung up everywhere across America and are serving a very real function in the continuing treatment of substance abusers.

Traditionally, the halfway house operates as a safe place where recovering addicts can live in an atmosphere of sobriety and understanding. They are expected to conform to the rules, which always mandate a drug-free life. The houses usually require attendance at AA meetings and in-house group counseling sessions. But most try to include some lighthearted events, too, offering group parties— barbecues, picnics, a family day on Sunday, and occasional excursions to beaches and sports events.

In the Costa Mesa area of Southern California, a number of excellent halfway houses are currently operating under the guidance of Nancy Clark, long recognized by the court system as a knowledgeable professional in the field of substance abuse. In describing her work, Clark says her clients can be put into two categories: the voluntary admissions, who come to her because their spouses or parents insist, and those who have been in trouble with the law and are ordered to live in one of her facilities in lieu of going to jail.

Unfortunately, Clark has noticed that a certain amount of tension derives from mixing voluntary people with court-ordered clients. The noncompulsory people sometimes display attitudes of superiority over those who were assigned by the courts: "*I'm* not coming from the court system—which makes you an alcoholic *and* a criminal." As though, she says with a smile, one alcoholic is so very much superior to another.

As to the mixing of sexes, Clark has found that having men and women interact for parts of the program provides balance and a sense of a normal community. But for great parts of her program, such as sessions requiring a more personal kind of sharing, she believes it works better to keep the men and women segregated.

She says, "Addicts always think they're unique. But they're not. When it comes to treatment, you need to look more at where they are now than which socioeconomic class they came from. When choosing treatment, class doesn't matter—only what drugs they've been using and how deeply they're into addiction."

The courts recognize that Clark is strict in her requirements for both sobriety and civilized behavior. She is realistic enough to know that she will always have a certain percentage of failures. But the successes! Ah, those are the people that make the job worthwhile. Her eyes light up when she speaks of all her former residents who are now living productive, drug-free lives, and she acknowledges that these are the ones who inspire everyone to keep going.

Individual halfway houses can vary greatly in atmosphere and the rigidity of the program. Phoenix House, with facilities in Los Angeles, Orange County, and Corcoran State Prison, is actually more than a halfway house; it is a strict, all-encompassing lifestyle, known to be among the toughest of the California treatment facilities. Although organized as a therapeutic community, the tone is at times harsh and the clients get heavy doses of confrontation and criticism in a group setting where the person under attack is not permitted to leave. One client was told, "Don't expect any affirmation from us."

Phoenix House seems to get the more hardened segment of the drug-abusing population, and the philosophy is that their residents need discipline to change their addictive lifestyles. A young mother who walked out of a group meeting under a barrage of criticism was given a severe penalty: for seven days she had to do menial work from 6 A.M. to midnight.

Yet along with its rougher, more confrontational side, Phoenix House encourages the active participation of families, who attend weekly parents' nights and openly discuss problems. And the center offers such positive experiences as outings to local entertainment events, the celebration of holidays, encouragement in job searches, dressing up for appearances outside the complex, and caring attention from individual counselors.

The program (originally modeled after Synanon) was designed for the resident with a strong ego who does well in boot camp. For those who stick it out to the end, the recidivism rate is low, estimated at less than 20 percent.

Delancey Street in Los Angeles is a somewhat gentler program. The original Delancey Street in San Francisco was organized around a group of hardened drug abusers who built their own facility and, having learned the construction trades, went out into the community with marketable skills.

The Delancey Street in Los Angeles occupies a reclaimed, four-hundred-room Hilton Hotel, where clients, some court-ordered, some not, learn marketable skills in three areas: physical labor, office or clerk skills, and people-interaction skills. Among the training offered in the physical labor arena are catering, moving company work, a range of construction and maintenance jobs, and the sale of Christmas trees.

Rick Wolder, the intake facilitator, says, "You know how Yale and Harvard get the top 2 percent of the population? Here, we get the bottom 2 percent." Yet Delancey Street has had great success in sending its two-year graduates out into the world with skills and attitudes that ensure most won't return to the criminal justice system.

Here there are no doctorates or criminologists offering advice. Rather, residents teach each other and, as in a therapeutic community, they work up through the ranks to ever-higher levels of respect and responsibility.

Yet their policies concerning family contact can be extreme. In an August 1, 1999, *Los Angeles Times* article by columnist Dana Parsons, a wife complains that she virtually lost her husband to the Delancey Street program. The article was entitled "Deal Was to Quit Drugs, Not Marriage," and the column begins, "Last December, Tammy Waters dropped her husband, Orville, off at a drug-rehab center near downtown Los Angeles and returned to their home in Orange. She hasn't seen or heard from him since."

After thirty days, Waters sent her husband a letter, only to have it returned. As of the date of the article, the silent period between wife and husband had already stretched to seven months. To her dismay, Tammy Waters had just learned that all contact would be suspended for still another eight months, for a total of fifteen. It seems that when the brochure said residents could write to their "family" after thirty days and phone them after ninety, they meant parents, not husbands or wives.

The counselors at Delancey Street are not concerned about such marital separations. They believe that a marriage distorted by drugs is a sick relationship anyway, and the drug user needs at least a year to reestablish himself. According to Bob Juencke, co-director of the Los Angeles site and a former heroin user rescued by the institution where he now works, "If they don't get themselves right, it does no good to send them back to their families."

Experts who understand the subtleties that distinguish one treatment program from another stress the importance of finding the program that best suits the needs and personality of the client. "Every wrong guess as to which treatment is best," says Nancy Clark, "is another hash mark for failure."

$\sim$

As successful as these support fellowships, treatment programs, and halfway houses have been with entrenched addicts, they all lack one critical feature: they are noncoercive. For the unmotivated addict who is not court-ordered, they offer a take-it-or-leave-it choice he probably can't handle.

Without a club of some kind hanging over his head, the stubbornly resistant addict will not stay long in even the best program. While it is true that unmotivated abusers can be treated successfully, programs have to be realistic about the missing link: first you have to keep them there.

This is not intended as a criticism of any of the programs or centers described in this chapter. It is simply a fact of life that the bullheaded, doggedly resistant addict who cherishes his one-sided love affair with chemicals needs an additional strong-arm element added to his treatment program.

The following chapter addresses an additional option for the addict who wants to change as well as a coercive version of it for the addict who thinks he might change someday—but certainly not today.

CHAPTER SEVEN

Therapeutic Communities: A Different Way to Grow Up

With so many Americans currently abusing drugs, it's surprising that the public at large knows so little about two important treatment options. One is drug court, a treatment program offered to a relatively small number of addicts caught up in the court system; the other is the therapeutic community (TC), widely used in a variety of settings, yet somehow unfamiliar to most people on the outside.

Since TCs can be either voluntary or coercive, they neatly span the gap between addicts who want help and those who don't. Most TCs operating within a jail or prison setting are, by definition, coercive. (Though a few accept only volunteers.)* Others, available mostly to addicts who are actively seeking help, draw from a population with a significantly different mind-set. Both can provide significant help to drug addicts, and both have been highly successful at changing lives.

Larry Hales, clinical social work supervisor at the Virginia Correctional Center for Women in Goochland, Virginia, describes in detail how a therapeutic community operates. Residence in a TC can be for as short a time as one year or, in the case of a handful of in-prison

---

* The first therapeutic community behind bars was put into place in the sixties. At the urging of Nevada's then-governor, Grant Sawyer, and Warden Fogliani, a group called Synanon was invited to start a therapeutic community in the Nevada State Prison. Also in the sixties, the federal government invited Synanon into the women's prison on Terminal Island in California. Both communities were very effective and markedly reduced both the violence in the yard and the recidivism rates of their participants.

programs, for as long as three to four years. Typically, the term is eighteen months to three years.

Limited capacity is always a problem. The therapeutic community at the Virginia Correctional Center for Women, for instance, currently treats only 48 women. However, plans are under way to enlarge that number to 120, which will then constitute one-fourth of the correctional center's total population.

The typical TC is set up to operate like a large family. Individual members are encouraged, helped, guided, and held accountable by their peers. Within the family unit are hierarchies, and the goal of the newcomer—though he may not know this at first—is to grow within the family. He is encouraged to change his value systems and his behavior, and to work his way through the various levels to ever higher positions of respect and responsibility.

As is true of conventional families, not all therapeutic communities operate exactly alike. But in general, the principles are as follows:

Most addicts come to the community with a set of values and rules, but they are not the ones valued by conventional society. The abuser doesn't know how to function in a society that won't tolerate drugs, alcohol, and crime. The goal of the TC is to resocialize the addict, placing a high value on the work ethic and a sense of personal responsibility for the addict and others. Addicts are taught immediately that what they do affects the entire community, and if the family is to succeed, each member must conform to the family ideals.

Structure is very important. The newcomer relates almost entirely to the person just above him on the ladder, a pattern that holds from the bottom up. Work crews are overseen by coordinators, who in turn report to an assistant senior coordinator. These people report to a senior coordinator, who reports to staff.

Most important, the newcomer learns to answer to his peers, to the people he lives with. His attitude toward them and his day-to-day behavior is under constant scrutiny, but then, so are other family members' attitudes and behaviors under *his* scrutiny.

In most TCs, there is an orientation phase that typically lasts thirty days. During this period the novice learns the rules, which are generally divided into three categories: the cardinal rules, the major rules, and the house rules.

The cardinal rules involve the safety of the whole community: no violence, no threats of violence, no drug abuse, no sexually acting out. Breaking any of these can result in immediate termination from the program.

The major rules deal with how the abuser relates to others—family members, his peers.

House rules are unique to each program and vary according to individual families.

The orientation phase, during which the novice is learning the rules, is very confrontational. Members hold each other accountable with verbal "pull-ups," which might go something like this: "You haven't cleaned your part of the room. I'm giving you a pull-up." The only response permitted is, "Thank you. I'll take care of that."

A written pull-up is more serious and reaches the next level of confrontation—the attention of the entire family. The family meets every evening, and written pull-ups are read aloud. Consequences and learning experiences are assigned by staff. If written pull-ups and learning experiences don't produce change, the family as a whole confronts the individual, who can only listen but can't argue.

At times such meetings can get quite emotional, with the confronters emphasizing how they feel and how the unacceptable behavior or attitude affects them. The focus is always on the behavior itself and how it impacts others—and what should be done differently in the future. An individual is "pulled up" for failures in things like cleanliness, general attitude, or rules violations, or perhaps for refusing to talk about himself in group meetings, or whining, or displaying what are called "leaky feelings"—too much moodiness—all of which are detrimental to the group.

The offender is given consequences for his negative behavior, such as extra house cleaning or kitchen duties. It's critical to the plan that consequences address the underlying reason for the aberrant behavior. It's also critical that family members follow through to see that consequences are carried out. As Hales says, "Now you have forty other people watching you, all hoping your behavior will change."

Almost all therapeutic communities employ some kind of encounter group therapy as an instrument of change. Sometimes called "the Game," it is always run by members of the family, though with a staff member present for guidance and direction. During the game, different individuals are singled out for the "hot seat" and advised of behavior or attitudes that don't meet family standards. Members continually work on each other's ego, attitude, and anger issues, with a strong emphasis on accountability.

Yet underlying these negative aspects, there is an attitude of support: I'm here for you. I'm watching you, but I care for you. You're a member of my family, and I want you to succeed. If you can stay clean, if you can last out the program, it's going to help me as well. You are my brother. We're in this together.

Encounter groups typically are thrown off balance when a member chooses to leave a voluntary facility. In the same way that a conventional family is disturbed by the member who rejects the rest, TC members suffer a serious sense of loss and rejection when a fellow member abandons them. Those left behind typically say things like, "And he was doing so well. I know he liked us. I don't understand what happened. Why would he leave?"

The dynamics of a TC are indeed like those in a family.

∼

Phase two of most TC programs lasts about six to nine months and encompasses a large part of the treatment for addiction. While the focus in the orientation phase, or phase one, is on learning rules, this second phase focuses on substance abuse, AA, NA, and other self-help programs. Members receive group and individual counseling and attend lectures and participate in group discussions about such issues as anger control, parenting, abusiveness, criminal thinking, and shame. Highly spiritual discussions often take place as clients learn to work the Twelve Steps.

Phase three, about nine months into the program, is a process of maturation and internalization. Members are beginning to conform to group standards, not because they are required to, but because it's the right thing to do. They are now seeing themselves in a new light, as individuals worthy and capable of accepting responsibility. The length of this phase varies with the individual, who is progressing at his own pace.

Hales notes that people vary in how well they react to different levels on the hierarchy. Most TCs find that people need to be moved back and forth—or up and down—not as punishment, but for more effective learning.

Phase four involves transitioning out of the TC. For some people this is a frightening period, knowing they'll soon be on their own without the close support of the "family."

Although all four phases emphasize the work ethic and job training—such as food preparation, clerical work, electrical work, and plumbing—at the Virginia Correctional Center for Women, Hales says it never feels like enough. Learning lines of communication—taking one's problems to the appropriate superior instead of trying to go to the top—has been discussed throughout as well. But transition to the outside means the individual will now have the entire responsibility for himself.

Recognizing the need for effective transition, as of this writing counselors at the TC at the Virginia center in Goochland are actively studying work centers and dorms on the outside, hoping to provide women with jobs and substance-free housing after they're released. They are also studying the Stay'n Out program in New York, a residential program that has had notable success at helping offenders transition back to society.

Hales notes that corrections facilities and businesses need to collaborate more in providing work for offenders. He said, "It's a win-win situation. The business gets workers at a reduced price, and the offender gets job skills he can take out into the community."

Hales is clearly excited about the many lives that are being salvaged through his TC; his enthusiasm for his job comes through continually as he describes what's taking place in the Goochland women's correctional center. He summarizes the TC by saying, "It's a tough program. But when they come out on the other side, they're responsible individuals with a strong work ethic. They're pretty good people. As we keep reminding ourselves while we're working with offenders—today's inmates are tomorrow's neighbors."

~

As noted earlier, individual therapeutic communities vary widely.

Peer One, in Denver, includes aspects that don't seem to exist in other TCs. For example, Peer One is housed in a couple of very large, elegant old houses on the outskirts of the city. From the outside, they have the ivy-covered look of old money.

It isn't unusual to see a group of men standing on the back porch singing—creating the impression that whatever else goes on within the walls, there must be a strong sense of camaraderie.

Yet Paul Thompson, the director, admits that it's not an easy program. He believes clients need to prepare for the real world, which consists in large part of things going wrong. "The washing machine overflows and soaks the rug. You get a traffic ticket. Someone gets sick. Your boss shouts at you. How do you deal with it?" He describes residents yelling at themselves in the mirror, and says, "We frustrate them at every turn." Since frustration will always be a factor in normal living, the men at the TC need to develop skills for handling it. "We give them the unexpected. How do they deal with no praise? We try to push their buttons." He sees his role as teaching clients to channel their angers and "suck them up."

Inside, it's not unusual to see a number of men sitting on chairs with their backs to the room, staring straight ahead at the wall. "They are supporting Monad," Thompson explains, a cryptic term that describes the grown man's version of "time-out." For the ten minutes—or perhaps an hour—that the man faces the wall, he's supposed to be meditating. A few do this voluntarily, while others are ordered to "Support Monad" by a senior client, a "senate" member, or a staff member.

A staff member explains that for most of his clients the chief issue is struggle: they struggle with their identity; they struggle with a fierce desire to do things their own way, despite all the bad consequences their way has brought them.

As in most TCs Peer One holds regular "games" for purposes of confrontation and group discipline. Twice a year, however, the game changes. Instead of occupying part of an evening, the game lasts forty-eight hours, with breaks only for meals. Aptly named a marathon, this overlong, intense session strips away outside distractions and reduces the players to a raw state of numbness and exhaustion—a state conducive to learning. The purpose is to break the men down emotionally, leaving them vulnerable for the lessons that follow.

The start of a marathon can be dramatic. In a typical marathon some twenty men are seated in a large circle around a room. The evening is spent throwing a barrage of criticisms at one or another of the participants—more often yelling at him. As the session grows heated, four-letter words start to flow: "Why the f— did you . . . How come you didn't . . . You know f—ing well that you . . ."

On one typical evening, the man under fire was mature—perhaps mid-forties—a slim man who was calm and quiet, but visibly reeling from all the verbal abuse. With his mustache, dark eyes, and beaten expression, he resembled a beleaguered Charlie Chaplin. To an outsider, he would seem unusually decent. Even in the face of all those shouted accusations, it was hard to imagine that he'd done anything to get excited about.

The session grew rougher; the accusers were now using the "F" word in every sentence and shouting at the tops of their lungs. Yet that frail man, finally worn down by the session, sat quietly in his chair looking down at his hands. At one point it seemed he might cry. And then, sure enough, he began sniffing and wiping his eyes.

At the end of the marathon, with everyone worn to a nub, the Peer One clients are blindfolded and led to a meadow and told to lie on their stomachs. The counselors drive away, and nobody knows when they'll return or what will happen next. Finally Thompson picks them up again, takes them to a hospital, and says, "Is this where you want to end up?" Then he drives them to a morgue and says, "Or you can end up here." At last he takes them back to the facility and says, "Or you can do the program here and end up having a life." Presumably, after such a wretched forty-eight hours, the lesson becomes unforgettable.

For hard-core offenders, such extremes of emotional trauma seem to be necessary. "Because of their warped values," a staff member explains, "we have to break them down emotionally and rebuild them with values that are socially acceptable. The trip to the morgue is just one of the things we do at the end of a marathon game."

Bill Ritter, the district attorney in Denver, says of Peer One, "The people we send there are often serious offenders. It is like the last option to prison, and they know it, and that helps Peer One with their successes. But you know, there are people who opt for prison over this." Even Paul Thompson admits that some of his men walk away, claiming prison is easier.

In spite of these harsh techniques, most clients seem to be thriving. The mood in the group dining room is one of cordiality and good spirits. For many, just being surrounded by a group of men who care enough to criticize is a new experience. Paul Thompson swears that Peer One saved his life.

～

The women's version of Peer One, called Haven, is housed in another large mansion a few doors down from the men's.

The women, too, have confrontational sessions, or "games," although theirs are usually gentler and mostly good-natured. While there is some bad language and occasional yelling at the victim on the hot seat, such moments are generally punctuated by embarrassed laughter, even giggling. For women, it seems, yelling does not come naturally. None of the women under scrutiny suffers unduly harsh criticism from her peers, and the facilitator, herself a recovering addict, is apt to laugh gently at those moments when the accusations grow most heated.

Some of the women tell their stories: Lori, thirty-seven, is on probation. She's had six and a half years of sobriety, then a relapse with Percodan. She makes the classic statement: "I thought I could do it on my own." During the course of her addictive life, she drank cough syrup for its alcohol content, slapped her husband's face, was on Antabuse (an anti-alcoholic medication) but managed to manipulate the drug—meaning she took it at times when it didn't interfere with her drinking. She says, "Here they work on changing our behaviors—but they also work on our issues, which has never happened to me before. It's a very hard program. The system [the courts] doesn't rein us in quick enough."

Another woman says, "All my life I've been a master manipulator."

Some of the women have children, and all have had serious drug problems, some for as long as nineteen years. One woman speaks of having a daughter who was molested by her husband's brother: "That was when I lost my feelings for my husband." Her past life included partying with alcohol and cocaine, then shoplifting, which she likens to sex. "I'd climax each time. I did it daily." She adds, "I wanted to die getting high." She'd been in prison and a halfway house, but neither gave her any tools for the inevitable day of release. Now, at forty-six, she says, "I really want to be clean and sober."

One of the women comments on the prison system: "It teaches you to be harder and angrier. It gives you less self-esteem."

The counselor notes, "The key is, how long they're here. It takes a woman up to sixty days just to feel like she wants to stay."

The women speak of their preference for segregated facilities. "We don't really want to be with the men. Women are raised *not* to be angry. There's a big difference between men's and women's issues. We feel freer here, without any guys."

At Haven, the women do all the housework and rotate through jobs. Periodically they elect a "senior sister" and a "house manager," who, in these positions of respect, are entitled to eat separately and be served first.

On selected evenings, as a treat, the women engage in a "dance encounter," a lighthearted session of freeform dancing and laughter, all to music of their choosing. It is impossible not to be swept up in the good spirits and laughter that accompany some truly creative dancing.

～

By contrast, few of these elements seem to be present in a Denver therapeutic community known as Cenikor. Near downtown Denver, Cenikor occupies several residences that are indistinguishable from the other middle-class homes in the neighborhood.

Like Peer One and Haven, Cenikor admits a certain number of clients who are referred by the courts. Unlike the others, however, Cenikor won't accept anyone who can't convince the staff he's ready to change. Potential clients are interviewed, but approved for admission only if they seem convincing.

The director and regional vice president of the Cenikor Foundation, Eugene Strauber, sums up his attitude in strong terms. "A lot of people are motivated intellectually," he says. "We see all kinds of motivation. For instance, they don't want to go to jail. But how committed are they going to be tomorrow? We get people who walk in here wearing a suit and tie. They think that will impress us. I tell them, 'Hey, go back out there and walk in like you normally are and we will talk to you. Don't come over here trying to impress us. I mean, I'm looking at the information here and you've got three felonies. What are you wearing a suit and tie for? What do you think you're coming here for—a job?'"

When asked what a mother could do to get a son into Cenikor, Strauber replied, "You can't *do* anything. *You* can't do anything. He would have to call, he would have to come out for an interview, and he would have to convince the people here that this is what he wants to do."

A link seemed to be missing. "But someone like my son wouldn't have the foggiest notion what you do here, so he wouldn't come prepared with a bunch of ideas like, 'This is what I want.' Because he wouldn't know what's involved."

"He doesn't *have* to know."

"All he'd have to tell you is . . . he wants to change?"

"Exactly. We're not looking for people who are shopping. You want to go shopping, go to the mall and see what kind of ties or suits they have, then pick and choose. If you call Cenikor, they're going to tell you what it's about, they're going to give you a brief understanding of what the program is and what the eligibility looks like. And then they're going to listen to why you want to come, what your interest is, and whether you're saying things like, 'It's too long. The program is much too long.' We'll say, 'Well, what have you been doing for the last ten or fifteen years?' 'Well, I'm drinking and doing some drugs and getting into trouble.' 'Okay,' we say, 'so nothing is working. What have you tried?' 'Well, I have been in this program and that program.' 'Well, this is a long-term program,' we say. 'This is a program that is going to help you change your lifestyle, change your thinking, change your values, change how you see the world and yourself in it. If that is what you're looking for, that's what we do. Now if you're looking for some quick fix for thirty days or ninety days, then you need to keep looking because you are not going to find it here.'"

He was asked, "And nothing that's thirty days or ninety days ever helps?"

"Not the person who's got a long-term problem. For a first offender it may work, but not for the long-timer. Scientists believe that for every year you use drugs, you need to be in a treatment environment like this for a minimum of a month. And that's minimum."

Strauber describes the interview process: "You know, addicts are not very truthful. They don't tell you the whole story. When you interview them, you start asking questions: 'How long have you been using?' 'Oh,' they say, 'about a year.' We say, 'I don't understand. It says in this thing here that you were in treatment three years, okay?' 'Oh, that's right; it's been longer than a year.' 'Well, you got arrested six years ago. When did the problems first start?' You play with these people, because they think they are going to pull one over. It's like talking to my thirteen-year-old.

"The point is, the problem started long before they ever used drugs. Drugs and alcohol are not the problem; they are symptomatic of something deeper. And until you get to those issues that evolved as part of growing up, you never really get to what happened. You don't know *why* drugs and alcohol seemed to be a good cure for what the pain was all about. So people don't start taking drugs and become addicted, and *that's* the problem. If it was, simple detox would be the answer."

It seemed pointless to argue that *everybody* grows up with thorny issues, but not everyone escapes into drugs. Strauber wouldn't have accepted the argument that, as often as not, it's the drugs themselves that become the problem—that after an addict uses long enough, dysfunction is added to his psyche, and he's not the same person he was when he was growing up.

Strauber probably would have agreed, though, on one important point: substance abuse is a complicated subject, and all generalizations are dangerous.

~

For those accepted into the program, Cenikor is free. Expenses are paid by the offender's own efforts. Everyone has a job, whether in one of the Cenikor industries or on the premises themselves, and the money goes to pay for food, lodging, and overhead. Some clients are enlisted to work in outreach programs at Denver's jails and drug courts. The work ethic is emphasized, and for the graduate, the years he spent working pay huge dividends in future jobs.

Since the staff believes that pocket money is often a trigger for drug abuse, in the first year clients aren't allowed off premises without a buddy.

As in other therapeutic communities, group therapy sessions and day-to-day discipline are handled by one's peers, who become role models as they work their way into ever higher levels of responsibility. Also like other TCs, individual problems and behaviors are critiqued and handled in the sessions called games.

Most TCs find that the best professional staff are graduates of the program. Strauber says, "When you turn around and look at this program through the eyes of the graduates who are running it, who have been through it, versus the eyes of people who are trained professionals trying to learn about therapeutic communities, they can't do it. We've tried. For twenty years I've tried to hire people in the community to work here, whether it is counseling or program stuff. I almost have to tell them to come in and do the program for us before I'll consider them for employment. They really don't understand the culture, and there are so many little things they wouldn't know and I couldn't tell them. They don't have the insight; they don't understand the behavior when they see it; they don't see the dishonesty when it's right there."

In two respects, Cenikor differs significantly from the other TCs discussed in this chapter. They don't allow negativity, and they don't permit profanity. It seems that the highly emotional, very intense shouting matches observed at some of the other TCs would not be allowed here.

The abusive TC encounter group, or "game," discussed earlier in this chapter originated with the earliest therapeutic community, Synanon, in the sixties. The idea then was that every addict was essentially egomaniacal: boastful, cocksure, and so thoroughly driven by denial of the harm of drug use that he would go to any length to defend his decision to continue using. Synanon believed that such a personality could only be reached by a harsh, in-your-face confrontational style that would penetrate the addict's drug fog and break down the psychological walls of denial by breaking down the ego that created and sustained them. As we have seen, many current TCs are structured on this premise, and certainly they are effective with a certain type of addict.

Cenikor and TCs like it, however, have a different view of the addict and his essential character and needs. They believe that beneath the cocky demeanor, many addicts are insecure, fearful, and psychologically fragile. The abusive approach may backfire with some addicts, psychically demolishing them. The abusive TC encounter group may succeed only in driving them further into themselves and out of the TC—and back to prison, where the crushing routine and isolation are preferable to the intense inner pain inflicted by the TC "game."

In our view, the truth is that all addicts are not alike, and one treatment method does not fit all. Therapeutic approaches that are effective with one addict may be relatively useless with another. Yet the proponents of each treatment model rarely admit that their philosophy does not apply equally well to all types of addicts and all forms of addiction. Family members who are seeking treatment for an addicted member would do well to make an effort to understand the psyche of the addict and find a program that is well matched to his needs—a program that will help him break through the powerful walls of denial without destroying him in the process, a program that will help ready him to successfully reintegrate with society. That program may well be a harsh TC, but it may also be a place like Cenikor, where the approach is less caustic.

Certainly the graduate who is about to leave Cenikor and reenter the community would be as well prepared as it's possible to be. Before he goes out on his own, the client must have his general equivalency diploma (high school graduation), a job, $1,500 in the bank, a place to live, support systems in place, and transportation to and from work. All of these requirements are part of the thesis of this book.

Eugene Strauber believes his program is the best in the business. For the substance abuser who is strongly motivated to change, Cenikor does seem to include most of the features that have proven effective with hard-core addicts. If all the factors work out in practice as well as they've been described, Strauber may very well be right.

∼

We've seen, then, that therapeutic communities operate equally well in voluntary or coercive settings. The next few chapters will address programs designed for the addict who stubbornly resists all forms of treatment.

CHAPTER EIGHT

Why Prisons May Fight Change

Not every addict wants to stop being an addict.

It is an unfortunate fact of life that a great many substance abusers resist any form of treatment. They are entrenched in drugs, they like how drugs make them feel, and they want to keep doing all the dangerous, thrilling things they're used to. They feel terrible when they don't use. In spite of having suffered some bad consequences, they can't conceive of a life that doesn't include their drug of choice.

To all of us who are "square," normal, or recovering, this attitude seems like the mind-set from hell.

Rick Faulkner, program manager at the National Institute of Corrections in Washington, D.C., talks about the problem of helping addicts who are not motivated to change. When asked, "Do you believe it's true that addicts can't be helped unless they're desperate—unless they really want it?" Faulkner answered with a laugh, "We've all heard that old adage—you can lead a horse to water but you can't make him drink. We in corrections have discovered another side to the saying, however. The horse may not want to cooperate, but you can run that son-of-a-gun so hard he'll *wish* he'd taken a drink."

In an hour's conversation, Faulkner discussed America's rush to incarcerate, pointing out how few positive benefits have accrued to inmates. He notes that the theory behind imprisonment has always been simply to get offenders put away and out of sight. "We never did expect it to do any good."

～

That hasn't always been the case, at least in California. There was a time during the forties, fifties, and sixties when the newly formed

California Department of Corrections (CDC) strongly emphasized rehabilitation, education, vocational training, counseling, and treatment for the mentally ill. Under the guidance of its first director, veteran penologist Richard A. McGee, who was appointed by then-governor Earl Warren, California became a model of prison management. According to the CDC's own publication titled *Fifty Years: Public Safety, Public Service,* McGee "developed and refined the medical-rehabilitative model of prison management." Later, Earl Warren, by then chief justice of the Supreme Court, wrote, "May 21, 1944, is a significant date in the history of our state, because it took California out of the dark ages in the field of penology and ushered in a period of enlightenment."[1]

In its publication, the CDC speaks of numerous innovations that came soon after the department's creation: the Deuel Vocational Institute; the Correctional Training Facility; the California Medical Facility (for mentally ill); academic and vocational education programs at all institutions; a trade advisory council; correctional industries (to employ inmates and work with representatives of private industry and labor); and group counseling.

In the department's second decade, mid-fifties to mid-sixties, as prisons grew in population, there was "increased focus on rehabilitation. By 1960 more than 10,000 inmates were enrolled in some kind of group counseling."[2] By the late sixties, however, these programs were phased out. The CDC felt that research could not demonstrate their effectiveness.

It is ironic that the CDC's newest and harshest declaration of purpose came in 1977, at a time when California was enjoying its lowest prison population in twenty years. Under the Determinate Sentencing Law of 1977, "punishment became the stated purpose of incarceration." The word *rehabilitation* was now markedly absent.

Since the late 1970s, every California statistic concerning prisons and prisoners has shown a dismal and alarming upward trend. California prisons are currently operating at 203 percent of their stated capacity, and the state holds the dubious honor of hosting the most crowded prison system in the country. Most disheartening of all, 60 to 70 percent of all inmates released from conventional prisons (meaning no training, rehabilitation, or drug treatment) will eventually return with new crimes.[3]

∿

In spite of isolated opinions like Rick Faulkner's, echoed by occasional editorials in newspapers and magazines, relatively few voices from the criminal justice system itself have demanded reform, urging a new approach to the punishment of addicts that might actually stand a chance of getting results. Thanks to being caught between the "hang 'em high" mentality of California voters and the frustrations of reform and rehabilitation, judges in Southern California understandably run for office on "get tough on crime" platforms and leave the issues of reform to the legislature.

In a recent Orange County election, sixteen people ran for election or re-election to the office of superior court judge. Of the sixteen, ten proclaimed their support of three strikes and the death penalty, and additional numbers labeled themselves "tough" or "no-nonsense." Only two gave favorable mention to the rehabilitative alternative known as drug courts. The problem, of course, is that the voting public has not yet caught on to the idea that supporting rehabilitation for addicts is in everyone's best interests.

Whatever their private, unspoken opinions, men and women who face the electorate to gain or hold jobs clearly don't want to be tainted by that most odious of all labels—"soft on crime." Rhetoric from the late eighties and early nineties still reverberates throughout our society, and the voting public is perceived as the next thing to bloodthirsty, demanding ever harsher retribution against criminals.

While most judges do hold more reasoned, personal views, and while the public is possibly less grim about incarceration than everyone thinks, neither side seems willing to tip its hand to the other.

∿

In the October 1998 issue of *National Institute of Justice Journal,* Dr. Alan I. Leshner, director of the National Institute on Drug Abuse, brings the scientist's viewpoint to a U.S. Department of Justice publication. After illustrating in convincing detail that addiction is a brain disease, he concludes by saying: "If we know criminals are also drug addicted, it is no longer reasonable to simply incarcerate them. If they have a brain disease, imprisoning them without treatment will be futile. If they are left untreated, their crime and drug use recidivism rates are frighteningly high. However, if addicted criminals are treated while in prison, both types of recidivism can be reduced drastically. It is, therefore, counterproductive not to treat addicts while they are in prison."[4]

~

Before we look at the positive side of this issue—and there is one—it's necessary to explore all the reasons why some jails and prisons may not welcome a "curative" approach used with their addicted offenders . . . why the thought of reducing the prison population might be a negative instead of a positive. If you didn't know it already—and most of us don't—jails and prisons are big business!

In a December 1998 article in *Atlantic Monthly* titled "The Prison-Industrial Complex," Eric Schlosser explores the reasons why in some quarters there may be scant interest in diverting the river of Americans being washed up into the prison system: a significant number of people have real money at stake in the continuing construction and operation of jails and prisons.

For instance, look at what large prison complexes mean to the telephone companies. Because prisoners aren't allowed to make calls in the normal way, *all telephone calls, even local, must be collect.* Thanks to having a captive audience that can't bargain or fight back or change carriers or protest to the Public Utilities Commission (PUC), phone companies, with assent from the PUC, have been free to set high rates for inmate calls, just as they do in certain other places, such as airports and hotels. In some facilities, MCI has been adding a $3 surcharge to every in-prison call. Pay phones that would normally generate $3,000 a year on the street are worth $15,000 in the prison setting, though to be fair, all of the jail's portion is reinvested in the inmate welfare program.

It is no wonder, then, that MCI was willing to install its inmate phone service, Maximum Security, in the entire California prison system at no charge or that it offered the California Department of Corrections 32 percent of the revenue as part of the deal. According to the *Atlantic Monthly* article, it's been estimated that inmate calls generate a billion dollars or more of revenue for U.S. phone companies every year.

But who do they generate it *from?*

Let's digress a moment and discuss this, because here's a topic that seldom sees print. Who pays that billion dollars a year?

The families of inmates, of course. The same people who are always penalized by the justice system—and in more ways than anyone knows.

For years I've asked myself, How can inner-city families afford these horrendous phone bills? How can they keep in touch and still eat?

I was always aghast when I saw our collect-call charges from Kirk; I often wondered if we were paying an unfair premium. But until I read the Atlantic Monthly *article, it didn't occur to me to dig any deeper.*

As part of my research, I did exactly that. Our July 1999 phone bill shows our son called eighteen times from a local jail, adding $59.23 to the bill. I called Pacific Bell and got their normal, collect-call rates. I added up the minutes and did the math. It seems a "civilian" making those same collect calls would have generated charges of $27.97—less than half! Calling from a phone booth, with no operator involved, he would have paid only $6.50.

Over the years, our family estimates we've paid some eighteen hundred dollars in collect-call charges to various phone companies—a high price for the cost of guarding callers and replacing damaged phone equipment. It is interesting to note that the big cost is always in the first minute of the call—meaning there is no way to escape this overcharging by limiting the number of minutes spent talking. M. W.

~

Phone companies are only one set of beneficiaries from the expanding prison system. Profitability spreads out in all directions. All the vendors who supply electric fences, prison bunks, bullet-resistant cameras, plumbing fixtures, and even such exotic items as "body-orifice security scanners" stand to make substantial financial gains from the growth of prisons. The *Atlantic Monthly* article states, "What was once a niche business for a handful of companies has become a multibillion-dollar industry with its own trade shows and conventions, its own Web sites, mail-order catalogues, and direct-marketing campaigns."

However, it isn't just commercial companies, architectural firms, and construction companies that benefit from prison expansion. Consider the huge numbers of people that the average prison employs. While admittedly the job of overseeing sullen, sometimes dangerous prisoners would hardly be called cushy employment, the pay is fairly good—the average starting salary for a California prison guard is $31,000 a year, plus benefits. From there the salaries go up, until a guard with a number of years tenure can bring home up to sixty thousand a year.

It is no wonder that small, impoverished communities, such as those in the north country of New York State, have fought long and hard to have prisons built in their area. In many remote parts of the United States, prisons are the best possible guarantee of year-round job security.

In recent years, sixteen correctional facilities of all kinds, from drug-treatment centers to boot camps, have been built in the north country of New York. With the prisons in one setting, and the prisoners largely coming from another (the urban area of New York), prisoners had to be bused in. Author Anne Mackinnon calls this northern incarceration area New York's "Siberia."

In the February 15, 2000, issue of the *Los Angeles Times*, in an article entitled "A Nation of Too Many Prisoners?" Jesse Katz writes, "Even the warden at the Louisiana Department of Corrections intake and classification center concedes that cost-effective alternatives, from electronic monitoring to diversion programs, could be used to shrink the state's incarceration rate—if the incarceration business did not have a financial interest in perpetuating itself."

Yet nobody believes there is any kind of evil intent out there to ensure that the prison business continues to expand and thrive. As Eric Schlosser says: "The prison-industrial complex is not a conspiracy, guiding criminal-justice policy behind closed doors. It is a con-

fluence of special interests that has given prison construction in the
United States a seemingly unstoppable momentum."[5]

In some ways, it might be better if there were an evil clique—a
malevolent group that dogged journalists could unearth, expose for
punishment, and bring to a halt. As it is, Schlosser's and Katz's conclusions are far more discouraging. With this kind of scenario in place,
there is built-in resistance to doing anything to reduce the unnecessary, high-security incarceration of so many nonviolent Americans.

Yet this inertia must be overcome. The best approach is to educate
and convince legislatures and the public that funds must be allocated
to lower-security prisons—and to the therapeutic communities that
will make them effective. If enough citizens knew that in-prison treatment facilities have the potential of saving taxpayers $20,000 to
$40,000 a year for every recovering addict who goes straight, there
would be a great public demand that significant jail and prison
money be put where it will do the most good.

∼

One last obstacle to the introduction of in-prison treatment programs needs to be mentioned here: the availability of drugs inside
prison walls. Though rumors have long insisted this is a fact, some of
us remained skeptical. How could *anyone* sneak anything inside,
when at least half the time the visitor can't touch the offender, when
the two are talking by phone and looking at each other through a
thick wall of glass? Even with face-to-face visits, women visitors must
leave their purses behind, and men have to empty their pockets, and
all go through one clanking metal door after another. Once inside,
the guards are always nearby, watching.

Yet it seems that even closely watched visitors find ways—that determined drug runners can be astonishingly ingenious. Drugs come in
through the baby's diapers, somebody's mouth, the cups in a woman's
bra. Or even through the felon's lawyer. Add to this the occasional
corrupt guard or, more likely, the trusted inmate who works on the
outside, and you find an all-too-steady supply inside the fence.

Tales of drugs in prison have been reported to us by ex-offenders
all over the country. One recovering addict said, "When you give

your son money in prison, you're buying him drugs. Never send him a penny more than he needs for dental floss."

A respected judge in Denver comments offhandedly about the problem: "As you know, drug trips are just as available in prison as they are on the street. It just costs more money."

Usually, though, when the issue is mentioned to people in authority, they become vague and change the subject. One district attorney said, "However it gets in, it gets in." Nobody wants to believe that the system breaks down.

Drugs behind bars, then, would certainly be a strong impediment to starting any kind of substance abuse program within a prison facility.

~

Yet despite these many obstacles—in spite of judges' justified fears of being labeled soft on crime, in spite of profits to be made from the prison-industrial complex, in spite of drugs finding their way inside prisons—it turns out that here and there around the country, a few dedicated individuals in corrections are actually trying new approaches; these pioneers already see their roles differently.

While occasional voices, including ours, decry the lack of alternatives to mindless incarceration of nonviolent addicts, a number of in-jail, in-prison substance abuse programs have been quietly making inroads in several states. While editorials cry out against too much incarceration in America, a handful of courageous leaders are bringing drug treatment inside the walls, where addicts can't get away.

Most such programs are new, only a few years old, but they're out there.

The jails and prisons that have dared to try new treatment programs are already changing the lives of addicted inmates. They're already taking the first steps toward reducing the nation's heavy burden of addicted offenders. And they're doing it for all the right reasons.

The following chapter describes some of the innovative in-jail, in-prison programs now available to nonviolent addicts.

CHAPTER NINE

Prisons That Work:
How They Save Addicts and Reduce Recidivism

For most people, the word *prison* evokes a bleak image. To the fresh arrival glimpsing a prison setting for the first time, it can seem nothing less than a landscape of despair. Guard towers with unearthly eyes stand vigil over treeless acres and rolled-wire fences. Gray cement fortresses turn windowless backs to the world, offering no chance that anyone will see in—or see out. Near the fences, nothing moves. Nothing even seems to live.

Inside, the atmosphere is less humane than most zoos.

Nobody has described this image better than author Sasha Abramsky in the June 1999 *Atlantic Monthly* article "When They Get Out."

In chilling word pictures, she describes a visit to the high-security Estelle Unit of Texas's Huntsville Prison. She speaks of a facility surrounded by rolls of lethal, razor-wire fences, of passing through a series of metal doors, each clanking shut behind her before the next one opens. She mentions the deep, hollow silence inside and the fetid odors that fill the halls, emanating from people who never see the outside. She notes that everywhere, security is controlled by computers, as in some futuristic horror story. "The security here," she is told proudly, "is better than Alcatraz. Alcatraz didn't have the electronic things we have now. The art of incarceration has definitely improved."

Abramsky talks of men confined in bathroom-sized quarters for twenty-three hours a day, the only interruption in their long, desolate days coming from food pushed through hatches in their doors.

And even this modicum of comfort sometimes is withdrawn as punishment. She speaks of minimal exercise, no more than three to seven hours a week.

With no sensory stimuli for months or even years, she says, "Many, quite simply, seem to go insane."

As grim as this scenario sounds—and admittedly it's from a high-security prison—versions of the same scene exist for the nonviolent prisoner who is being "processed" after transfer to a new facility.

Kirk, too, has spent several weeklong periods in what amounts to solitary confinement. He speaks of arriving at a new prison, and because he wasn't yet "classified," spending twenty-three hours a day in a cell, released only for meals. He says, "We didn't get any exercise. We didn't have TV. They wouldn't give us any books. We couldn't make phone calls. And we didn't know when it would end. We just sat there in the cell. For hours. I thought I was going to go nuts."

Over the last few years, this has happened not just once, but three times. His father and I were outraged. How dare they! We couldn't adjust to the inhumanity. The unfairness. The utter stupidity. How many humans, I wondered, could endure a week of this? I'm not sure I could. To make the stupidity even more blatant, Kirk wasn't even being punished! It was just an administrative thing. M. W.

～

Not all prisons are like this.

As the title of this chapter suggests, what follows is a discussion of lock-up drug treatment facilities within jails and prisons that are actually doing good instead of harm.

This book was conceived on the premise that such facilities are an important answer to the problem of overcrowded jails and prisons—and would save a significant number of nonviolent substance abusers from spinning endlessly through revolving doors.

Throughout the country there are pockets of people who agree with our premise. Quietly, without fanfare, they are busy treating substance abusers in a jail or prison setting. They're seeing favorable results coming out of lockup programs—and mostly with addicts who are resistant as mules, who absolutely, positively don't want help.

~

All of which suggests a generalization—always risky when it comes to human beings. Men and women whose daily lives consist of rescuing others seem to become transformed themselves. To anyone who has toured numerous lockdown drug facilities, it's obvious that jobs within such institutions attract staff members with unusual dedication.

The same attitude prevails everywhere. To a person the counselors and staffers love what they do, wouldn't change jobs with anyone, wish the whole world could visit their facility, hope others will soak up their message.

~

Before we discuss specific institutions, we must offer a caveat about inmate outcomes: as of this writing, all of the listed facilities that include treatment programs, with two exceptions, are too new to have reliable outcome data. The following descriptions are given as preliminary anecdotal observations, not yet backed up by statistics. While each facility is promising in its own way, it will take a few more years to provide the "proof" that skeptics demand.

The results of therapy programs cannot be tabulated like scientific data unless identical standards are established for identical time periods. Furthermore, it's probable that different approaches will succeed better with some individuals than others; only time and careful analysis will tell us which treatment methods work best for whom.

Indian Creek Correctional Center

Since chapter 7 ended with a comprehensive discussion of therapeutic communities, we'll start by describing what may be the second largest lock-up therapeutic community in the United States: the 950-bed facility in Chesapeake, Virginia, called Indian Creek Correctional Center.

Indian Creek is, first and foremost, a prison.

An initial, quick view of the facility is not cheering. The whole area is bleak and treeless, and beyond the administration building are row upon row of high fences, all topped by curling razor wire. It's obvious that whoever is inside is supposed to stay there.

In fact it is the very coercive nature of the place that raises grave doubts in the mind of Eugene Strauber, who runs Cenikor in Denver. When told about Indian Creek, he dismissed it out of hand. He insists that people who are kept in a therapeutic community by force cannot be getting much out of it. He theorizes that what you see are surface changes, that the inmates do what they do because they're forced to. By contrast, he says, at Cenikor every client makes a daily decision to remain with the program, thus strengthening his resolve to stay clean for life.

Clients may indeed benefit from making daily decisions to stick it out at Cenikor, but the staff at Indian Creek is equally convinced that their program works.

Any negative feelings that might stem from Indian Creek's grim exterior evaporate once an observer is inside. Within the walls, Indian Creek does not have the feel of a barbed wire community. Staff members are forthcoming, upbeat, and eager to talk about the program. Pithy, positive messages hang on all the classroom walls. It doesn't take long to soak up the prevailing mood. From the warden, Pat Terrangi, on down, emanates a powerful message: *We're the best. We're changing lives. We have a mission. Give us a wreck of a human being and we'll turn him into a restored, drug-free man.*

Throughout their stay, inmates are treated with respect. They are called "Mister," and they're listened to by staff. As in other TCs, they're encouraged to work their way up through the hierarchy to ever-greater positions of responsibility, to ever-more respect. The terms *cadre* and *coordinator* are reserved for those high on the ladder.

The central idea behind this practice is that a man responds best to pressure from his peers. As in all TCs, those on the lower levels are advised and disciplined and cajoled by those just above them—keeping in mind that this is a "family" and the health of the group is affected by the lowliest member.

In its own literature, Indian Creek defines itself as "an intensive, long-term institution-based treatment program for incarcerated substance abusing offenders." Since these are neither voluntary admissions nor first-time drug abusers, they aren't the "easy" cases. Most have such serious offenses as a long history of breaking and entering. To be accepted into the program, inmates must have at least three years left on their sentences. And long sentences aren't generally given for minor infractions.

The clients progress through five phases, described in an abbreviated form as follows:

Phase one: orientation, learning the rules.

Phase two: resocialization and "sharing." ("This is hard," says one of the counselors. "Guys don't want to share.")

Phase three: internalization/maturation—a change from staff control to internal control. Here the inmate is thinking, If I do this, I'll have a different lifestyle. Inmates in this phase are focusing on their own treatment plan. They're learning about enablers and beginning to consider the people they've hurt. As facilitators, they now lead other groups.

Phase four: preparation for reentry into society. This includes job interviews, housing placement, and peer support groups.

Phase five: post-release. The client continues to attend peer-support and self-help groups in the community. Indian Creek has a transitional specialist who works with the probation officer in each county to design home placement, to help with jobs, and to assist with maintaining quality peer-support groups.

In most respects, Indian Creek resembles other TCs, except that each phase is considerably longer.

A daily schedule lists all the classes offered in phase two. Courses include such subjects as "The Group Process (What Is Group?)," "Life Skills/Peer Support Group," "Introduction to Criminal Thinking," "The Addictive Disease Process," "Shame—Where Does Shame Come From?" "Guilt," "Anger," "Dealing with Physical Violence," "Raised to Be Bullies," "Self-Esteem," and "Men's Issues: 'I Act Like a Man.'"

On the walls of each classroom—all small, seating perhaps twenty or thirty people—hang inspirational messages and exhortations for

change. The Twelve Steps of AA are prominently displayed, plus inmate drawings and posters.

As in most TCs, regular confrontation groups are a tool for addressing client deficiencies and problems. Here, as elsewhere, staff
and counselors are a mix of recovering and nonrecovering people.
"You have to have a balance," one counselor explains.

Once a month, inspirational speakers are brought in from outside—usually a paroled inmate who comes with his parole officer. As
a further spur, inmates meet weekly with peer-support groups including members who are within ninety days of discharge.

"Our TC is a microcosm of society on the outside," a counselor
offers. "Here they learn life skills. They learn about making restitution. They learn to beware of enablers who may sabotage recovery.
They learn what recovery *is*."

With a heavy emphasis on some fifty-one values, including truth,
love, honesty, fairness, patience, humility, the community endeavors
to resocialize its members. And along the way clients learn dozens of
Indian Creek concepts: "People need people, not drugs and alcohol"; "Remember the rock you crawled out from under"; "Act as if,
feel as if, be as if"; "Nothing changes if nothing changes"; "There is
no situation so bad that one drink won't make it worse."

In the belief that decent clothes enhance self-esteem, clients are
required to be properly dressed: boots shined, laces tied, shirts
pressed and tucked in. Men are also encouraged to iron their clothes.

No society is complete without its celebrations, rituals, and cere-
monies, and Indian Creek has its share, all led by inmates, who
make posters and plan the details. Clean-and-sober parties are regular events.

When a client is ready to move to a higher phase—"fly up" is the
term—an assessment group called a "Wings Panel" decides whether
he's ready. Everything about the inmate is considered: his demeanor,
his dress, his hair, his attitudes. He is asked questions, which differ
from phase to phase. In phase three, for instance, the client's perception of himself is probed: has he given much thought to his future?

~

Change is the operative word at Indian Creek. When they first arrive, clients aren't happy. Most didn't choose to be there, and they bemoan the fact that they've been assigned to a place where they'll be scrutinized and prodded. They long to be at some other facility, where it's "three hots and a cot" and little else, or a mindless job that requires no self-examination.

Though this may seem contradictory to earlier observations that inmates prefer to be "busy," the kind of "busyness" required at Indian Creek is not what most have in mind. Clients would rather have nothing personal expected of them—no self-examination, no studying, no inner conflicts, no peer pressure to change. Often they grumble that they want to quit the program. Some actually do request a transfer. The staff gives the impression to outsiders that a transfer is possible under some circumstances. "We don't give up on them easily, though," a counselor says. "We do everything in our power to persuade them to stay. We know if we can just keep them, change will happen."

For those who stick it out to the end, the rewards are incalculable. Over and over, staff members hear the words that make the job worthwhile: "This is the best thing that ever happened to me."

Similar thoughts are expressed by Julius Franklin, a warmhearted bear of a man who often serves as a guide to outsiders. "There's no place I'd rather work," he says. "Every morning I jump out of bed, eager to get here. It's a great place to be."

The final assessment comes from parole and probation officers. "After an inmate's been there a few years, you don't recognize him. He's a different person. Anyone who graduates from Indian Creek would fit in anywhere."

Detention Centers:

Tidewater Detention Center for Women
Southampton Men's Detention Center

Judging by the diversity of drug treatment facilities currently available in the state of Virginia, the Virginia state legislature, which established the programs, believes that the greatest number of people will be served by the widest range of treatment options.

In any case, the approach used by the Tidewater Detention Center for Women in Chesapeake, Virginia, is different in every way from Indian Creek. Tidewater is a paramilitary facility whose aim is to bring discipline, self-awareness, and intense inner scrutiny to women who've had little of this in their lives.

Tidewater's mission statement says, "The mission of Tidewater Detention Center for Women shall be to provide intensive rehabilitation training through the application of discipline, the ethic of work, the instilling of pride, and the benefit of instruction and education for all probationers entrusted to its care. . . ."

From the outside, the facility seems friendly and relaxed, with lawns and trees leading to the administration building and dormitories.

Inside, however, the relaxed atmosphere disappears. Strict discipline is the order of the day, and indeed, even the superintendent, Irene Green, has the look of someone long accustomed to giving orders. Her graying hair is cut in a short, no-nonsense style, and her trim figure and upright carriage suggest military discipline and firmness. The voluntary program started in July 1998. Superintendent Green explains that it serves as a final correctional facility for women on probation—or as an alternative to jail or prison. The offenses that bring women there are usually the result of drug or alcohol problems. Having led aimless, self-destructive lives, the women are considered good candidates for a program that emphasizes rigid, no-nonsense rules and military discipline.

Many of the women have been abused by husbands or parents, and the majority are parents themselves—hence the center offers parenting classes that cover such issues as how to listen to your kids and how to be responsible parents, as well as corollary topics such as food, cleanliness, timeliness, budgeting, and job issues.

The core of the program, however, is military—with twice-a-day marching, drills, and vigorous exercises like jumping jacks. Through it all, silence is paramount. Nobody is allowed to speak, even during the scheduled free time.

"Not even at night?" Green was asked.

"They don't speak at all," says Green. "If they did, they'd be talking about trivial or destructive things. We want them reflecting on themselves, figuring out what's wrong with their lives. They need to focus on self-improvement.

"This is harder than ordinary jail," she adds. "Unlike jail, everything here is structured. It's a shorter, but tougher time."

It soon became obvious what she meant. There is no recreation built into the program—no television, no radio. The women are given one hour of free time at night to read or study for their GED (high school equivalency test), but even their books are restricted to self-improvement or the Bible.

Self-image is paramount. Nails must be cut, hair for African Americans left unbraided, uniforms kept neat, boots polished. Even the underwear comes with rules—all white, cotton only.

The women's days are mixed, divided between classes and work. Part of the group draws kitchen duties; others labor in the laundry or out in the yard. Still others get the preferred assignments—spending part of a day out in the community parks or along highways, where they perform such tasks as cutting grass and picking up debris. But even out in the community the rule of silence is maintained. The women are not allowed to talk to anyone they might see or meet.

Within the day's routine, silence is broken only on those occasions when Superintendent Green or a visitor appears in one of the dayrooms or bunkrooms. The minute Green is spotted, the nearest woman shouts at full voice, "Superintendent on deck!" Immediately the rest join in a shouted chorus, "Ma'am, good afternoon, Ma'am!"

Green says crisply, "Good afternoon!" to which the women reply, still at a shout, "Ma'am! All right, Ma'am!"

If Green's visitor thinks to mutter a quick, "Good afternoon," the group responds with a second, "Ma'am, good afternoon, Ma'am!"

This ritual follows Superintendent Green and her guests wherever they go, always in full voice and always in unison.

Exercise and drilling are an integral part of the day. A platoon of women, all dressed in burgundy jumpsuits, performs a drill that involves jumping up and down from their chairs. The chairs are arranged in a block and the leader yells, "Platoon, attention!" As one, the women jump up and stand in front of their chairs, chins high, chests forward, arms down, eyes straight ahead. The leader yells, "As you were!" and the women quickly sit down again, still staring straight ahead. To the nonmilitary eye, four or five of these would seem sufficient.

Not so. If the group is considered less than perfectly disciplined, the women must do endless repetitions of the jump-up, sit-down routine, always with eyes fixed, backs stiff and straight, until it would seem their legs would give out and plop them on the floor.

Green is asked, "Aren't a lot of the girls rebellious?"

"Not rebellious. Fearful."

In a nearby bunkroom, a few women sit on chairs, all silent, all quietly polishing their boots in little pockets of isolation—as though each is a loner who prefers her own company.

As Green approaches, she is acknowledged with the usual shouted greeting. Then the women return to their jobs. Not one glances up or shifts her eyes from her task. The nearest woman keeps her head down while she focuses on a black leather boot. Polishing, polishing, polishing. As though her boots are her universe, as though they are all that matter in life.

In a letter, Superintendent Green writes, "The 'chair drill' you saw is a special drill for a platoon of detainees who have not yet learned to act quickly and simultaneously . . . for a platoon that displays a lackadaisical attitude and needs reinforcement."

She adds, "Most of our training is not as repetitive [as the chair drill], with the exception of the military drill. That portion . . . which includes right face, left face, about face, must be repetitive in order to train the detainees to execute those movements the same way at the same time. All of this is done so staff can move a large group from one point to another in an orderly fashion.

"One of the learning tools that we use to encourage detainees to execute military moves correctly is competition between platoons. The platoon that executes the moves without any mistakes gets a 'Hoo

Rah' from all. The detainees in the platoon that wins feel very proud of themselves."

The average stay at Tidewater is four to five months. From there the women go home, or to a diversion center for job training, or back to jail. The women who complete the program gain an unaccustomed feeling of team spirit and leave with a certain pride, knowing they were able to stick it out.

I later ran into one of the graduates at a diversion center, and she spoke of her months at Tidewater as having been a good thing, the first time in her life she'd ever been disciplined.

"And what about all that silence?" I asked. "How did you stand not being able to talk?"

"It wasn't so bad, actually." The woman grinned at me. "It sure got me into a lot of thinking." M. W.

∼

The men's equivalent of Tidewater is in Capron, Virginia, and is called the Southampton Men's Detention Center. One of a number of different correctional facilities within the same region, the men's detention center is run on the same military principles as Tidewater. (The men's version actually came first.)

Marching, drills, military haircuts, and strict discipline are paramount, all on the order of a boot camp. Because the age range of clients at Southampton is so much broader than in boot camp—a few men are in their mid-fifties—the physical training is less arduous.

As with the women's facility, the program is voluntary and the probationers are not allowed to talk. Since the facility is essentially a farm, the men spend six to seven hours a day being farmers. Silent farmers. They grow crops, tend cattle, and work in the fish processing plant.

Evenings are filled with drilling, marching, and classes. Along with substance abuse programs run by certified counselors, and NA and AA meetings, the men attend classes in parenting ("Fathers Who Care"), anger management, and the Breaking Barriers program—a videotaped course for addicted offenders used extensively throughout Virginia. With minimal help from outside facilitators, they're also encouraged to run a self-help group among themselves.

In preparation for life back home, the probationers attend life skills classes, learning everything from personal hygiene to how to balance a checkbook.

Again like farmers, they are up by five every morning and in bed by ten. They commit to staying with the program four to six months, knowing the regimen will be hard, the drilling intense, and the silence difficult to maintain. Furthermore, they will see their families only twice a month, on Sundays.

Since the detention center has been in existence for only three years, follow-up statistics are scant. But John Loving, the director, sees what little data they have as encouraging. "Recidivism is much lower than traditional incarceration," he says.

Russell C. Schools Jr., a certified substance abuse counselor at the center, talks about alcoholism. "Education alone won't sober up an addict," he says. "It's a disease." In recovery groups that meet twice a week, the men write their own recovery programs. Schools always reviews the plan, and if it's too thin, he beefs it up. He notes that all addicts think alike, that all are quick to say, "I'm not an addict; I can quit whenever I want." The hardest job is convincing them that because of their unique genetic makeup, they'll never be able to drink in a controlled fashion. "It's hard to give up something you love," says Schools. "Nothing is ever enough for the con in recovery. Addicts will go through real pain when they're recovering."

He finds fence-sitters are often the ones who have the biggest problem making it, those who only half-believe they have a problem. His job is convincing the addict where he stands. "If he wonders if he's an alcoholic—he is."

Relapses are more frequent in the beginning, Schools says. Yet even the alcoholic who's been dry for years is at risk. After a long period of sobriety, rationalization is right there, ready to bring him down. "I've been clean for twenty years. I'm okay now. I can have one beer," is how the thinking goes. It's a recipe for disaster.

Schools says the typical alcoholic is more afraid of the pain of abstinence than the consequences of screwing up. And he finds age to be a big factor. The older the alcoholic, the more amenable he is to treatment. Furthermore, it is always easier to treat men if they are addicts first and criminals second. "The criminal personality," he says, "is tough to get through to."

He concludes by saying, "People change most with spirituality and relationships." Which suggests that Russell Schools, like so many others, finds Alcoholics Anonymous the best path to recovery.

Diversion Centers:

Chesterfield Men's Diversion Center
Diversion Center for Women at Southampton

Not all prisons look like prisons. Chesterfield Men's Diversion Center is located in a rural, woodsy area not far from Richmond, Virginia. In spite of its having a chain-link fence topped with razor wire, the center has a benign exterior, with the harsh aspects of the fence blurred by the forested look of the surrounding area. It would be easy to imagine that the razor wire is there to fence out deer rather than fence in people.

Inside, Jim Bruce, Chesterfield's superintendent, typifies the staffers who spend their days trying to bring change into the lives of addicts. A quiet, soft-spoken man, seemingly unemotional, he has an understated zest for his work—yet his attitude about the program, his co-workers, and the men in his charge is clear. He says there is nothing automatic about a diversion program like his. Sometimes addicts can be helped, sometimes they can't. He believes it all depends on the passion and devotion of the staff.

When told, "It's obvious how much you care about what you do," his expression scarcely changes and he answers almost matter-of-factly. "You have to have a fire in your belly." Running through all the staff at the Chesterfield Diversion Center is that same attitude, that same fire in the belly.

It is ironic, Bruce says, that his diversion center evolved out of the nation's current "Get tough on crime" philosophy. In a special session of the Virginia state legislature in 1994, parole was abolished for violent offenders. As part of the package—a part not much talked about—a number of diversionary programs were established around the state. The idea was to divert nonviolent offenders from prisons, thus making room to keep violent offenders longer.

The result has been what seems to be an almost-accidental experiment in the effectiveness of alternative programs for addicted offenders. Whatever the legislature had in mind, exactly, these "offshoot" programs have taken on a life of their own. Bruce believes they are beginning to prove that the remedy for the *addiction* crime wave was never a get-tough policy, as legislators believe, but rather its opposite— programs that include compassion, respect, and in-depth treatment.

Though Chesterfield is Virginia's first diversion center to open its doors, it has only been operating since 1997. It took the criminal justice system a number of years to get all the alternative programs up and going.

In this center, as elsewhere, most of the clients' criminal behavior stems from a variety of addiction problems. The current population consists of 114 men, nearly all of them substance abusers.

What began as a coercive work-release program has evolved into a plan where most of the clients are referred from the courts, often without having spent time in jail or prison. In this sense it is truly a diversion program. The focus is on prevention, and those who fail during their stay will probably spend time in jail or prison.

The men are expected to remain twenty-two weeks, but at the end of that period, a review committee may decide that some need an expanded program—up to six months or even longer. Bruce says, "It takes time to get a man's attention."

After a six-week orientation, clients are expected to work in the community, paying room, board, child support, and court costs to the center. In effect, their wages are split three ways: between the Central Corrections Office, restitution, and a savings plan against the day they'll need a down payment for rent.

Among the many positive features of the Chesterfield program is the availability of jobs. "We have more employers than we can satisfy," Bruce says.

"They don't mind hiring convicts?"

"Not if they come in with a clean, honest, straightforward appearance. Our local personnel managers really want them." A number of nearby businesses stand ready to employ clients: fast-food restaurants, medium industry, light construction, an oriental noodle factory, and a factory that prints cotton cloth.

The men leave each day with a sack lunch and are allowed to have sixty dollars in their possession to spend at the canteen. They are distinguished by their clothes. The newer offenders wear blue jumpsuits, the seasoned inmates khaki work clothes.

The six-week transition period can be an eye-opener for newly arrived inmates. Most are caught by surprise, unaccustomed to being treated with respect. To those fresh from the penitentiary, the atmosphere seems unreal, not to be trusted—and no doubt temporary. It takes time for newcomers to "thaw out" enough to open up and start responding to therapists.

The transition period includes classes on substance abuse and sessions built around the Breaking Barriers program. Early in their stay, clients meet Dr. Carole Hannigan, a small, grandmotherly woman who emanates wisdom and charm. Hannigan assigns the clients to small groups—five in each—and, with other counselors, guides them through a process of self-examination, reorientation of destructive thinking patterns, and eventually preparation for employment.

Hannigan notes that most of her clients have had a lifestyle devoid of the elements necessary for positive self-esteem. With a lack of job skills, and often coming from a dysfunctional family, the newcomer is both aggressive and negative. And past incarceration hasn't helped. She says, "Prison surroundings and prison personnel tend to reinforce the negative self-image with which inmates enter the system." All too often they see themselves as victims, which translates into distorted thinking patterns. "With limited expectations and perceptions," she says, "offenders easily return to their former lifestyle."

Here, clients feel safe. At all stages in the program, Hannigan keeps in mind that these battered men have fragile egos and defeatist attitudes. Gradually, as they write their autobiographies and discuss well-known characters on the outside who exemplify traits she wants discussed, the men begin to open up—both with her and their peers.

Each day, Hannigan works with the men on self-esteem and all the other self-concepts: self-worth, self-respect, self-confidence, and self-image, reaching them through discussion, quizzes, exercises, role-playing, and journaling.

A discussion on communication invariably touches on the anger issues so common to substance abusers. Through role-playing, they recognize and identify their hostility, gradually learning more effective, less aggressive ways to communicate.

Throughout, Hannigan coaxes inmates to understand that making choices based on integrity will actually enhance the quality of their lives. She helps them realize that every day they must make decisions and that how they decide each issue as it arises works for or against them. She shows them how they are ultimately responsible for what happens to them. Hannigan says, "This population has a tendency to rationalize their situation and avoid responsibility. They don't realize they have choices in life."

It is Hannigan's goal to make clients aware of how their thinking influences their actions, which in turn leads to consequences. Her hope is that their belief systems will change for the better—and that, with time, these new beliefs will become internalized.

∼

The second phase is career development. Here Hannigan presents a unique viewpoint, explaining the differences between a job and a career and emphasizing that merely having a job is not enough. She leads clients through a typical career path, in this case that of an auto mechanic, illustrating with graphs how a man can utilize training, apprenticeships, certified mechanic tests, community college courses, and experience to progress from a single job opening at Pop's Place to a variety of possibilities and salaries at companies like General Motors or Lexus.

Too often, LBWA—Living By Wandering Around—has been the

lifestyle of these men, she says. As they begin considering "real work," they're inclined to talk about starting their own businesses. "They're so unrealistic," says Hannigan with a smile. "Their plan is to sit back and watch others work. They don't know that the boss is the gofer. He's the one who comes in early and stays late. He's the one who makes everything else possible." For those who "get it," Hannigan and her counselors open up whole worlds of new possibilities.

Toward the end of the program, the clients' probation officers are sent a letter summarizing the program and a copy of the goals and objectives of the clients. A portfolio containing the self-goals and objectives written by the resident himself, a career plan, and his daily journals are retained by the client. Before he leaves, he is asked to write a kind of hopes-and-aspirations letter to himself, place it in a self-addressed envelope and give it to the counselor. The letter is mailed a year from the date the client leaves the facility.

~

Carl Smith ("Smitty"), the recovering ex-inmate described in chapter 6, has become an integral part of the center's counseling team, bringing insights that can only come from a man who's "been there, done that."

Smith plays an important role in offering clients a dual viewpoint, a look from both sides of the fence. After sharing the details of his past life, he says, "My reason for teaching this class is strictly selfish. It is quite gratifying for me when I see one of you leave here and do well. You deserve to do well. The problem is, you have some screwed-up ways of thinking, because no one ever showed you another way."

Carl then offers what he calls the "New Math." It goes like this:

Hey, I wanted the same things I saw everyone else with, didn't you? A house, a car, a big-screen TV, with a Nintendo, of course, not to mention a job. Did I say job? No, no, what I meant was a career. I've had lots of jobs, cause I needed the money. That's what it takes to get all those things, doesn't it? I mean, I see Mom and Dad plus other family members with these things, but I never stopped to look at how long it took to get them or what action they took. I just knew I wanted them, didn't you?

See, we only do what we know. So, if all we see is "Guido" on the corner selling drugs and hanging out drinking, there's a 95 percent chance we'll do the same thing. Why? Because we all have this lure of fast and easy money . . . and women, cars, and clothes. These are the things we want, right?

The only problem is, once we get them, they really don't mean that much to us. If they get ripped off or they break or whatever, we don't care. We figure we can just go buy another one. After all, we can make the money in no time, right?

What happens when Mom and Dad's TV goes out or the car breaks down? They have a fit. Why? Because it has value to them, it has meaning. Why? Because they had to put out some effort to get it. They had to work for it.

Now most of us who have been in the business usually think along these lines: I can do it for just a little while and get out. Ha. As soon as I get X amount of money, I'll quit. Yada, yada, yada. Sound familiar?

Okay, I'll give you this, you might get away for a while. In fact, let's look at you this minute, especially you younger guys—I've noticed you seem to think this way. Let's say you're out there, and you're out of school, either you graduated or you left. You need money cause you still want these things, right? So what do you do? You go to "Guido" and you pick up a package and start twirling.

Now imagine you get away with it for three or four months. I know these figures may not be right or exact, but bear with me just for the sake of argument. Maybe you've saved $5,000. I know it might be more than that, but figure what you've spent partying and chasing those skeezers around, since you're not used to having a lot of money. So now let's see, $5,000, I'm going to buy something. What's first? I know, a big-screen TV. Oh yeah, and a Nintendo and a bunch of games. What did I spend? $3,000, no problem. I'll use the $2,000 that's left for flash money, you know, just to show off.

Now here comes Joe Splivey, you know the one—there's always a Joe Splivey, isn't there? He says that the stuff is no good and that he didn't get off, and he wants his money back. Well, we know what we're going to tell him, don't we? Get out of my face. I'm trying not to hear it. Nobody else came back, so F— off.

Now he's hot, what does he do? He jumps on the phone and calls the Man. "Yeah. He's out there now, he's got a pocket full. He's wearing a blue Reebok running suit."

What happens then? Here comes the jump-out. Now you've got your first beef, and with the zero tolerance that the courts are taking with drug and driving offenses today, chances are you're going to get, uhmmmmmm, five years, but because it's your first time, you might get three suspended. Okay, you've got two years to do, twenty months under the new law and no parole. Well now, that $2,000 you had left . . . if the police didn't confiscate it, it's gone. You had to have money for the canteen, didn't you? So Mom's been feeding that money to you here and there over the two years. Cigarettes, sodas, small five-inch-black-and-white TV (cause it's cheaper), maybe even a Walkman.

Now you're out, what have you got? A small check and a bus ticket, plus a boot in the butt good-bye. And that's it.

Now you're home, and what have you got? A two-year-old TV that you never got to watch and a Nintendo that you never got to play—if they still work. So, you still want those things, right? Okay, so what do we do?

What we know. "Hey, Guido."

"Hey, man, it's good to see you back. Hey, I know you need a little help. Here, take this package and let me help you get on your feet." So, what do we do? Like I said, what we know. We take the package and run with it, thinking, I know what I did wrong last time. I just won't do that again.

Now a year goes by and you're rollin', you've got a bomb. Everybody is coming to you. You've got a smoker. It's the best thing out there. You've been dealing with these Colombian nationals, getting the real deal. Okay, let's say you've saved up, uhhhmmmmm, $50,000. Now we've got a little room to move, huh? Did I say move? Well, $50,000, now we can get us a car so we can style and profile—you know, showboat. Now we don't want to get too crazy, we really worked hard for this, didn't we? So we're off to the dealership. Let's say, again for the sake of argument, with the tax, tags, and title and the insurance, we spend $40,000. Not too shabby, huh? Plus, we've got $10,000 stashed.

Now, poor old Joe, he can't sell his, cause everyone is coming to you. But his dope man doesn't care, he's putting on the pressure, he wants his money. Joe's in a tight spot, so what does he do? You know what he's thinking? "Man, I gotta get this fool outta here. I can't sell S____."

What does he do? That's right, he's back on the phone. "Yeah, he's out there now. That's right, he's wearing a blue Reebok running suit."

So we know what the deal is now, don't we? Here comes the jump-out crew, and now your butt has another beef. Let's see, second-time felon and again for drugs. No question this time, ten years. And under this new law with no parole, we're talking nine years and two months before you get home again. Oh wait, I forgot, we have another charge. We've got that suspended time from before—what was it, three years? I think we can tack that on as well. We actually have thirteen years to do. And that $10,000 you had stashed, well, the lawyer got that if the police didn't confiscate it.

Here we go again, we finally make it back to the street. We come home this time and what do we have? A fifteen-year-old TV that we never got to watch and a Nintendo that we never got to play, if either of them still work. Drat, I forgot the thirteen-year-old car that we never got to drive, if Mom or Pop hasn't sold it. Or little brother or cousin hasn't tore it up. Otherwise, the only thing we've got is a small check and a bus ticket and another boot in the butt.

Now, let's look at this a minute. We've spent about fifteen years in the penitentiary for about a year and a half of the so-called good life. And we've still got nothing.

But then you've got some poor slob like me who, let's say, makes $20,000 a year. Well, how much have I made in fifteen years? That's right, $300,000. And I've been out here where I could chase them fillies around. You've been in the joint tossing off in the shower. I'm driving and you're walking.

Do you see something wrong with this picture? Does it add up to you? It doesn't add up to me. Oh and by the way, this is all information that I got from all of you. When I say that, I mean 90 percent of the guys I've had in class thought this way. Just so you know, I call this New Math. Mainly because I put this together from information from young guys, who in essence are new to the planet, not just the game.

I hope it means something to all of you.

～

Conversations with the Chesterfield inmates themselves suggest that Jim Bruce, Carole Hannigan, Carl Smith, a Lt. Bell, and the rest of the staff are accomplishing most of what they've set out to do. The changed attitudes of the men are unmistakable.

Kenneth S., a vigorous-looking forty-three, notes, "I was always on heroin." Yet here, in the diversion center, he is about to earn his GED. "I'm getting new values," he says. "Here, I'm treated with respect. They call you 'Sir.' They check how we think, so we can see where we were wrong."

Kenneth says he is mastering life skills, preparing his transition to the outside. For the last six weeks, he's been learning how to write checks, how to fill out W2 forms, how to balance bank accounts and understand bank statements, how to make out deposit and withdrawal slips. He admits he's also learned about personal hygiene: "flossing my teeth, using deodorant, getting my hair cut and my mustache trimmed."

J. Wilson, probably in his late twenties, was caught for possessing narcotics with an intent to sell. His grandmother raised him and his sister. "Mom and Dad had problems—they could hardly keep their heads above water. . . . Grandma did her best, but I was hardheaded. I went to detention homes, and my grandma, she got discouraged. She didn't want me to call. So I write her letters once a week. These people here have changed me a whole lot. I came from the penitentiary. I got no respect there. They called me Wilson. Those people, they'd stab you in the back. They didn't care. They'd throw you in the hole for no reason. They'd try to rile you up, try to make you lose your temper so they could beat you up. They used their badges to take advantage of you."

Wilson adds, "I feel comfortable here. Nobody ever provokes me, they treat me with respect. They're trying to help. It's a better life." He says he has three boys, and he now has a chance of supporting them. "I'm making plans for when I get out. I'll go into the welding trade. I came here with a big attitude. Now my attitude's improved. I'm committed to staying clean." When he speaks of using drugs, he says with a shake of his head, "Ain't nothing there."

Another man, Jim T., whose seamed, beat-up face makes him look considerably older than his forty years, talks of all the facilities he's sampled during his years of using drugs. Most recently he'd been in a paramilitary detention center where, for five months, he wasn't allowed to talk. "Yet in between, I always worked," Jim said. "I've lived two different lifestyles."

He grew up in a drug neighborhood, raised by his grandmother, mother, and stepfather—yet he was never taught responsibility or accountability. Jim says, "Nothing touched me. I knew I was not an addict. I could quit anytime."

All the prior treatment centers left him untouched. "I talked the talk, but I didn't walk the walk. I liked using drugs. I just didn't like the consequences."

When Jim wasn't using cocaine, he was drinking alcohol. Yet he never considered himself an alcoholic. "My head knew, but my heart didn't," he said.

Finally, to get cocaine, Jim began selling. For that he went to prison for four years. He believes prison did him some good. He was a model inmate, constantly reading. Once out, though, he violated probation immediately. He says now, "Nobody can do any more for me. I know it's up to me. I have to change my perceptions, or I'll go right back to the same old lifestyle." He grins ruefully. "I've got a master's degree in mistakes."

The stories all have a similar ring, whether related by the inmate in person or laboriously written on paper.

In his autobiography one young inmate writes:

"Through all of this, I find it ["using"] is not worth it at all. It took all of this to open my mind. But this one thing I will do, I will use the tools Carl (and others) have planted in me. And I thank the staff for helping me get my life back on track. I see all things like I never thought or seen them before."

Another says,

"So here I am in here, still away from my family, hoping and praying we can work things out. But I have a different outlook on life today. I want to make something out of my life. I am now thirty-nine years old. What I'm learning here is to better my skills. I have learned a lot since I've been

here. *This is not like any other place I've ever been. This program helps people care for themself. It shows us how to pay bills, to grow within ourselves. The teachers here are more than teachers, they are friends, someone you can depend on. Someone who cares about you, the person inside you. So to me, my life wasn't a life until you are able to fully understand yourself. Well, with the help of this place, I can now care about myself and others. That was hard for me, once. I learned how to forgive myself and others. Even some of the inmates here, I have learned something from them.*

"*It's been plenty of times I wanted to give up, but the inmates won't let you. When I go back to the outside world, I know how to apply what I've learned in here— to take and apply it to the streets. I never thought I would enjoy learning the way I have enjoyed learning here. So someone should really honor this place, because it's a good place for hard-core inmates.*

"*I would strongly recommend this program to anyone that have a problem with themself. Mrs. Bell, sweet but yet so strong-minded. Mr. Smith, cool and firm. Mrs. Bell keeps the peace and order. She shows love and concern. Mr. Smith been where we've been, so you can't pull the wool over his eye.*

"*But both of them are, and will be, loved for many years to come.*"

~

The women's version of Chesapeake is the Diversion Center for Women at Southampton, in Capron, Virginia. From its hilltop perspective, the visitor sees a large complex of prisons, boot camps, and detention centers, all spread out across an isolated part of Virginia.

Patty Bass, the director, personifies the women's version in much the same way that Jim Bruce represents Chesapeake, though the two could not be less alike in personality. Patty Bass brings liveliness, good humor, energy, and at times sternness to the women under her care. It's inevitable that her charges would be caught up by her intensity and forcefulness—even by the unusual blueness of her eyes. When Bass speaks, always at a rapid pace, they listen. It would be impossible not to.

Director Bass makes it clear from the start that her Diversion Center for Women is not intended as a diversion from drugs, but rather a diversion from the penitentiary—in keeping with the legislature's original intent. "Yet," she admits, "some 80 percent of our women do have drug problems."

In this relatively small facility—at present only fifty women—the same spirit of kindness, compassion, and respect prevails that is seen in other Virginia facilities. The clients call their director Mrs. Bass and aren't fooled by her sometimes stern, sometimes joking manner. They know she cares about them. They also know she expects a great deal from them—that she thinks it's about time they pulled themselves together and started living by a new set of standards.

Bass makes the rules clear from the beginning: drinking or using drugs is cause for immediate dismissal—so is any assaultive behavior toward other women. So far only one client has ever been sent away— for slapping.

After a mandatory four- to six-week treatment program, the clients find jobs in the community. For the remainder of their five-month stay, group sessions with a certified counselor must fit in around the women's work.

A typical group counseling session consists of six or seven women sitting around a table in the cafeteria discussing their problems with a counselor, speaking freely of grievances and feelings.

One woman, who seems much younger than her actual mid-forties, suspects she has a medical problem. Though frightened, she refuses to admit what the problem is. Mostly out of fear, she begins to cry, and another woman puts an arm over her shoulders. "Now that I'm not on drugs, I know something's wrong. But I'm afraid to find out what."

The male counselor, a tall, scholarly-looking man with a gentle demeanor, says softly, "You can't put this off, you know. It isn't necessary to tell us, but you must find out what's going on. These women are here to help you."

La Sallya, a beautiful woman in her late twenties, turns away defiantly. "I don't want to care about her. I don't want to be depressed. I have to be strong." The others ignore this outburst.

A third says of the sick woman, "She should be an example. She's the oldest. I hate it when she sits around and mopes."

They go on to other issues. One of the heavier women, Cindy, accuses another of not sharing her food. The accused, Danielle, snaps back impatiently, "'Course I won't share. You're already fat. I used to be 350 pounds. I was miserable."

Another speaks up quickly, "I was once 400 pounds." Suddenly the session has become, Can you top this?

Cindy says angrily, "You don't have to remind me every day that I'm fat."

Danielle responds, "My father made me feel bad about myself. He made me hate myself."

A calm young girl says to Danielle, "And now you're doing the same thing your father did."

The counselor, turning back to the woman with the medical problem, says, "If you let this go, you know, it's going to get worse." And then to the group as a whole, "How will you help her?"

"Comfort her."

"Talk to her."

The counselor, again addressing the sick woman, says, "If you don't deal with this, what do we do?" A pause. "Perhaps she can give *us* permission to deal with it." Another pause. "Will you give us permission to break confidence and go tell someone?"

The sick woman gives a barely perceptible nod.

After some additional sharing, the group disperses.

$\sim$

Two of the women stay on to share their life stories.

Cathy is only nineteen. Earlier, she was in a paramilitary detention center, which she admits gave her new self-control and new respect for others.

Her short life has been sad and full of trauma. She says, "I can't go back to the trailer park where I lived. I stole there." Worse, her stepfather is now controlling her home situation and doing it badly, putting her two younger sisters at risk for serious problems. "My real dad was always drunk," she says. "He was a bad alcoholic. He beat my mom."

Even today she can't accept that her parents lied to her—continually. "I was the adult around there. I had to get between my mom and dad, to try and save my mom." With no warning, her desperate mother suddenly left the home, and Cathy says sadly, "She went away without me or the kids. I felt deserted. My mother was gone for a year."

"She didn't try to call you?"

"No. Not even once. I felt abandoned. It was like being rejected. Finally I ran away. I did drugs and hung out with the wrong crowd. I was caught breaking and entering. I stole a car. I was drunk, smoking marijuana. I tried just about everything."

"Now that you're in diversion, what will you do?"

"I want to go to college." She smiles, a thin smile. "I always got good grades. I learned how to study. I hope I'll do well in college."

Another girl breaks in with a quite different story.

Lindy, a thin young woman with big eyes and a soft, sensitive face, talks about her addictions. Only twenty-eight, she's been in jail for the last fourteen months. The jail did have a substance abuse program, but it was voluntary.

Before jail, she forged prescriptions for oxycontin (morphine). She and her husband took a variety of prescription drugs, including Percodan. "Without dope I couldn't get out of bed. Your body just shuts down. I was stealing to get dope." In early 1997, the police found the prescriptions, and she was given probation.

She says now, "That first time I should have gone to jail." She thinks back. "You're real scared the first time you get caught. But I got off. The doctor went to court with me and gave excuses. He kept me from suffering any penalties. But jail . . ." a dark look comes into her eyes, "that was a reality check."

Lindy's opinions are reminiscent of comments from Chuck Griffith, the commonwealth's attorney for Norfolk, Virginia. He makes the point that society has lost its will to make people responsible. Alhough he concedes that most people who commit a first crime aren't inherently evil, once they break a law they're in a new category. "The very first time," he says, "we should lock people up for a few nights, instead of giving them a slap on the wrist. Even if it's the bank president. Even if he loses his job. Immediate punishment is a great deterrent."

A quick reply: "Well, maybe a short stay . . . a really short stay, like a night or two, wouldn't be all bad. Just for shock value."

"That's right," he says. "For shock value."

Lindy goes on with her story.

"After three months clean," Lindy continues, "you get your feelings back." She hesitates. "I guess that's why you start in the first place—to drown your feelings." It is only toward the end of the session that she reveals what those feelings are, that she'd been sexually abused by an alcoholic father.

Lindy adds, "I wouldn't have been ready for diversion until I'd done jail. Now, after jail, this program is working." She says thoughtfully, "Even while I was in jail, I went to the substance abuse program voluntarily. But my sentence was too long. Three months would have done it. A short sentence works just as well as a long one. After that, I needed a structured program on the outside. Even now, I still need discipline."

She says with unusual candor, "Now I'm kind of scared. All these years I've partied and schemed to get dope. I haven't held a job in four years. I haven't lived a responsible, normal life. I need to relearn my work habits. It'll probably take time."

"But you'll do it?"

She nods, and her intentions are clear. But it will doubtless take a lot of hard work and perseverance if those intentions are to be realized.

~

The Old and the New:
Programs from Delaware to California

Thanks to the 1998 book *Crime and Punishment in America* by Elliott Currie, a wider readership now knows about the Key program in Delaware. As one of the earliest in-prison substance abuse programs to attract media attention, the Key program was initially much acclaimed, and the concept seemed to be one of those great breakthroughs, like penicillin. Lately the name has popped up in other contexts, and it's clear that Delaware has become a model for the rest of the United States.

The Key program enjoys two major distinctions: not only is it one of the country's first chemical dependency programs behind bars—in operation now since 1988—but it's also one of the best tracked, with the University of Delaware currently keeping outcome statistics, as it has from day one. When an ABC News program reported jubilantly, "A whopping 74 percent of felons don't come back!" their claim was based on long, reliable records.

It's no exaggeration to say that Delaware's Key program has enjoyed a remarkable record, producing an exact reversal of the expected rate of recidivism. Among the nontreatment institutions that keep track, 60 to 70 percent of released felons do come back, following an arrest for a new crime. In fact, it's probably Delaware's Key program that has inspired a number of jails and prisons around the country to try new approaches.

As in other therapeutic communities discussed in these pages, the residents start with a thirty-day orientation period and gradually work into ever-higher positions of respect and responsibility. The various levels are flexible; clients move up at their own speed.

The program lasts nine to twelve months, and it's one of the most intense in existence. Substance abuse treatment takes up the entire day, from 6 A.M. to 9 P.M., with breaks only for meals. Though about half the clients are there by choice, residents never find this kind of intense self-scrutiny comfortable or easy. As in all programs that dig deep into the addict's psyche and demand change, there's a period when the offender wants to bail out and forget he ever heard of the place.

Thanks to the high success rate of the original Key plan (Key North at Gander Hill Prison), Key programs have been implemented in other parts of the state, treating some five hundred clients in all. The Delaware Department of Corrections enthusiastically backs the project and helps assess clients for referral.

Among inmates who make a written request for treatment, Counselor Ray Barneman has noted a pattern. "They often have a moment of clarity," he says, "usually late at night, when they're lying in their cells, thinking. They realize that life is passing them by . . . that people on the outside are actually living decent, normal lives. Suddenly they think, I need to do something. How long the moment lasts, I don't know, but it's often enough to get them here."

As in other prison programs, treatment clients are segregated from the general prison population, with dorms and meeting rooms that reflect a noticeably friendlier atmosphere. Resident-made posters and murals decorate the walls, spreading messages of encouragement and hope. "Here," said Barneman, "we try to turn negatives into positives." The client who painted a beautiful mural for the original walls when the program first began came back as a relapsed patient eleven years later to paint another in a new facility. "You see," said the counselor, "your relapse may have had some purpose after all."

When the resident's sentence is up and he leaves prison, he has the option of going to the work-release Crest program for six months and after that to a third level, called, generally, aftercare. Statistics have proven that the best results come from attendance at all three levels. Yet, strangely, it's what takes place outside prison walls that seems to have the greatest impact on whether the client succeeds in the normal world. For this reason, most in-prison programs now focus heavily on aftercare. Clearly, a good prison program can change an addict in significant ways. But what happens later makes the ultimate difference.

～

A second in-prison program, this one in Southern California, shares Delaware's record for longevity and enjoys even more dramatic results. Amity, a small program within the very large R. J. Donovan Prison in San Diego, is actually able to claim a recidivism rate of 15 percent, which means of those who complete the program, 85 percent never return—possibly the best inmate success rate recorded anywhere.

The R. J. Donovan Prison sprawls across a number of barren acres near the Mexican border south of San Diego. Surrounded by vast, rolling plains, all treeless, its exterior fits the bleak prison image.

Community Resources Manager Pete Flores is a knowledgeable guide for the visitor who is cleared to visit the Amity portion of the facility. As in most prison tours, the guide and his visitor pass through a number of locked gates and guarded checkpoints, showing IDs at each station. In the vast bare-dirt yards that surround the buildings, scattered clusters of prisoners can be seen exercising.

While the largest part of the prison is occupied by the usual mix of inmates, the drug treatment units are relatively small, with meeting rooms reserved for those being treated for substance abuse. Amity's intimate group sessions are held in what appears to be a temporary building. As of this writing, Amity can accommodate only two hundred inmates, but the program will soon expand to four hundred. The usual stay is between nine and twelve months.

Across the country, in-prison programs seem to be equally divided between the coercive and voluntary. Amity is strictly voluntary. Inmates apply when they're two years away from parole, but even so the wait can be as long as six months. Currently, 139 men are on a waiting list.

Unique to this program, Amity accepts criminals who have committed serious violent crimes. The leader of one of the groups had, eighteen years earlier, killed a man.

The program is structured as a therapeutic community, with encounter groups that encourage the venting of hostility, so that the typical meeting involves inmates who shout at one another, often with profanities.

Which brings up an interesting, separate issue. Whether voluntary or involuntary, therapeutic communities seem to come in two varieties: those that allow, even encourage, abusive language during encounter groups, and those that don't. Cenikor and Indian Creek do not allow profanity. Peer One, Haven, and Amity do.

Which works better?

It's our opinion that profanity and verbal abuse can only damage an already fragile ego. However, certain experts believe differently. It's our hope that an objective study will help prove who's right.

Given the fact that Amity is part of a prison setting, the intimate room where the encounter groups are held seems unusual: not only is there a colorful area rug on the floor, but the chairs are reasonably comfortable. The usual encounter group consists of twenty or so inmates sitting in a circle, with two counselors, both recovering drug abusers themselves, serving as facilitators. In the scene described below, both counselors were women.

Typical of the conversations aired during encounter sessions is the following exchange. (Unfortunately, these are only fragments. No tape recorders are allowed, so it's necessary to listen hard and scribble as fast as possible—and later change the names, of course.):

Bill, a young Caucasian man with a crew cut, begins by expressing his relief that his grandmother forgave him before she died. "She told me she was proud of me for putting myself in Amity. I feel new hope now. I haven't been going to Monday groups. I was too upset over my grandmother's death."

George (short, a bulldog of a man, balding and irritable): "That's just an excuse. You're like naturally shitty, you know it? We could use better behavior from you on the floor. That's just one example, Bill, of what happens in life. When is something gonna go wrong on the streets that flips you over?"

Jerry (thin, with glasses and narrow mustache, quiet and philosophical): "How are you going to restrain yourself on the streets? Out there, you'll get deeper in trouble."

George (making a pugnacious face): "You had an incident with Flores. Another with Tim. It wasn't your grandmother. You just didn't have the nerve to show up here."

Bill looks grim and defensive. He's clearly on the hot seat, with the others accusing him of not functioning according to group standards.

Jerry (pushes his glasses up): "Small stuff will always come up. You've got to control your anger. What happens when you're out, and there are guns on the street?"

George: "Your temper is your problem. Big time. When are you gonna work on it?"

Jerry: "And you're always ducking too. When people call you on stuff, you give them nine different excuses."

George: "You keep throwing things off on other people."

Bill (breaks in furiously): "I'll deal with my shit!"

George: "You'd better. Those resentments are gonna kill you."

Bill: "I'm going home soon. I'll be okay then. I know I'm gonna see old friends. But I won't hang out with them."

Jerry (thoughtfully): "There's a general expectation that you guys who are leaving will go to the ranch." (The ranch is a four-month halfway facility out in the country.)

Bill: "I'm not going to the ranch! I'm going home to my family!"

George (stubbornly): "So pick your top resentment, okay? You've got a gangload of resentments. Throw out a major one."

Bill: "You think I'm a fake and a fraud."

George: "That's a start. So get the list out!"

Bill (now turning defensively to Todd, across the room. Todd is a handsome, self-assured man.): "I notice that you think you're better than you are!"

George (belligerently): "Go on—get out your resentments!"

Bill (to Todd): "Why was you gonna quit the community? (then to a counselor, sitting by saying nothing) "One resentment would be with you! My latest resentment is over a job change slip. And over the thing about my mustache."

George: "People think they can act shitty in here. But we're going to respond back. We get people to listen sometimes by being shitty ourselves. You're getting shitty about a mustache. It'll grow back!"

Ozane (Ozane is the leader, an enormous African American man with the demeanor of a wise, patient grandfather. He seldom speaks, but when he does, everyone listens. He clearly enjoys great respect from the others.): "You're well-liked, Bill, but you won't say what's bothering you. You need to say it here. When you get out, you'll be frustrated, and first thing you know you'll get a beer. Then you'll go get your drug of choice."

Jerry (mildly): "It's good you want to be with your family, Bill. But you have to tell them the facts. Your recovery comes first."

Ozane: "So, Bill. When are you gonna stop being an emotional coward?"

This question is followed by a long silence. Nobody seems able to respond.

Bill finally says: "I am an emotional coward, in a way. But I do deal with my shit with some people."

Ozane: "No. You choose to deal with things besides yourself. You take one step forward and three or four steps back."

Bill (speaking again to Todd—not yet heard from): "Todd, you always try to prove yourself better than everyone else. You always make yourself look better than the rest of us."

Ozane (mildly): "Why don't you like Todd?"

Todd (a superior smile): "I've been here two years without smacking anybody."

At this moment, the rest of the group gets very confrontational, all picking on Todd.

Then Bill says, "I'm all yelled out."

Ozane asks Bill, "Do you feel better?"

Bill laughs weakly.

Ozane: "You're on a roll. Go on. Get it out. Air your resentments."

Bill: "Here you get laced and embraced. I know when Todd leaves and goes to the ranch, he's gonna hit a corner. I can tell by his attitude. So I give him a pull-up. I try to live up to the expectations of the group."

Jerry: "Did Todd hurt your feelings, Bill?"

Bill: "He kind of did. We were friends once."

Todd: "Only three people I've let get close to me. Now Bill tells me I'm gonna hit the corner when I get to the ranch. I don't need friends like you."

Bill (suddenly furious at Todd): "Why do you act like you know it all? Like you've got no time for anyone? You're a piece of shit!"

Ozane: "Why does what he says affect you? Why do you take his words and make them gospel? You internalize everything he says like it's the truth."

Todd (with his faint superior smile): "You know, you could talk to me, Bill, if you wanted. You see me every night. I'm playing cribbage and doing pull-ups."

∼

And so it goes—the men boring in on each other's weaknesses, exposing problems, encouraging others to vent their hostilities. And from time to time, Ozane, the leader, breaking in to offer a new way to think.

Afterward Pete Flores comments on the session. "You don't know how unusual that was," he says, and his awed tone suggests he considers it something of a miracle. He explains that men in prison are vulnerable and quickly learn never to give out information, even to their roommates. Everyone in this setting knows that other inmates are manipulative and will use information as weapons. "You learn to keep to yourself," he says. "You keep your mouth closed. Everything you say can be used against you." He explains that after an inmate gets burned, he withdraws. He keeps his thoughts private and never reveals anything.

Furthermore, men who take abuse are seen as weak and become prey for predators. "If you and I are in line at the grocery store, for instance, and we get bumped," says Flores, "we turn around and say, 'Excuse me.' Not so with a man in prison. He has to respond to any slight or perceived disrespect with abusive anger, or others will gang up on him.

"You can't expose your fears or worries, it's too dangerous," he says. "That, too, makes you look weak. Men in prison develop a hard shell around them. And when they get out, they're antisocial."

∽

Pete Flores opened my eyes about the changes we've observed in our son. As his imprisonments increased in length, we saw most of his former softness disappear. Whereas Kirk once laughed readily, and with genuine pleasure in the people around him, his laughter is now rare and tinged with sarcasm. No longer relaxed and easy to have around, he is nervous and on edge, always ready to explode. To our dismay, he takes instant affront at words not intended to provoke.

Where is the young man our friends once described as "such a nice guy"? Where did his deep reservoir of anger come from? How could the gentlest, the most easygoing of all our five sons change into the scariest, flintiest member of the family?

After I met Pete Flores, I began to understand. M. W.

∽

Somehow the men in the Amity program acquire the strength to break all the unspoken prison rules; they muster the courage to confront each other and, more important, confront themselves. In sessions held twice a week, for a total of ten to twelve hours a week, the men open up, coming to know intimately the others in their group. They feel safe. Since the group is static—the same people remain together for the length of their prison stay—trust is eventually established.

As one of the women counselors describes the dynamics: "It's the most amazing thing to see this in a prison environment—guys sharing. Spilling their guts. Hugging. People who don't understand the prison culture don't know how extraordinary this is."

The payoff is phenomenal. Considering that the Amity program includes violent criminals, its recidivism rate is nothing less than astonishing. For those who spend an additional six months at the Amity Ranch, the recidivism rate is *under* 15 percent—nearly unheard of!

Yet even for those who don't go to the ranch, a nonresidential community center offers the men a way to stay connected.

As for the leader, Ozane, his manner of dealing with the others seems both wise and statesmanlike. He states matter-of-factly and without bitterness that he comes up for parole soon. One can only hope things will work out for him.

～

Corcoran Prison in Northern California is a name that evokes dread in the minds of criminals. Once the site of riots, shootings by guards, scandals, and extensive outside investigations, it is slowly gaining a different image. Who would imagine that a new prison, adjacent to the old one, would one day be a leader among in-prison treatment facilities? Or that it would be known for its humanity and wisdom?

Yet this is exactly what has happened.

Opened in 1997—the same year that so many treatment facilities opened their doors in Virginia—the new California Substance Abuse Treatment Facility and State Prison at Corcoran (CSATF/SP) was given a boost when John Stallone, who helped start the R. J. Donovan Prison, came up from San Francisco to become clinical director and help run Corcoran's new treatment facility. With him came Elaine Abraham, also from Donovan.

With a head count of 1,500 substance abusers, few there by choice, Corcoran has tackled a thorny problem, creating the largest treatment facility in the United States and doubtless the world's largest therapeutic community.

For the felon who meets certain eligibility criteria—drug use without violence or gang membership, and at least a year left on his sentence—the program offers real hope of rehabilitation.

As with most of the prisons scattered around California, Corcoran is miles from anywhere and does not offer a welcoming face to the world. An electric fence surrounds the compound, complete with chilling statistics. Lest anyone think the prison might be soft enough to let down its guard, the literature mentions that the 5,100-volt fence can deliver up to 650 milliamperes—and that 70 will kill.

Inside, precautions against escape are never far away. Even personnel well known to guards must present their IDs at every checkpoint as they move about the facility.

Yet deeper within, the atmosphere changes. Compared to normal prison conditions, the living is better in every way. Instead of forty men to a shower, the number drops to ten. Instead of dorms housing fifty or a hundred men, the facility has small rooms with four single beds to a room. In such relatively intimate quarters, inmates develop a sense of responsibility for, and pride in, their living space. And indeed, personal cleanliness and clean living quarters are stressed, partly as a matter of self-esteem.

Two outside groups, well known in California for their work with substance abusers, provide treatment within the walls: Walden House and Phoenix House, both therapeutic communities. Inmates get twenty hours of treatment per week in a program that lasts six months to a year.

Treatment consists of four phases: orientation, therapeutic community, pre-reentry, and aftercare. In addition to individual and group substance abuse counseling, inmates participate in classes that cover all the traditional areas of therapeutic communities: anger management and conflict resolution, life skills, relapse prevention, abuse issues, criminal thought processes, self-esteem, Twelve Steps, and a number of classes devoted to the problems of reentry. Random urinalysis testing ensures that the inmates stay substance free.

Unlike other in-prison facilities, the treatment contractors offer up to ten additional hours of structured, optional treatment activities, such as family counseling and recreational activities, which may include physical activities, art, and music therapy.

The inmate's day consists of four hours of work within the facility and four hours of treatment. Vocational training is offered in no fewer than twenty-two different trades. Such fields as auto mechanics, upholstery, air-conditioning, plumbing, and carpentry help give the client marketable skills for the outside—always a major concern for counselors, who recognize that treatment often fails if the substance abuser can't find employment.

The fourth phase focuses heavily on aftercare, which is voluntary. Here as elsewhere, counselors feel that what happens after the prisoner leaves is almost more important than what happens inside.

~

It appears Corcoran isn't one of the "swearing at each other" facilities. When clients speak up, they are low-key, respectful, but always honest, freely discussing their mutual problems as substance abusers. One man says with a wry smile, "It's our best thinking that got us here."

The leader of one of the groups is an older man, dignified and assured, himself a former drug abuser. He tells the others, "The minute you get back in your comfort zone, that's when you slip." He calls the penitentiary environment a war zone. "People try to bring old habits in here." He looks out at his audience sternly. "Hang on to what we're trying to tell you. You may *never* get this opportunity again!"

Another inmate speaks up. "There are a lot of talented people behind bars. I've got a problem with people telling me, Once a dope fiend, always a dope fiend. I don't like people saying, 'Hi, I'm Jerry. I'm an alcoholic.' I'm *not* an alcoholic. I'm not drinking anymore, so I'm not an alcoholic."

The leader responds by noting that the label serves as a reminder that the problem is always there, even in the absence of drinking. He adds that a therapeutic community operates within the principles of AA, but as an *addition* to AA. He further describes the operation of a TC: "It's about taking back our personal power. The TC is not meant to induce fear. AA uses those statements to remind us, 'This is a blind spot.' The therapeutic community is here to add new truths to AA and NA. We're at our best when we're part of something—part of a family. Here, it's inmates helping inmates. There's a lot of respect here."

Private interviews are granted with two inmates who have progressed through the hierarchy and are now leaders, or facilitators.

Dale Piute is a Native American who, for the last six months, has been a facilitator. He once lived what he himself terms the typical reservation life. He says, "I was an alcoholic who beat women." He was married at age fifteen to someone he now labels "a good woman." By then he was already deep into drinking, having started at age eight. "All my relatives began drinking early, and most of them have already died of alcoholism." He smiles ruefully. "I'm about the only one left."

Now age forty-five, with the heavy-jowled look of a much older man, Piute feels like a longtime survivor. But it hasn't come easily. He looks back on a youth that he calls "a disaster." After six confinements by the California Youth Authority, he says he was tired of being in trouble and tried to stop drinking.

But then he was imprisoned again in 1975, "drunker than a dog." The escapade that landed him in jail began with his test-driving a new car and ended with a kidnap of sorts, since he was caught with the new car and the mechanic still inside.

That day he vowed to himself, "This will be my last time ever in jail."

Once out, Piute was able to maintain his sobriety for sixteen years! But his very pride in all those sober years became his downfall, for he was lulled into thinking he was safe, that he was okay to drink again.

He wasn't. Three times Piute was caught driving drunk, and now his hangovers turned into momentous events, lasting a week instead of a few days. He thought to himself, "I don't want them putting handles on me and lowering me into the ground."

Finally clean again, he considers himself a functional alcoholic. But he still doesn't trust himself and has decided he no longer dares drive a car. He has a strong message to give inmates about becoming complacent with their sobriety.

~

The second interviewee is named Terrence S. A thin, restless man, he'd been imprisoned five times at California Rehabilitation Center, which he dismisses as having been useless in helping him reform. "There's more dope there than on the street."

His drug of choice was methamphetamine, but he feels he has escaped its clutches. He's now with the aftercare program as a resident demonstrator. Eventually he wants to help children.

Terrence points out that it takes dedicated personnel—at Corcoran or elsewhere—to deal with addicted inmates. Newcomers to the program are difficult to reach because they don't understand how a therapeutic community functions. On the other hand, some of the more sophisticated inmates actively try to undermine the program.

Odd as it seems, Terrence now feels uncomfortable on the outside; he says he can no longer endure an unstructured life. "It's like a madhouse out there," he says. "Everyone's loose. I went to a party, and I had to turn around and go home. I couldn't stand it." He knows what's wrong with him; by his own admission he's become "institutionalized."

Another counselor explains the term. Sometimes an inmate like Terrence, who lives too long in a structured environment where he isn't allowed to make choices, finds that freedom has lost its appeal and is simply frightening. Without rules, predictability, and routine, such a person feels adrift and uncomfortable—even terrified. This label can apply to children, as well, when they are raised too many years in a rigid group environment.

Terrence feels confident that in his current setting he's gaining control of his life. He has learned his relapse traps, which include his old neighborhood and his old girlfriend. "I've cut her loose," he said. "I had to. She'd bring me down again."

At last he feels he's been given the tools to make a new, decent life. He declares proudly that all his attitudes have changed.

His last thoughts are of the counselors who introduce and explain the substance abuse program to newly arrived prisoners—those who can still choose whether or not to participate. "They should help people make the right choice. Maybe these new guys should be kidnapped. They've just gotta know what's here."

～

Jane Silva, supervisor of one of Corcoran's units, speaks about her job in a way that's reminiscent of Jim Bruce, superintendent of the Chesterfield Men's Diversion Center in Virginia. It was Bruce who explained in his low-key way that success with addicts isn't automatic; it depends on the passion and devotion of the staff. "You have to have a fire in your belly," he said.

In a quiet voice, because much of hers is a whispered conversation during a group meeting, Silva evinces that same spirit, that same "fire in the belly." If the inmates at Chesterfield regularly single out their counselors for having helped change their attitudes and their lives, it seems probable that those at Corcoran will do the same with Jane Silva.

Silva is eager to explain the many positive things that are happening in her prison unit. "Here, we integrate the races," she says, looking around at the mix of whites, Latinos, and African Americans sitting together at the meeting. "We break the convict code that keeps the races separated. There aren't any gang bangers here." She smiles. "They get pretty comfortable. Sometimes they even forget where they are." (As though this weren't a prison.)

In a tour of the facility, she points to the walls, where a variety of pictures and posters are hanging. "The inmates do their own artwork," she says. "The guys can point to it and say, 'That's my work up there.' And another thing. We celebrate all the holidays here."

The theory is that holidays help make the days meaningful and keep clients connected to the outside world. Marking important occasions is just another way of instilling hope, of showing respect for inmates and the rituals that matter to them. She adds, "Once a year we throw a barbecue in the yard, with the staff serving the food. It's a very healing experience."

She describes the staff in more detail, explaining that Corcoran regularly hires ex-inmates as facilitators—a policy that wouldn't be approved in other prison settings. "Our facilitators have to interview for the job," she says. "They have to be smart. As they parole out, we take more interviews. It's good for the facilitators themselves. They serve as role models for the others."

She adds, "We're always bringing new staff into the cluster." Like counselors everywhere, Silva believes that a mix of recovering addicts and counselors with no drug history provides the most comprehensive treatment.

Even among the noncounseling staff—the career professionals who do the administrative jobs that keep the facility running—there's an attitude that Corcoran's substance abuse facility is a preferred assignment. "We like it here," says one of the officers. "We have fewer accidents, fewer sick days, and far less stress. It's a great place to work."

~

Eventually, of course, the inmates serve out their sentences. But they don't just "leave"—they graduate. Jane Silva describes what happens at graduation. "The men make graduation hats and everyone wears them. It's quite an event. I've heard guys say, 'It's the first time I've ever finished anything in my life.'"

She speaks vehemently about the need for aftercare: "Without it, their outside needs are not being met. The men can't handle the sudden freedom, the lack of controls. They're used to constant supervision and 'three hots and a cot.' We offer them 180 days of continuing care. And 180 more if they relapse.

"We plant seeds while they're here," she says. "We talk to them about the importance of aftercare. Even though it's voluntary, about 50 percent of them do end up attending programs on the outside. We used to be 'to the gate.'" She grins, adding with pride, "Now we go beyond the gate."

She sums up the program: "Here, you've gotta have heart. You've got to have faith in what you're doing. If you can get them involved in their own recovery, it's theirs!"

At the end of the day Silva makes the statement that rings out above all others: "We believe in them. We believe in them until they believe in themselves."

~

Hoping to confirm that its program works, Corcoran has hired students from UCLA to do long-term statistical studies. So far, the studies show that without treatment, seven out of ten inmates return to prison. With treatment, seven out of ten Corcoran offenders leave and don't come back.

~

In spite of the caveat offered earlier that most of the facilities described are too new for reliable outcome statistics, it's important to mention once more the two exceptions—Delaware's Key program and R. J. Donovan's Amity program—both carefully tracked and both with astonishing, provable success rates. A skeptic need only look at the carefully kept statistics from these two institutions to deduce that the other facilities will soon be able to report similar results.

In-jail, in-prison drug treatment programs *do* work. We just need the public will, the political will—*the guts*—to try them. We have to believe that it's a disgrace to throw human beings away like refuse, when, with some effort, we can reclaim them.

And here a last point needs to be reiterated: The success of most of these programs depends to a great extent on the dedication of staff. The attitudes, the generosity of spirit, the determination, the personalities of the people who run the programs seem to make the largest possible difference in whether they work. Just as a bad or good teacher can make any subject boring or fascinating, bad or good staff members are key to how well a drug program is accepted by those who need it.

In essence, when it comes to programs, leaders are everything. They make all the difference. But we knew that all along, didn't we?

~

The following discussion takes us beyond jail or prison walls to additional resources within the community. What is available to help a recovering ex-inmate connect with treatment upon release from prison? Too often, relatives and friends—and the prisoner himself—have no idea where to go, first for counseling, then for treatment.

On a local level in Orange County, California, research has unearthed two programs little known to most Orange County residents. The Great Escape program, for instance, offered in the Orange County jail, gets so little publicity that it takes on the feel of a secret society.

Great Escape is a prerelease planning program that offers inmates connections to recovery sources on the outside—but only to those men and women who want it. Apparently many do. Counselors are often stopped in the halls and asked, "How can I get in? Will you put my name on the list?"

Yet not many names ever make the list, partly because there isn't enough space—the groups are small, only ten to fifteen inmates in each—and partly because the prisoner has to meet certain criteria. The offender cannot be a security risk or considered uncooperative by those in charge. The names of inmates who've created problems just aren't "seen" by those in authority.

In four different facilities—O. C. Central Jail, Theo Lacy, the new Intake and Release Center, and James Musick Facility—Great Escape groups meet several times a week for one to two hours at a time.

In these small meetings, counselors help inmates make plans for their release. Prisoners are told about post-custody options in outpatient treatment programs and shelters. As an extra service, a counselor will pick up offenders on their release dates and transport them to temporary housing. Outside, two contract providers offer forty-two-day substance abuse programs, with separate meetings for men and women.

Ron Webb, program manager of the Orange County Alcohol and Drug Abuse Services, says of the programs, "Once inmates get out, they need to be connected to a program for an extended period; it takes longer than a few days to reach them. Our local hospitals used

to provide excellent services, but unfortunately they priced themselves out of the business. Nobody can afford fifteen thousand dollars for a relatively short thirty-day program."

During the 1998–1999 fiscal year, Great Escape served 1,487 inmates, with 472 actually connecting to post-release treatment. The
largest number, 385 men, went to Cooper Fellowship, while 31 women
chose New Directions, both live-in programs. An additional 56 attended county outpatient clinics.

∼

If Orange County is typical of other communities, additional programs might very well exist to help those on probation or parole adjust to normal living, but again, those who need them most may
know the least about them. In this county, for instance, the Friends
Outside program is available to help ex-offenders find housing and,
even more important, jobs. But who's ever heard of it?

In addition, for offenders needing encouragement, guidance,
and a helping hand, the local Volunteers in Parole organization,
comprised of volunteer attorneys, stands ready to mentor ex-felons
one-on-one. Among the mentors in Orange County is Rich Pfeiffer,
the former hang-gliding champion, now lawyer, whose remarkable
story is featured in chapter 4.

The lesson here is that offenders, or families of offenders, cannot
assume that their own area is devoid of resources. Almost every metropolitan community has programs that will help ex-offenders find
treatment, housing, and jobs. You just have to track them down.
Attending local AA and NA meetings, talking to other offenders and
their families, and seeking out judges in the nearest drug court
would be good places to start.

∼

Which brings us to a last, and vitally important remedy for stubborn,
addicted offenders whose addictions haven't yet gotten them into
deep and serious trouble with the law: drug court.

Chapter 10 is devoted to exploring this highly effective new
program.

CHAPTER TEN

Drug Court: The New Kid on the Block

Drug court is a relatively new but vital program that gives stubborn addicts a push toward cleaning up their lives. It's a plan for emptying jails and relieving overcrowded courts. It's also an opportunity for judges to slow the tide of repeat offenders.

Yet how many people have ever heard of it? Not many, it seems.

The authoritative book *The Real War on Crime*, published in 1996 by the National Criminal Justice Commission, makes no mention, anywhere, of drug court. Though drug courts began in the late 1980s, they were simply too new to be widely known when that book was being written.

Even today, drug courts are little known by the public at large. A few informal polls of students, writers, and friends uncover only a handful of people who have ever heard the term. And fewer still who know much about how they operate or what they do.

$\sim$

The theory behind drug court is that an addict whose behavior brings him to the attention of the police may do better with intense monitoring and a judge's supervision than he'll do in jail or prison.

Soon after his arrest, the offender who isn't already in deep trouble with the law may be offered the alternative of going to drug court instead of jail. There, all the people who would normally deal with him in the court system unite to push him toward sobriety outside prison walls. By "all the people," we mean the district attorney, the arresting officer, the public defender, the probation or parole officer, the treatment counselor, and, of course, the judge.

Drug court is a unique and intense effort by a group of people working in concert—an effort not lost on the offender who is the subject of all this attention. He has, in effect, a personal cheering section willing him to succeed, while at the same time he knows there's a threat of imprisonment if he fails.

Donna Boone, Ph.D., the drug court coordinator for the state of Virginia, describes drug court as a process of catching drug offenders "at a teachable moment"—the crisis of arrest—when they've just been caught committing a crime and are still feeling guilty and contrite.

With little fanfare, the first drug court started in Dade County, Florida, in 1988, when Attorney General Janet Reno, then Prosecutor Reno, spearheaded the formation of the first real drug court in the United States. The idea was to use the authority of the courts to force substance abusers into treatment.

Instead of simply ordering an offender to get help—and hoping he would—as a few judges were doing, the court would now keep close track of him, week by week. The court drew up some simple rules: abusers would have to report to specific treatment facilities; they'd have to give frequent urine samples; they'd be ordered to meet regularly with their probation officers; and they'd be required to report back to the judge on a regular basis.

In a sense, the judge became the most important person in the offender's life. For the first time, in some cases, a parental figure was watching over the addict, demanding that he stay sober, forcing him to be responsible and take control of his life.

～

Watching a drug court in action for the first time is a memorable experience. Typically, the judge begins his day at 8 A.M. in his chambers, which is where Judge Junius P. Fulton III, of Norfolk, Virginia, starts the process.

All the offenders on the day's docket have earlier been "sentenced" to Norfolk's drug court. All have voluntarily given up certain rights and pleaded guilty to using drugs or alcohol, agreeing to cooperate with the court in exchange for escaping a jail or prison sentence. All are now participants, with varying amounts of time left on their sentences.

Gathered in the judge's chambers at that early hour are the various professionals mentioned earlier—individuals like the prosecutor and public defender who would normally be adversaries in such a procedure. But here's where drug court takes an amazing turn. It isn't the judge who decides what should happen next to these offenders. It isn't the district attorney who has the final say, or the probation or parole officer. It isn't the treatment specialist or public defender.

It's everyone—all of the above.

As a group, this disparate collection of people who traditionally have conflicting interests gets together and discusses in rational terms what punishments, sanctions, or rewards should be given out this week to each offender. For purposes of drug court, the group operates as a team and will remain a team as long as they're working with the drug court judge.

This precourtroom phase in the judge's chambers is almost always an informal procedure. In Norfolk participants drink coffee. In Denver they loosen their ties and take off their jackets. In Phoenix someone brings doughnuts. In South Court, Orange County, California, they have bagels.

One by one, the difficult cases are reviewed by the group. The judge listens as the various officials who've dealt most recently with the offender make their reports. The probation officer, for instance, may note that the client has or hasn't appeared for the week's required meetings. The treatment counselor briefly describes a bad or good attitude. Someone from the day reporting center reports on a "clean" or "dirty" urinalysis (UA) (evidence of drugs or alcohol in the urine. Not showing up for UA is considered a "dirty urine"). The district attorney mentions the client's failure or success in attending the required number of AA meetings.

Any or all failures or successes are taken into account, and the team decides what punishment or sanctions, if any, to impose. If the offender has had a bad week and his offenses warrant it, the judge, with group approval, might decide the miscreant needs a weekend in jail or perhaps additional AA or NA meetings added to the five-times-weekly requirement. Or some weekend hours of community service. Or, if the offender is truly out of control, the treatment specialist may recommend a month or two in a live-in center for more intensive drug treatment.

At Norfolk's in-chambers meeting a counselor remarks that the client is suffering with a toothache, and someone says, "We've got to get him to a dentist and get that tooth extracted." Fortunately, Norfolk has a number of community services available for recovering offenders.

Today's drug court is truly unique. Gone is the adversarial climate that once prevailed in such cases. The public defender no longer fights to get "the best deal" for his client. The district attorney isn't pressing for ever-longer incarceration. The probation and parole officers aren't trying to put the offender back in jail. Instead, the group as a whole decides what's in the best interests of the offender and what punishment or reward will bring him back in line. And so it goes for each of the addicted people scheduled to meet with the judge later that morning.

By necessity, decisions are quick. The total time spent in the judge's chambers is somewhere between thirty and forty-five minutes. Since no one feels any need to stand on principle and argue, a decision on each case takes only a few minutes. All the participants have been through this before. They know what works. They have a unified approach. There's a spirit of satisfaction in the room; the climate is one of accomplishment and teamwork rather than controversy.

At the end of this short session, the judge slips into his judicial robes and heads for the courtroom. There, most of the professionals who've just been in chambers sit back and listen as the judge speaks to the offenders, one by one. The moment is one of great solemnity. The offender standing before the judge knows this is the moment of truth; whatever he's done in the past few weeks, he's aware that everyone knows it. He's been watched and monitored. Now, if he's been good, the judge is going to tell him so—in front of everybody.

The judge leans forward. "I see you've been following the program, Mr. Brown."

Matthew Brown nods. He may be dressed in a tank top—rarely—or he may be wearing a clean shirt and jeans. He almost certainly isn't dressed in a suit and tie.

"Your treatment counselor tells me you've had a good attitude," says the judge. "Your UAs this week and last have been clean. You've attended all the AA meetings that were required of you. You've met with your probation officer. That's good. And by the way, Mr. Brown, how is your new job going?"

"Fine, your honor."

"No problems at work?"

"No, sir."

"Glad to hear it. We note that you're due back here in two weeks. Keep up the good work, Mr. Brown. You've had a fine month. We'll look forward to another report like this when you return."

"Yes, sir."

"Your name goes into the pool." (In South Court, Orange County, a raffle for theater tickets or the like is held at the end of the session—a unique reward system for good behavior.)

A nod. "Thank you, your honor." Mr. Brown walks back to his seat.

Like a stern, but fair-minded parent, the judge has given his charge the best reward an offender can have: a few words of praise and public recognition for staying clean and sober. If the meeting marks some kind of milestone—a certain number of clean and sober weeks or months, the courtroom breaks into applause.

One of the more memorable clients in South Court is a woman in her late twenties who stands before Judge Ron Kreber holding her year-old baby. She is smiling and her posture is proudly erect. Her skin is clear, her eyes bright. She's been clean more than a year, and as someone confides proudly in a whisper, "This woman had a drug-free baby."

The judge says, "Ms. Smith, you're still doing well, I see."

The woman nods. "Yes, your honor."

"How's the baby?"

"He's fine, your honor."

"Job okay?"

"Yes."

"See you at graduation, then. Your name goes into the pool."

"Thank you."

The woman is due to "graduate" soon in a solemn, drug court graduation ceremony. There, the offenders who have completed the year-long program successfully will be honored in an occasion as momentous as any in their lives.

In a sense, drug court graduation has greater implications to the clients' lives than most other milestones. They have achieved the nearly impossible. From the starting point of a worthless life steeped in drugs, they've wrenched themselves free and, over a period of one to two years, have become clean and sober citizens.

The drug court ceremony reflects this noteworthy accomplishment. Graduates break down and weep as they express their thank-yous to judges, counselors, probation officers, and even the police officers who arrested them. Relatives get choked up, too, describing what it means to reclaim a wife, a father, a mother. As the graduate speaks, surrounded on stage by family members who love him, cheers and cries of support come from the audience—many of whom are recovering addicts awaiting their own graduation day.

The district attorney publicly drops all charges, and from that moment, the graduate is expected to be a normal, productive member of society. Everyone concedes nothing is more inspiring or moving than a drug court graduation.

~

How did drug courts come about?

In the mid-1980s, when cocaine abuse swept the country and flooded the prison system with an excess of inmates, people who had to deal with the problem became desperate; *something* had to be done.

Legislatures, judges, and even President Ronald Reagan reacted by taking a hard stance and declaring a "war on drugs." Reagan said, "The American people want their government to get tough and go on the offensive." He promised that police would approach the drug problem "with more ferocity than ever before." Addicts were viewed as willful scoflaws who needed to be stopped at all costs and taught a lesson. The solution of the day was an uncompromising posture: lengthen sentences for all offenders and scare everyone into submission.

Police officers, district attorneys, and judges were given a mandate: find more drug abusers, take a tougher attitude, set an example by locking them up longer. Mandatory sentences were decreed by legislatures, removing discretion from judges. The bench could no longer consider extenuating circumstances when handing out punishment. Looking back, some of us believe it was a lot of good people making bad decisions for the right reasons.

∼

Unfortunately, the net result was a still-greater flood of abusers into jails and prisons—far too many for existing facilities to handle. Even double and triple bunking couldn't solve the problem. By the late 1980s and early 1990s, violent criminals were being released early to make room for nonviolent addicts.

States like California tried to "build out" of the problem, spending tens of millions on more jails and prisons, only to be hit with a new reality: more millions would be needed to operate and maintain the new structures.

Meanwhile, the volume of prisoners continued to rise. The problem was, the war was being lost. Punishment, by and large, has never worked well with drug abusers—who rarely think about consequences as they're getting high.

It took trying a number of things that didn't work before those in charge decided a new approach was needed.

∼

Out of sheer necessity, some communities began trying to deal with chemical abusers separately. And faster. Since these were the people causing all the jail overcrowding problems, it seemed logical to approach them with different solutions.

With support from the federal government, some jurisdictions developed expedited drug case management systems (sometimes called drug courts) to speed up the process and reduce the time between arrest and conviction. The net result was not exactly helpful: though drug cases did move through the system faster, habitual users simply went through the revolving door at an accelerated rate: use, go to jail, get out, use again, go back to jail.

Judge William Meyer, a Denver judge who is recognized nationally as a leader in the drug court movement, explains his reasons for wanting change: "I got sick and tired of seeing the same people in front of me, and doing the same things, and seeing that it wasn't getting any results at all. It is my firm belief then, as it is now, that ultimately what we were doing just didn't work. So I thought we needed to at least try something different." He adds with the hint of a smile, "Is it Einstein or Kipling that said, 'Insanity is doing the same thing over and over and expecting to get different results'?"

⁓

Eventually it became apparent to a number of people that the criminal justice system ought to be cooperating with treatment providers, since they all had the same goals—to get people to stop using drugs and, as a consequence, to stop committing crimes. By then, almost everyone in the field realized that drugs and drug-related offenses were the most common causes of crime in nearly every community.

Often enough, judges *wanted* to send offenders to treatment instead of jail or prison, but their hands were tied.

In the mid-1990s, when I begged a judge to let us put our son in a costly inpatient program at our expense, he explained honestly that he'd get in trouble if he did. He said, "Your son can go to a program after his prison term."

When I mentioned this incident to treatment provider Nancy Clark, she said, "That never works. The guys won't do it. After they've been locked up, they want their freedom. The last thing in the world they'll agree to is more restrictions. You have to catch them at the front end. You have to make treatment part of the sentence. Then *they'll cooperate and do what you want."* M. W.

~

Many authorities believe the personality of the judge is the single biggest element in how well the system works. Statistics have shown that different judges get somewhat different results, even when the rest of the treating group remains the same. In fact, before drug court was really established anywhere, a retired judge in Sweetwater, Oklahoma, took it upon himself to come back to court and meet with a group of drug offenders once a week, cajoling and pushing them to straighten out their lives. Just that small amount of judicial pressure and attention worked miracles. A large percentage of the offenders were so awed by the judge's interest in them that they changed their behavior and turned themselves around.

Judges who sit in drug courts are nearly always enthusiastic. They like the team concept. They like the harmony that results from everyone having the same well-defined goals. They like being part of the solution.

Best of all, they sense the positive impact they're having on offenders' lives. It's more than the power of the black robes, more than the flags and glitter of the courtroom setting. It's their words and their style, reaching across the bench to nudge someone in the right direction.

No longer does a judge hand down a sentence and then lose track of the substance abuser for all time. Instead, he is *involved* with him, monitoring his progress by the week and the month. Before his eyes, the offender slowly changes: he loses his unhealthy complexion, his watery eyes, his hangdog expression, his attitude of defeat. He begins to stand a little straighter. He shows hints of future poise. Like a once-wayward son, he waits hopefully for the judge's comments.

One judge says, "Sometimes I feel like I've got fifty-four children."

Another notes, "I am a cheerleader. My job is to motivate people." And indeed, judges often demonstrate their enthusiasm by reaching out to shake hands with successful clients. Others hug the participants at graduation.

~

Although drug courts have existed for only a few years in most states, statistics show that they are having a significant impact on recidivism. While figures vary from court to court and better record keeping is needed everywhere, in every court results are positive and significant. Even in the least effective courts, fewer addicts come back into the system than before, and all the numbers are moving in the right direction.

Advocates of drug courts cite a number of reasons why they work:

1. Instead of having his case drag on for months, the offender gets into the system quickly. The court catches him in that vulnerable moment when he has just been arrested. Feeling guilty and scared, he's ready to listen to reason. Consequences are immediate, making punishment seem related to the crime. The same speed operates when he relapses. He is caught immediately and brought to the judge's—and everyone else's—attention.
2. As much as possible, treatment is fitted to the individual—to his personality and to the severity of his problem.
3. The offender reaps the benefit of a number of expert opinions as to what will work best for him.
4. Drug court creates an environment where the rules are clear and definite. Every offender knows what's expected of him and what will happen if he relapses.
5. The abuser is constantly reminded about the need to stay clean and sober—by meetings with his probation officer, visits to the treatment center, frequent urinalyses, required meetings in AA, and those all-important follow-up meetings with the judge.
6. The offender is kept in line by the constant threat of punishment if he fails. He knows punishment will be swift, fair, and certain. By

pleading guilty to drug offenses and agreeing to the program, he knows he can't fall back on an attorney to "get him out of trouble."

7. Along with escalating sanctions—punishments—if he fails, the offender has hope of rewards if he succeeds . . . and in fact he sees people rewarded every week by judges who are pleased with an offender's progress. (Most judges make sure that all offenders witness the process—that they see handcuffs come out for those who seriously fail and praise offered to those who succeed.)

8. Everything that's expected of the client is measurable and definite. He must show up regularly in court. He must have clean UAs. He must attend a specific number of meetings and counseling sessions. The requirements are easy to understand, and there is no room for manipulation or cheating.

9. The system takes into account the relapsing nature of the disease. Judges, treatment counselors, and prosecutors *expect* that abusers will relapse a few times. Instead of kicking the offender out of the program for a single failure, or even several, they tighten the screws, raising the level of punishment. The offender knows he will be kept under scrutiny, even when he relapses. He knows he'll be given repeated chances to do better.

10. The system values honesty over perfection. The client who admits he's failed and intends to do better impresses everyone more than the manipulator who tries to beat the game.

As Donna Boone says, "Drug court is the most intensive supervision that the criminal justice system has to offer."

∼

Drug courts don't operate exactly the same in all states or even in different communities within the same state. Some confine their services to first-time users, while others will take anyone whose crimes are nonviolent and tied to a history of substance abuse.

Drug courts vary, too, in how many additional services they offer offenders. In Norfolk, Virginia, a community services board provides treatment services at a downtown location. In a program called

Second Chances, several members of the Norfolk community board deal with other important issues, such as finding clients jobs and a place to live. One of the directors sometimes transports offenders to jobs or calls potential employers on an offender's behalf.

This same helpfulness extends to the probation and parole office. Officer Christopher Pate says he, and others in his office, sometimes call potential employers to vouch for ex-offenders, pointing out they will be keeping tabs on the offender and will handle the situation if the offender somehow fails.

Among the adjunct programs offered to drug court offenders in Virginia is Virginia Cares, a statewide program intended to help ex-offenders transition back into society.

~

Richmond, Virginia, has established what may be the state's most active drug court. Knowing this, a group of concerned doctors called Physician Leadership on National Drug Policy filmed the Richmond drug court to produce a videotape that profiles the lives of two graduates. Called *Trial, Treatment, and Transformation,* the film is an emotional study of judges and participants in a courtroom setting, providing dramatic evidence that drug court works.

Not far from the court itself, the Richmond Day Reporting Center offers the other half of the program, staying open late each night to provide individual and group therapy, counseling, drug screening, advice, and peer support.

In a long discussion with counselor Diana Keegan (who appears briefly in the film) we agreed that drug abusers have traditionally received scant, if any, help for their problems, that instead they've been warehoused— literally "put on ice" to get them out of the way. "We're a nation of zoo-keepers," she says wryly. "We've fooled ourselves into believing if you build better prisons, faster, it's a solution."

We were preaching to each other, of course, but we agreed that locking up drug offenders is no solution at all, that it is, in fact, worse than nothing. Let the prison term be long enough, and prisoners come out as animals—angry, antisocial animals. M. W.

Keegan makes another point: "Ironically, if the only consideration were the safety of the community, stashing people out of sight and filling them full of hatred is ultimately the most dangerous thing we can do."

Diana Keegan notes that the majority of offenders who reach drug court are initially resistant. Luckily, the success of rehabilitation does not depend on the client's attitude when he arrives. Drug court has a quiver full of arrows, ready to ping away at the client until he changes his beliefs and his behavior. She adds, "We raise the crisis on the client until he's willing to try something different."

∼

In an evening group session at the Richmond Day Reporting Center, men and women who are participants in Richmond's drug court willingly discuss their behaviors and problems. About twenty offenders are in the room, all in different stages of recovery, though most are nearing the end of their program.

Daniel, twenty-seven, says, "My drug of choice was heroin. But I've been clean now for a year and two months." Everyone claps, and he pauses, then lists all the places he's been locked up. "The court's been very patient. My mom's been saying prayers. I've kept my job now, for a year—something I've never done before in my life." He looks around at the others. "This is the first outpatient program that's really helped me."

Tiffany, thirty-two, says she's used alcohol and cocaine. "This is my second time in a program. I went to Tidewater Detention Center first."

"Where you couldn't talk?"

"That's right. We had to be silent. But it helped me. I've been clean ten months. I feel my life is back on track."

Duncan, thirty-one, claims only six months of sobriety. "This is my second time around. I was an inpatient at Rubican—you know, the therapeutic community. I kind of grew up there. Drugs really screwed me up; they sent me to jail. The biggest influence in my life was having a sponsor and all those outside meetings. I need the fellowship. I get support from my wife too. I have four children." He looks around proudly. "I'm supporting them now."

Pete, twenty-five, has a surprising background. "Alcohol and marijuana got me stealing. But I have a $1,000-a-week job now, working on cars, painting them, fixing them up. Someday I'm going to finish college. I plan to major in philosophy and physics. In high school I did public speaking—I was the state champion. I'm not married, but I'm supporting my four kids."

Kate, at twenty-six, seems to be the star among the women. Shy and self-effacing, she admits she's used heroin and marijuana for ten years. But now she's been clean fourteen months. "This program has taught me how to set boundaries. For years I was a street person. I have three kids, and I have custody of them now. If you ask what I do, I guess I'm a mom a good part of the day. But I work too. I want to get my CNA [certified nurse assistant] certificate. I plan to work as a companion while my kids are in school." *She smiles shyly.* "I try to teach them to be responsible."

The male star is Doug, forty-nine, clean now for two years. As a Vietnam vet, he'd tried everything—cocaine, heroin, alcohol, marijuana. He'd been sent to three different inpatient programs, including the diversion center at Chesterfield. There he gained self-esteem and new, positive attitudes and emotions. "I'm still on parole," *he says,* "but my family can see the change in me. All these meetings here, and outside, are really helping. It helps me to facilitate other groups. When you've been clean awhile, that's what you have to do. Addicts have to help addicts. We really understand the losses."

~

Later, Diana Keegan explains how the group operates when they have no visitors. "We usually have an open discussion. We encourage them to tell us about their day and we try to assess their needs." She seems to be saying, *We're the parents they come home to at night.*

She continues: "This group is more advanced. The people here are working toward transition. They're at the stage where they need to face issues of the past, the pain and problems they've caused others."

She considers her role as a counselor. "We give them intense, day-by-day support. It's hard, though, and some won't finish." She adds with a smile, "When they first come in, our program is like a set of training wheels. One bolt at a time, we take off the wheels. In the end, they're pedaling by themselves."

~

The drug court in Denver, which began in July 1994, has accumulated impressive statistics. The research branch of the Division of Criminal Justice for the state did a study that involved 1,200 people. For those who completed the drug court program, recidivism was an astonishing 10 percent—which means 90 percent were not rearrested.

Adam Brickner, coordinator of the Denver drug court, defines the whole system: "They're calling it therapeutic jurisprudence, which is this idea of using a court system as treatment. That's a big change. My biggest concern is that drugs have always been treated as a criminal problem and not a health problem."

He begins by detailing Denver's history. "Judge William Meyer was extremely instrumental in getting the drug court started here. . . . It was really his vision that made it happen. There were so many drug arrests in Denver, and they were all getting treated differently by different judges—each with his own philosophies and personal feelings about drugs and alcohol and criminal behavior. The idea was to get one courtroom that dealt with the same types of offenses in a standardized manner."

Responding to a comment that perhaps drug court hasn't caught on, philosophically, across the country, he agrees that drug court, nationwide, is spotty.

He adds, "It's a real idea of restorative justice, where you keep the community and the offender connected. You keep the offender *in* the community, where the offense happened. You try to fix him where he is. The old method was to pull the person out of the community, try to fix him, and then put him back and see what happens.

"Well, anyone who understands human behavior knows that's not going to change anything. When they go back to the same old world, it's hard for them to resist the urges they didn't resist in the past. Basically, past behavior is the best predictor of future behavior. If you don't give addicts the skills they need to change themselves, why would anyone expect different results?"

He offers insights into how treatment counselors approach abusers: "When we talk to offenders, we say, 'Society has always allowed you wiggle room at every age. Kids can cry in a crowded train and nobody is going to do much. But when you're an adult, you can't do that—people are going to react differently. Offenders have a certain amount of wiggle room as well. The problem with committing crimes is, you start to use up that wiggle room. The closer you get to the edge of what's acceptable, the less you have, and the more you are going to be mistrusted and disrespected, and the fewer mistakes you are allowed to make—because you have already made so many all the way up.

"'So once you cross over that line and get into the felony world and they put you in prison, you've used up all your wiggle room, and you have to earn that back. You can't just return to the community and say, "I'm a different person now; I've changed. Treat me like you treat everyone else." It's unfair to expect other people to change just because you have.

"'You can't count on people giving you a break just because you insist you've changed. You have to prove it.' This is a speech I gave quite a lot to offenders when I was working with the employment program. I told them, 'You have to start in the lower-level jobs and work up. But it helps if you are in the right field, if you love what you do. If you're passionate, whether it's about dog grooming, or photography, or whatever, you can make your job a career.'"

As to the problems of ex-offenders finding jobs, Brickner says that Denver is handling that issue with the Continuum of Care Center (CCC). "We work with employment, life skills, and aftercare. We have a lot of programs that are unique to the Denver drug court. Until recently, we were the only court that had this kind of employment program connected to it."

When asked how an ex-inmate overcomes the problem of telling the truth on an application, Brickner says, "That's one of the things we cover. We say to the offender, 'You have to learn to internalize what you've done—you have to accept your crimes, and then you can offer the truth to the employer.'

"We try to help them present themselves in such a way that the employer can't let them walk out the door—because here is some-body who is honest, who has made some mistakes but is willing to work with me and tell me what is going on in his life. That is one of the things we stress.

"It isn't easy, though. Most people are embarrassed and ashamed of what they've done. How *do* you tell a potential employer you have a felony on your record? Well, you tell him matter-of-factly. You men-tion what you've done to change. You tell him you're in treatment now, you are dropping drug tests twice a week, and you'll be more than happy to give your supervisor the name of your treatment provider. You tell him you're working on your issues . . . and how many people will they meet who can say that? And maybe the em-ployer is thinking that the other people on his assembly line, he doesn't know whether any of them are users or not. We are hoping the interviewer is thinking, 'This guy is being honest about this stuff. It's very refreshing.'

"In our Continuum of Care Center, we spend a lot of time con-centrating on the individual. We put him through a battery of assess-ments—aptitude tests and interest assessments. We try to find out what he really wants to do, and then we help him find a career in that field.

"This is why we don't spend a lot of time doing job training. I've heard of programs that will train the person to be a welder. The training is great, but only if the person wants it. If he doesn't want to be a welder, you can train him for ten years and when he gets out, he is going to be a cook somewhere. He'll take his welding certificate and never use it. For me, the important thing is that the individual does what he likes to do. People tend to stay in jobs longer if they love the field."

The conversation veers to what makes people eligible for drug court.

Brickner explains that about 75 percent of Denver's drug offend-ers do end up in drug court. The prerequisite, however, is that the individual must be arrested for drug possession and his charges must be drug charges. If he is able to stay out of trouble for two years, the charges are dropped.

He admits that the prerequisites mean a certain percentage of substance abusers are left out. Unfortunately, the drug courts would be overwhelmed if they included everyone whose crimes might be a result of drug abuse. "Our courts are inundated enough just with the people who have drug charges," Brickner says.

"What about offenders who commit crimes, such as breaking and entering, that they might not have committed if they weren't high? If these people didn't happen to have drugs on them at the time of arrest, would they get to drug court?"

"No," says Brickner. "They have to be in possession of a drug. That has to be the reason they're picked up."

Bill Ritter, the district attorney of Denver—another man of vision and strong commitment—describes in detail how the presentencing assessment part of the Denver drug court works. He says the court requires guilty pleas of everybody, but then they put offenders in tracks: a prison track, a probation track, and a deferred judgment track. People in the deferred judgment track might have their felonies dismissed if they comply with the drug court. Those on the probation track, the more serious offenders, wouldn't get dismissal but are nevertheless put in treatment, though possibly with some jail time. Landing in the prison track means the offender is definitely going to be incarcerated. However, offenders are able to move between tracks, indicating that the system has flexibility.

Ritter says, "Addiction is a tricky subject, as you know. I'll stand in a community meeting and I'll say that addiction is a very complicated issue, and if you have a friend or family member who suffers from substance abuse, you know what I am talking about. And virtually every head in the room is nodding in agreement. There is a far greater level of community understanding about the complexities of addiction than we give people credit for.

"And then you move to the second part, which is, Well, if it's so complex, it demands complex responses—something that is more thoughtful than simply incarcerating addicts or putting them on probation until they relapse. The relapse is so chronic that ultimately they are jailed or imprisoned.

"Having said that, what we try to do is build a response—hold people accountable, first, by requiring guilty pleas. For those that get the advantages of the treatment program, we *keep* them accountable. We accept relapse as part of that. But we don't accept chronic relapse. We don't accept three or four years' worth of relapse. Over time you have to pay the fiddler. But we do accept some level of relapse, and then we punish it pretty quickly with a day in jail, or two or three days, and we incrementally increase the sanctions so that they know we mean business and this is not a game we're playing.

"I have heard more offenders than I can count in a drug court graduation saying, 'First of all, I wouldn't stay clean. Then I decided I had better start staying clean for this judge because he keeps putting me in jail on Saturdays and Sundays, and that really disrupts my weekend. And then over time, because I was staying clean for the judge, I felt how it was to be clean, and I stayed clean for myself.'"

Ritter admits that all programs for addicts are bound to have their long-term failures. Then he adds, "[Drug court is] phenomenally better than any probation court, because we are managing the offender with close scrutiny, treating him like you treat a bad child—by punishing him immediately and then saying, 'Okay now, let's go on.'"

As Adam Brickner did before him, Ritter mentions the employment program. He says it's shortsighted to think recovering addicts can manage without help in this department. "There are a lot of things we can still do, but the fact is, we are trying to use all the leverage we have in the criminal justice system to address this complex problem. And it's so much better than what we did prior to 1994, where it really was a revolving door. We still have people in the drug court who get a second offense. The difference is, we are making a serious effort to look at that problem. We are not always going to be successful, but we are doing a far better job than we ever did prior to putting this drug court in place."

When asked if the success of drug court makes him feel pretty good, he nods and says quietly, "It's the right thing to do. It does make me feel good. I have to give a lot of credit to my chief deputy, Greg Long. Bill Meyer was the judge interested in it. I was the DA interested in it. But the guy who was the glue of the program is Greg Long, my prosecutor, who has a great understanding of addiction."

It seems clear that drug court works, in large part, because of the dedication of people like Adam Brickner, Bill Ritter, Greg Long, and Judge William Meyer.

~

Le Anna L. Day, the Continuum of Care Center manager for the Denver drug court, talks in more detail about CCC. As good as the drug court concept was from its inception, until CCC came into being, a vital link was missing. "Two years ago," she says, "offenders were going through the program and then relapsing at the end. We had no aftercare for them. No employment. No continuous support system. We just weren't supporting their sobriety."

Sobriety *is* the client's responsibility, she concedes, but her group helps give the client the means to make it work. Le Anna Day started the aftercare group when it became obvious that such a plan was needed. She says, "The location is crucial. We made sure it's in the same courtroom where they're sentenced. We're trying to make this a healing place." AA and NA speakers come in weekly, as well as representatives from Al-Anon. Since so many offenders have never had steady employment, CCC's goal is stability. The organization helps the offender with the assessments mentioned by Brickner, then makes calls to potential employers. As a spokesperson for the job seeker, Day can point out that the offender is in treatment, that he's being checked for drugs, that he's complying with court requirements and working on his issues—all the necessary factors mentioned by Adam Brickner.

"These people are now being responsible," says Day. "Some of them hadn't been responsible in their entire lives."

The Continuum of Care Center does more, however, than help with the client's career search. As an additional incentive for him to work with CCC, the client is excused from some of the fines and fees he's accumulated from drug court. Anyone who works at one job for three months gets a credit of $1,000. If he completes eight modules of the skills program, he is forgiven $400. For each AA, CA, or NA meeting he attends, he is credited with an additional $25.

Day says, "After a while they're invested in the program—they're no longer coming for the money but for their own purposes. Once their efforts are no longer court-driven, or fear-driven, they become self-driven."

Around town, storefronts have been set up as additional places for offenders to come for help. "We call these the weed and seed offices," says Day.

A new phase of the program is coming soon—the alumni group. Day anticipates that the alumni group will serve as mentors and will help with fund drives. She calls these the "Give Back" projects.

As is so often the case with such programs, Le Anna Day's personal enthusiasm is one of the ingredients that makes it all work.

∼

Ed Mansfield, chief probation officer in Denver, has additional thoughts on Denver's drug court. He says, "We know the clients we deal with. They don't have much going for them. They started using drugs out of poor self-esteem or they used drugs out of boredom, but whatever it was, they had nobody saying anything positive about them.

"So now all of a sudden they've got somebody who is taking an interest, even if it's a judge or a probation officer. Somebody is holding them up to standards and saying, 'Hey, you've got to be responsible for what you do,' and then saying a big 'Okay!' when they do something good. And if they lapse, if they slide back a little, nobody says, 'Well, that's it, we are throwing you away.' Instead the judge says, 'Well, okay, we may punish you a little bit, but it's okay to make a mistake.' These people are not going to make it all the way at one time, but at least they're moving forward, because something in their lives is positive."

Mansfield talks about the innovations taking place in Arizona, which will be covered in the next chapter. As he is finishing, he says,

"When you look at the Denver court and then go down and look at the Maricopa County court, what you have are two courts that are both successful, but each with a slightly different approach. I think you can have all sorts of different approaches if you have a certain core thing—and that's the judge's involvement with the clients. That is the *most* important aspect. Also, that your message is consistent—in other words, that the punishment and rewards are consistent and humane. By humane, I am saying that if the person relapses, you don't throw him away." As a final thought, he says, "The prosecution and the public defender need to buy into the program too."

~

For all the obvious benefits of drug courts, and in spite of the dedication of the people serving them, there is still a frighteningly large hole in the system. If some jurisdictions include only the people caught using or selling, instead of screening all offenders to see whether drugs are part of the problem, they are missing great blocks of addicted offenders.

All too many abusers commit drug-related crimes against property without having the substance in their possession. They pilfer from businesses and stores—all because of drugs long since consumed. For this they go to jail or prison, and the core problem is never addressed. We propose that, in the absence of an in-jail or in-prison treatment program, a modified version of drug court could combine incarceration with a follow-up stint in drug court.

We are not the only ones concerned about this. Denver District Attorney Bill Ritter says, "We went from about 1,000 cases a year in 1993 that were felony only, to 2,300 cases last year that were felony drug cases. And so you have to do what's possible within the resources allocated to you. We've been fortunate to have as much as we've gotten. The city has been wonderful in terms of providing resources, the federal government has been wonderful for the same reason, and the state has been wonderful. Having said all that, we could still do far more. If we had no limit on resources, I would build a court system that's oriented around drugs and alcohol at the misdemeanor level *and* the felony level. Any probation person would have a treatment orientation—to the extent that you assessed him and then determined whether there was a drug or alcohol problem. Over time we could make a significant difference."

And Ed Mansfield says of Judge William Meyer: "He's almost on a mission with drug court up here. He wants *every* drug abuser sent to drug court."

In a booklet entitled *National Drug Court Institute Review,* Summer 1998, author Steven Belenko, Ph.D., writes:

> Interestingly, although it is generally thought that drug court targets "first-time offenders," many drug court clients have substantial criminal histories and many years of substance abuse. While the drug court can be an effective intervention that stops or delays the onset of a chronic career of drug abuse and criminality, such "first-timers" are generally not sentenced to prison. It is the older, more "experienced" offender for whom successful treatment intervention can have the greatest impact on prison populations and generate the most substantial savings in reduced crime and criminal justice system costs.[1]

In the same booklet, Judge Jeffrey Tauber writes:

> Critics sometimes argue that drug courts are soft on crime and therefore should be limited to first time or "less serious" offenders; that drug-using offenders should be removed from our communities and given long jail sentences. The facts, however, demonstrate otherwise . . . *the average drug-using offender spends an average of three months in jail but 24 months on probation and living in your community.* It makes no sense to limit drug court programs to the least serious drug-user on probation, when more serious drug-using probationers are exactly the ones who most need the comprehensive judicial monitoring, probation supervision, frequent drug testing, treatment services, and immediate sanctions that a drug court provides.[2]

~

Among the features that distinguish one drug court program from another, the most unusual may be in Orange County, California, where sheriff and probation officer teams from South Court make random, unannounced evening calls to offenders' homes. Not only are the clients observed and tested for signs of drug use, but their rooms are searched for hidden supplies of drugs and alcohol.

Strangely, instead of causing anger and resentment, the calls have a friendly overtone and seem almost social. The court has been wise in its choice of callers. One of the teams, for instance, is a man-woman combination, both of whom are personable, good-natured, and naturally friendly. They arrive, not like the gestapo, but with an air of casualness and goodwill, and consequently they are greeted like friends.

The two describe their clients as being receptive and say they encounter little resentment. In fact, Deputy Sheriff Bill Beam says, "Even when I have to arrest someone for being under the influence, they're never hostile. I think in some ways they're glad to get caught."

One evening I went on a ride-along with Deputy Sheriff Bill Beam and Probation Officer Maureen O'Bryan.

Though the two arrived at clients' homes with smiles and an attitude of friendliness, they were clearly there on business. Yet nobody we visited seemed at all disturbed. As we talked, Deputy Sheriff Beam took blood pressures, then slipped away with the male clients to get urine samples. O'Bryan did the same with the women.

It was a fascinating evening. Contrary to my expectations, the apartments and homes we visited were not in slum areas. At our first stop, an attractive apartment complex in Laguna Hills, we were greeted by two snarling dogs. Beam suggested the woman put her dogs in the kitchen.

My first surprise was stepping into a sunken living room onto bare cement. Whether the place had ever been carpeted, it wasn't now. And it seemed nobody had bothered with housekeeping of any kind. We sank into a sagging sofa, only to sense that something was whooshing around overhead. Looking up, we saw two cockatiels streaking across the room. Between the birds, the dogs, and the accumulation of debris, it was hard to pay attention to what the female client was saying.

When Beam explained later that she was new to the program, I understood. All about her was the look of a recently sick abuser: stringy hair, sunken cheeks, grayish pallor, indeterminate age. Yet she seemed glad to have us there and talked willingly about her efforts to stay sober. I suspected she was happy to have friendly callers of any kind.

At the next apartment, we met a youngish crew-cut man who'd been clean and sober for some time. He talked rapidly and with enthusiasm, and proudly showed off his wonderfully neat bedroom.

I was trying to figure out the man's age and finally asked when he was born. To my surprise, he said, "Uh . . . early to mid-1960s." I tried not to laugh, wanting to ask, You mean it happened more than once?

Our last stop brought unexpected drama. We arrived after ten and woke up our client, Manuel, a tiny, solemn-faced Mexican national with dark, shaggy hair. He came out looking sleepy, wearing hastily zipped-up pants and no shirt or shoes. Deputy Sheriff Beam and Officer O'Bryan encouraged him to discuss his background.

Manuel explained in broken English that he'd lost a brother in a freeway accident. He'd also lost his wife and four-year-old daughter in another accident at nearly the same spot a few years later. Seeing him weighed down by these multiple tragedies, we could only watch sympathetically.

But then Deputy Sheriff Beam went off to search the bedroom and unexpectedly found another brother. After a few minutes Beam came out to the living room. "Your brother told me your daughter died a natural death," he said gently. "She was sick from birth."

Our Mexican friend looked despondent. "No. No. An accident. An accident. Never sick."

"And your wife is still alive," Beam persisted. He stood off to one side and a little behind his client, as though to seem less confrontational.

The little man's face sank further. "My mother in Mexico, she say the same thing. But not true. They died here."

"Why would your mother say something if it's not true?"

A look of desperation. A shrug. "No se. No se."

Beam disappeared again into the bedroom. When he came out, he said quietly, "You and your wife are not living together. Is that why you say she's dead?"

"*She wouldn't give me any more babies!*" *Manuel said vehemently.* "*She wouldn't give our daughter a brother.*"

"*So now you say she's dead?*"

No answer.

"*Manuel, you have to be honest with us. We can't have a relationship built on lies. Your wife is still alive, isn't she?*"

Slowly, slowly, the little man nodded, his chin almost touching his bare chest.

"*And your daughter died of a disease. She was sick for years.*"

"*No. She was never sick. Never sick.*"

"*Your brother says she was. Why would he say that?*"

Manuel shrugged with an air of defeat. He had been clean and off drugs for a decent amount of time, but now our two visitors were worried about him.

"*I don't think we should press any more,*" *said O'Bryan under her breath.* "*We don't want him to get so upset he relapses.*"

"*Okay,*" *said the deputy sheriff.* "*You're right.*"

Deputy Sheriff Beam moved closer and patted his client on the back. "*You're doing fine on the program, Manuel,*" *he said.* "*Just don't tell us any more lies, okay?*"

Manuel nodded sadly. Like a gentleman, a bare-chested, barefooted man of honor, he showed us to the door.

Afterward, we all agreed that the slow unraveling of the tragic tale had been as dramatic as any Mary Higgins Clark mystery. And as unfathomable. We could only conclude Manuel's story had been concocted as his way of dealing with a wife who refused him what he saw as his husbandly rights.

The evening had been an intriguing glimpse into lives that were in some ways better, in some ways worse than I expected. But there was no doubting the spirit of goodwill and decency that brought the deputy sheriff and the probation officer into those lives. M. W.

~

In the October 11, 1999, issue of *Newsweek,* Judith S. Kaye, the Chief Judge of the state of New York, provided a judge's perspective of drug court. She pointed out that court-ordered treatment works: a defendant in drug court is two times as likely to complete a treatment program as one who seeks treatment voluntarily. Given the nature of addiction, this isn't surprising: few people walk into drug or alcohol treatment and complete the program without *someone's* footprint on their backsides.

Judge Kaye acknowledges that some people think such personal attention from judges undermines the traditional distance of the judiciary and may therefore compromise the dignity of the office. However, given the massive caseloads caused by nonviolent drug offenders, she sees few other viable alternatives. And besides, she argues, anyone witnessing the celebration of a drug-court graduation, as she did recently, would probably feel that the decorum of the court matters less than the reuniting of formerly addicted mothers with their children. Judge Kaye reports there were many tears of joy at the ceremony, and that quite a few of them were hers.

For many people involved in drug courts, the salient issue is not decorum but effectiveness—and meaning. As Judge Kaye puts it: "With a problem-solving attitude, we can make a real difference in the lives of litigants and in the communities in which we all live. And in the end, that comes pretty close to the dream that drew so many of us to the law, and to judicial service, in the first place."[3]

~

With such a variety of substance abuse programs being tried here and there in a number of communities, one would think every addict in the country would sooner or later find his way to significant help.

Unfortunately, this isn't the case. So far programs are too few, too small, and too selective. Large numbers of addicts never reach them, and if they do accidentally land in a program for a short while, the communities haven't allocated sufficient resources to chase them down when they relapse. Yet we somehow find enough money to build more nontreatment jails where we can stuff addicts out of sight.

It's hard to imagine why mindless jailing, which has proved so ineffective at changing drug offenders in any positive way, remains such a popular solution. Perhaps it's a matter of expediency; simple incarceration is so much "easier." When you throw someone in a nontreatment jail, you don't have to think about him anymore. You don't have to deal with his problems, his needs, his sickness, his twisted psyche. You don't have to be imaginative. You don't have to set up special courts and then find ardent judges, cooperative DAs, and tolerant probation and parole officers who are willing to try something new.

You simply warehouse the offender, the way you'd warehouse yellowing documents and files. You stow him away and conveniently forget that someday he'll come out.

～

One state in the union won't do that anymore. One group of citizens in one part of our country got fed up with treating addicts like so much expendable trash. Alone among the union's fifty states, Arizona decided to do everything differently—to try all the effective means they could think of to bring their addicts back into mainstream society.

And so it seems important to devote a whole chapter to Arizona's noble experiment.

CHAPTER ELEVEN

Arizona:
The Great Social Experiment

For years, politicians in Congress have misread the American public. Ever since the mid-1980s, they've believed the people were squarely behind them in demanding harsh punishment for substance abusers of every stripe. They fill the airwaves with rhetoric about strict laws and think they've got a mandate to be as tough-minded as possible.

This may have been the case once, but it isn't anymore. Far too many of their constituents have had sons and daughters caught up in a downward spiral they were powerless to stop. A large percentage of voters now know the futility of trying to punish away a disease.

In fact, by and large, Americans are more compassionate than they're given credit for being. They're kinder, more forgiving, and a great deal wiser than most politicians think.

Judge William Meyer of Denver cites an interesting experiment in which a cross-section of the public was given the facts in a number of criminal cases and then asked what sentences they'd impose. In every case, the punishments meted out by the public at large were more lenient than those that would have been handed down by a judge.

Which brings us to Arizona—an outstanding example of Americans fighting back on punishment issues. There, the citizens became fed up with throwing an endless stream of drug offenders into jail. Through a complicated initiative on the ballot (the now-famous Proposition 200), the voters of Arizona mandated that first- or second-time drug offenders charged with simple use or possession be given treatment instead of prison.

Local law-and-order advocates were so shocked, they put the issue out again, and for a second time the citizens voted for drug treatment over punishment. Thus, by public edict, Arizona became one of the leaders in treating a majority of drug offenders with a variety of programs instead of jail and prison. (Offenders involved in sale or trafficking were excluded.)

~

A first, up-close look at what is happening in Phoenix, Arizona, comes from Ed Mansfield, now the chief probation officer in Denver. His look back at the years when he was the drug court manager in Maricopa County, Arizona, brings forth some interesting information.

~

Ed Mansfield describes some of the differences between Denver's drug court and the programs in Phoenix. Originally, Phoenix had a strong probation program as opposed to a drug court program. Even now, with all kinds of treatment programs greatly expanded in the state, much of the treatment in Arizona takes place through the probation department instead of through drug courts per se. Drug court has a strong presence, but so do a great many other plans and solutions.

Both Denver and Phoenix provide most of their drug treatment on an outpatient basis, but with specially trained counselors working within the criminal justice system. For those offenders whose needs are greatest, both cities refer a small percentage of clients to inpatient facilities, usually run as therapeutic communities.

Of all the justice system treatment plans so far reviewed, it would appear that Arizona has the country's most extensive presentence screening process. Substance abusers fill out detailed questionnaires and are interviewed privately for as long as an hour. Evaluators consider which drug or drugs the defendant has been using and for how long. They look at his criminal history. They evaluate his personality and mind-set. On the basis of all this information, they decide which treatment program will work best for him. To everyone's benefit, the counties offer a range of programs to choose from.

~

The structure underlying Arizona's drug treatment program is diverse and complicated. But with the mandate out there from its citizens, Arizona seems to be leading the way as an innovator among the states.

The best news is, treatment programs enjoy a steady stream of money, at least for now. Thanks to certain provisions of Proposition 200, treatment and education funds are allocated from luxury taxes on liquors, without the need for additional taxes.

With a variety of programs in place, Arizona has become a kind of mammoth social experiment on the effectiveness of substance abuse treatment. At all levels, people are deadly serious about their jobs. Treatment specialists attend outside conferences and seminars, intent on gaining more knowledge, determined to tap in on whatever research results can be found from anywhere else.

Counselors have long since decided they will not use anything unless it's known to "work." And indeed, the words *Research shows . . .* have become a kind of bible, a guide to what will be used and what won't. Nobody in the field wants to waste time trying things that haven't succeeded in other places. Furthermore, everyone providing treatment is given intensive training in methods that have already proved effective.

Knowing that the costs of such treatment programs (versus incarceration) and the amounts of money saved or lost would be closely scrutinized, the Arizona Supreme Court has been mandated to keep careful records and is required by law to issue a yearly legislative report.

In the year 1997–1998, by the Supreme Court's own detailed statistics, treatment programs—in lieu of jail and prison—saved the state of Arizona a whopping $2,563,062![1] In human terms, the statistics are equally impressive. The supreme court makes the following additional points:

1. The state of Arizona provided services to over 2,600 *more* substance abusing probationers than in fiscal year 1997.

2. Approximately three out of five probationers placed in drug treatment successfully completed it in fewer than ninety-five days.
3. Three out of four probationers placed in drug treatment remained drug free and paid at least one co-pay to offset the cost of their treatment.
4. The program diverted 551 adults from state prison at a savings of $2.5 million.

～

Such data, remarkable as it is, don't cover the whole story. Consider the 551 adults who, instead of costing the state incarceration money, are now helping reduce the welfare rolls by supporting their families—and are also paying taxes. Think of all those people—2,600!—who needed treatment and are now getting it. Most important, consider all the families whose newly "clean" members are giving them new hope.

～

Zachary Dal Pra, deputy chief over the assessment and program development, describes the exhaustive assessment process used to funnel substance abusers into one program or another. When a man or woman in Arizona is arrested for anything at all, he or she is thoroughly screened. But if the individual has addiction problems, the screening goes deeper. By assessing family factors, personality type, and the kind and intensity of drug use, Dal Pra can answer the question, What are this individual's risk factors?

Dal Pra says, "Risk means risk to re-offend. And the research in that area is getting pretty good. We're learning what factors lead someone to commit crimes. We've learned how likely it is he'll go on abusing chemicals. All in all, we've learned more in the last ten years than we did in the prior thirty years.

"At first it was hard to get staff members within the criminal justice system to understand. There are some prosecutors and judges who think, Because I put this man on probation and told him to go to treatment, and ordered him not to use, if he uses again, by golly, he's going to prison. But it isn't that simple."

Dal Pra's second, and most important, job is finding the program that fits the offender. He says, "In the community corrections field, we call that 'responsivity.' What we're trying to do is match. We look at the learning style of the individual and decide which program fits him. For instance, women have different needs than men in substance abuse treatment. That's a responsivity issue. Women may need transportation to treatment, for example, or child care. So responsivity is a big sort of buzzword now."

Dal Pra talks about years past, when a number of programs were running simultaneously but nobody was comparing notes. "We had substance abuse programs, drug court, women's network, and some other programs . . . and we weren't sitting down and saying, What are you doing in drug court that seems to be working? And what are you doing in women's network that we can use? So all of us got together, and this is what we came up with: that treatment works best when it's client-centered, when it's driven by assessment, when it's matched to specific client risk and needs. High-risk offenders, for instance, really need the highest intensity treatment. And time.

"At the other end, those low-risk, first-time offenders, who probably aren't going to commit another crime, don't need our intensive services. They need drug education and some support. It all works when it's research-based and when it's supported by thorough case management." He gives an illustration: "You can't just pick out one factor, for instance, that the offender is unemployed, and address only the unemployment; you also have to consider his living environment, his family needs, all those other things that contribute to his using.

"We've broken our offenders into three major categories," he says, "low, medium, and high risk. The high-risk offenders are those antisocial, longtime substance abusers who need cognitive restructuring and cognitive treatment."

When asked if he is talking about therapeutic communities, he answers, "Some. Yes. Big portions, though, can function in the community, but they still need that in-depth type of treatment. So we provide it in-house. We've hired counselors, clinicians, ourselves, for those high-risk populations."

The medium-risk offenders, he says, are mostly referred out to community providers. Drug court gets both medium- and low-risk groups. "We think working together as a community, as a criminal justice network, is the way to go. We can't just do it on our own."

But all this still isn't enough. The program leaders went to the jails and talked the sheriff into starting an in-jail program called the Alpha Program. Dal Pra says, "The sheriff loves the program now. I think it brings him great publicity. But it's also done real well—it's a good program."

The Salvation Army provides a treatment program called Harbor Lights. And now Maricopa County is starting a program called Reach-out, which begins providing extensive assessment in jail while the offender is awaiting treatment to open up outside. The goal is to reduce total jail time.

~

John MacDonald, communications officer in the Arizona Supreme Court, provides additional insights. "There's a great aspect to our funding stream [taxes on alcohol sales provide a steady flow of money] that makes programs readily available. So there's no waiting list."

MacDonald also talks about addiction from a judge's viewpoint: "I don't know that I've ever seen any real hard statistics, but if you talk to judges anecdotally and say, 'Okay, how many of the people in criminal court who come before you, what percentage of these cases are drug involved?'—they'll tell you, all. A hundred percent of them! Involved in some way!"

He explains why most legislators are so apt to vote for prisons instead of programs. "Legislatures operate in a two-year time frame," he says. "You can see results quicker with policing and interdiction than you can in substance abuse programs. Before that term as a legislator is up, you will see that jail cell be built and somebody sitting in it! A prevention program is maybe a five-, ten-, twenty-year investment, whose results are far less easy to record."

John MacDonald had recently attended a congressional hearing in Washington, D.C., on the decriminalization of hard drugs. MacDonald's colleague was there to speak about Arizona's approach to the situation. "We expected to get sandbagged," he says. "Instead, we found the congressmen quite receptive to our ideas. I think they were really listening."

When asked whether he thinks Congress is lagging behind public opinion, he says, "Oh, they absolutely admit that. The chairman of the committee, John Mica from Florida, came up and said, 'We in Congress are so far behind where the public is, that's why I'm holding these hearings—so we can catch up and find out what's going on out here and start to make decisions.'"

~

It's a short step from this formal approach to the in-the-trenches insights of Randy Rice, manager of substance abuse programs for Maricopa County Adult Probation. A man of boundless energy and keen perceptions, Rice is willing to discuss his programs for as long as someone will listen. His enthusiasm is absolutely catching.

Part of Rice's job is to oversee the Community Punishment Program (CPP). He quickly explains that the term *community punishment* is a misnomer meant to satisfy a once-conservative climate. He says, "Back in 1989, the notion of treating addicts was addressed by the local RBHA [Regional Behavioral Health Authority]. But the criminal justice clients (the people who were more than addicts, but also criminals) were out of the system. Lack of understanding, lack of resources. They were viewed as the problem children by treatment providers, who didn't want to deal with criminals in groups. So once they had a criminal history, there was nothing for them. I think the Community Punishment Program came out of a lot of lobbying of the legislature that said, Look, we've got tons of criminals sitting in jails that have substance abuse issues, and nobody will service them—because they've got a criminal history.

"So, in 1989, community punishment was born, as a kind of grassroots deal. With that title, we were able to get some jail and prison funds. We had three counselors who came together and developed programming, based on what already existed. We began running groups, and keeping progress notes, and developing client charts.

By '95 we were up to seven counselors, but still pretty much operating from the same perspective, the same principles. And it wasn't unique. There was no dialogue with RBHA.

"So our journey was, Shouldn't we partner with the community-based programs and create something that they don't want to do—that is, serve clients they don't want to serve? And provide complementary, rather than duplicate care? Namely, fill in some gaps.

"During that same period, about '92, our drug court started—one of the original six drug courts in the country. Now, of course, there are 400 plus.

"The original drug court design was pretty similar to the CPP design—except they had a judge involved. Again, we were all just kind of winging it. But we knew there was a need out there, that these high-risk people needed help therapeutically, not punitively. And that was our start.

"In '95 or '96, we were invited to the National Institute of Corrections in Longmont, Colorado. They had a conference, and it was this crazy little conference titled 'Effective Interventions for the Criminal Substance Abuser.'

"We were doing really well by then. About 70 percent of our clients were graduating from CPP, and we felt great. I went up there with my ego full of glow, thinking, I'll go up there and teach these guys how to do it.

"All these researchers were there, names you'll probably recognize: Paul Gendreau from Canada, Don Andrews from Canada, James Bonta from Canada, Dr. Ken Wanberg out of Colorado, Alan Marlatti from Seattle (an expert in relapse prevention), and all these really humongous leaders. All there to provide data on treating criminal substance abusers. All in this one four-day conference.

"I had my microcassette recorder and my pad of paper, and I can tell you that within the first day I realized that what we were doing here in Phoenix wasn't even close, nowhere near what the research was saying to do.

"So I kept listening, and kept writing, and kept taping, and I basically came back to Phoenix with my tail between my legs and realized that we had a lot of work to do if we were going to provide meaningful treatment for these high-risk offenders. We needed to make a lot of revisions."

When asked what he came up with, he says, "Well, it was very cool. Steve, here [Steven Davis, supervisor of the Community Punishment Program] was on the team at the time, and when I came back and started telling him what the researchers said, his first inclination was to say, 'No way,' because there was such a strong movement here in the Twelve Step Minnesota Model, and the conference experts were suggesting an added approach for criminal offenders. They were saying, you need to *join with* the Twelve Step program, not just duplicate it.

"Here's what they suggested we do: they said we should develop treatment around a cognitive, behavioral, social learning format. And what that means is, you're going to challenge thinking. You're going to confront the criminal's attitudes, values, and beliefs—those that support both his drug use and his criminal behavior. You'll attack both issues together."

When it's suggested that this might really be a therapeutic community, he says, "Well, a therapeutic community is an environment where they live and learn to adapt to healthy coping skills, a healthier lifestyle. You can put anything in a TC; you can have a Minnesota Model TC, or you can have a cognitive behavior TC. Any of those things."

Steven Davis speaks up. "Our big shift here made it almost uncomfortable. Since I became supervisor, we don't have any staff left from when we were doing strictly Twelve Step. I'm the last one. But what made it most disconcerting was that we went from being a substance abuse–focused treatment program to a program that focused on *all* aspects of the offender's life that were out of order—including substance abuse, the criminal behavior, and other abusive behavior."

Randy Rice again: "So all of a sudden substance abuse went from being the whole pie to just a piece of the pie. That is, substance abuse went from being the whole focus to some of the focus.

Because we were then talking about, Why do you use substances? What is the thinking that goes behind the use? Why do you commit criminal acts—and what is the thinking that goes behind that?

"That was a difficult transition for a lot of people, and we lost our whole team; we had to develop a whole new team."

"Doesn't your team need to address childhood traumas, too—in case the problems lie there?"

"Not exactly," he says. "We focus on their *belief systems* about what happened in their childhood. Today's belief systems. And this is important. The program that the NIC [National Institute of Corrections] endorses is very here-and-now oriented. They don't suggest we do a psycho-drama based on childhood or developmental trauma.

"And what's unique about this—what we had to learn— is that the treatment we're delivering today *is not the same treatment you should give somebody who is not involved in criminal conduct.* It's special treatment for people that have the criminal mind-set, *plus* are using drugs and alcohol. And boy, that shocked us, because we had assumed that you provided the same intervention regardless of background.

"But when you start thinking about how complex the antisocial thought structure is—when our client is entertaining criminal behavior *and* he's contemplating drug use—it does increase the intensity of what needs to be delivered.

"To put it in a nutshell, the research says there are four areas we need to concentrate on: they're called the Big Four, and this is from Paul Gendreau. They also said this is the order in which you address things:

"The first thing you do is attack those attitudes, values, and beliefs. And teach the client skills that *change* those faulty attitudes, values, and beliefs—especially when he's in a high-risk situation where people around him are using. Then he's got his best chance of making a good decision and not using.

"But if we don't address the basics, then anything else we do *may* work, but there's a huge chance it won't, because they're still sitting in the same mind-set. 'Well, I want to feel good.' Or, 'I want to escape.' Or, 'I want to have fun.' Or, 'I want to do whatever.' So we challenge that first. We've redesigned Community Punishment Program around that whole idea."

When asked how long the CPP counselors spend on that area, Davis responds, "Probably about three months. The clients attend one month of pretreatment as an introduction to basic cognitive, behavioral concepts, challenging attitudes, values, and beliefs. Then we hit them hard, for two months straight, before we do skill building in phase two."

Rice continues: "The second area you want to attack is their antisocial associates. Who in their life is supporting more crime? Who in their life is supporting more drug use? You can see the logic. We have to get them to challenge their *own* attitudes, values, and beliefs before we can start saying, 'Now who are your friends? And don't you think you should make a change in your friendships?'

"In the historical Minnesota Model approach, that would be one of the first areas you'd get into—getting rid of the old neighborhood, the old friends. But if you don't have the right mind-set, it won't work.

"The third area we attack is their criminal history. We begin to talk about, 'What is there about cracking cars that is so exciting to you? What is there about drug dealing you really enjoy?' Whatever their criminal history is, we start plugging into what motivates it. 'What is the element about your crime that makes it so great for you? Why do you like to forge checks? What's the point? What are you getting out of this activity? What's the payoff?'

"The last area we work on is the personality variables that get them into trouble. Their impulsivity, their problems with delayed gratification—I need to have stuff right now! And that leads into the idea of substance use: 'So drugs are one of those things that you're using chronically and compulsively, because you don't have any ability to delay gratification.'"

"Do you attack their inability to cope with stress? Or frustration?"

"Absolutely. That's the next piece of the pie. So what I've told you so far is all the cognitive behavioral piece. We challenge all the thinking, the attitudes, the feelings.

"But the next part is a social learning model. Here we do skill development through rewards and recognition—instead of through punishment and consequences. Which means we're teaching skills to cope with stress, to cope with authority, to cope with interpersonal communication, all kinds of interpersonal stuff. We deal with a variety of feelings: frustration, anger, grief, and loss.

"We get into high-risk situations. How do they cope with being at a party? How do they cope with seeing an old buddy? How do they cope with driving by the bar, every day, on the way home from work? We approach all that from a social learning perspective, which means we do it all with rewards.

"And that's the powerful thing. The research shows that offenders respond to rewards, not punishment. So when you're talking jail, that's not a deterrent. They don't care if they've got to go to jail."

"You mean, when they're looking at a little mound of crack, and they know in ten minutes they're going to feel great, really great, jail is the furthest thing from their minds? Isn't that sort of like the rest of us? That we live our lives eating too much, not exercising, without thinking that we're hastening our death?"

"Exactly." Rice pauses before going on: "What we provide is natural and logical consequences, versus punishment. We say, 'Okay, if you drive by that bar tonight and you go in, what's going to happen?' We talk through it. We do tons and tons and tons of role-plays."

"All with rewards, not punishment?"

"That's right. We do lots of role-playing for high-risk situations. Our treatment groups will sometimes begin with a joint that is found on the floor by clients coming into the room. It is interesting to watch the group just start grinding, because there's a little marijuana cigarette in the room. We walk them through it and the whole idea is, we want to support self-efficacy. That's the big buzzword for the '90s. It's the notion that they can be taught that change is possible. And here's *how* you change.

"We had to restructure everything we did in our program. For our population, we need to teach them *how* to live a different life. Not just, Here's what you can have. Or, Here are some principles to live your life by. But exactly *how* you go about changing.

"We even put them in high-risk situations. Steve has taken his group to a pool hall, a bar. We take them there under our guidance, and we say, 'So what's happening? How are you doing?' Because we *know* they're going to go back to those places someday. So they might as well go back while we're helping."

Randy Rice sums up how he feels about research: "We made a decision out of that NIC conference that we would not do anything in this program—anywhere in the department—that wasn't research-based. We'd give everything a try.

"What we're seeing, so far, are a lot of really encouraging outcomes. The clients are more receptive. In fact, the retention rate has improved. But more importantly, the long-term results are much better. We don't have as many dropouts. The clients *enjoy* what they're getting out of group now, because it fits."

Steven Davis breaks in. "We've developed an interesting system. The plan says, once you start CPP, you are ours until you die. Or until you successfully complete. Or you go to prison. So 72 percent of everyone who starts finishes without any issue.

"About 17 percent are terminated halfway through the process. They go to jail, and then they come out and start all over again. We lose about 8 percent to prison and 2 percent to death. If you go to jail, when you come back, you're still ours. You can't get rid of us."

Rice backtracks to the subject of traditional treatment programs: "We believe that AA, NA, and the Twelve Step program should be valued, recognized, and utilized as it was designed. Which is as a support system for people who have decided they're ready to stop using. Not mandated from a court bench, which is what was happening here.

"We used to have judges that were ordering ninety meetings in ninety days. But what's the point? You've got a guy in front of you that's plugged in to using drugs, and now because you're a judge and you're sitting on one side of the bench and he's on the other, you tell him to go to all these meetings.

"But will he go? No. He's not gonna go, he's gonna fake it. Once we work with them, we introduce them to AA meetings and say, 'Look, here's a good support system that will help you make it through long-term recovery.' Then they're much more amenable to going and plugging into AA and the Twelve Step program as it was designed."

He backtracks again to how Arizona drug programs were run before the days of research. "Historically, we made all our treatment decisions by offense type. Kim [Kim O'Connor, clinical supervisor, Adult Probation Department] had a whole hodgepodge full of people in drug court. Steve had a whole hodgepodge full of people in Community Punishment Programs. And we didn't know who should go into what.

"If you were an offender, and you did something really bad, you went into a long-term therapeutic community. Or if you were a heroin user, 'Oh, my gosh, that means you're sticking a needle in your arm; that's really bad, you need to go into long-term treatment. Not because you need long-term treatment, but because we think you're doing something really serious.'

"Later, through the conference and through some of the research, we realized we needed to do everything by specific assessment of the person. So now, Steve's CPP program is designed for the high-risk, high-need, antisocial offender.

"And the same with drug court and other programs. Now we're doing treatment matching. We match the level of care to the client's level of need.

"We restructured and designed curriculums. Another piece of the research said, 'You can't just wing it anymore. You've got to have a book, a design, a direction for groups, so you don't waste your time.'

"So now we've created programs that are matched to somebody who's lower risk than the CPP client would be, and a little bit lower need. Yet we still introduce the thinking paradigms, we still introduce ways to live your life differently, we still do skill-building, but it's at a different level and a different intensity than for somebody who's really high risk, high need, and basically unamenable to treatment."

Randy Rice thinks back again. "There used to be a day, back when we were starting out, that we'd deny certain people treatment because they 'weren't in the mood.' So we'd say to the facilitator, 'Whoops . . . has bad attitude, not in the mood for treatment.' So they were kicked out.

"Now the research says, 'No, that's our job. Our job is to motivate them.' So we've designed a whole program that does nothing but get the client prepared."

Steven Davis speaks up again: "Let me give you an example. This morning we did a farewell group for a client. This is a young lady who's been in the program for ten months.

"She is a twenty-nine-year-old black female who was born and raised in South Phoenix and started smoking crack when she was eleven years old. She's been a prostitute, she's been in and out of shelters, she's got nineteen arrests and eleven felony convictions, all since she was eighteen. And she has a juvenile record that's like fifteen convictions long, in and out of detention and jails as a juvenile.

"In the time she's been in the CPP program, by attacking her thoughts and her attitudes and her beliefs, she decided that first, she needed to move out of that environment, so she got herself into a halfway house. While she was at the halfway house, she got herself a job as a toll marker, because it's really tough for convicted felons to get work.

"She saved all her money, paid her bills, saved up some extra money, and got herself her own apartment six months later. She then got a promotion at work, to supervisor. The company has since expanded, so she has become manager of her own field office, with 150 employees. She says she went from wearing jeans with holes in them to wearing slacks brand new off the rack—and that's a huge deal for her.

"In the process, she lost five children—five of her own babies. Two of them died and three were taken by Child Protection. But in her recovery, she's been successful at getting all three kids back. As we were saying good-bye to her this morning, she said, 'The most impressive thing that's happened for me in CPP is that I learned how to live. And I only could have accomplished that by learning how I was screwing up my life with how I was acting.'"

Davis says, "We hear lots of testimony like that. She'd been through our Twelve Step program three different times. And it hadn't worked for her, because she never attacked the criminal thinking."

Randy Rice talks about the problem of relapse: "We now have programs called Lapse/Relapse Intervention, which involves a whole new treatment concept. What do you do with clients when they get out of treatment and use again?

"Do you put them right back in the same treatment, or do you do something different? We decided, under the guidance of Alan Marlatti and the research he's done, that we need to give these people an intervention when they use again. We say, 'Okay, what happened?' And the exciting thing is, there are assessment tools for this. The tools say, 'Here are the high-risk situations that will get this person in the most trouble. Here is a treatment plan for that.' And we do real short-term work.

"For instance, if somebody's son goes through treatment for six months, the research says, 'No matter whether he went to residential, whether he went to a therapeutic community, whether he went to outpatient, or whether he went to short term, in ninety days he will probably use again at least once.'

"The research says that it doesn't matter how intense the treatment is, they will all have a real struggle with relapse within ninety days.

"The question is, what do you do then?

"Do you tell them, 'You've failed treatment because you've used again, and now you need to go back and do a whole other six months, or a whole other therapeutic community, or whatever you did before?'

"Not really. We've designed lapse/relapse, which basically says, 'Now let's give you training to help you *use* the skills you learned in treatment.' And the clients love that, because they say, 'You're giving me credit for what I learned.'

"And we're saying, 'absolutely.' And we use a mountain climber analogy. We tell them, 'Picture yourself in this scene. I'm a mountain climber, I've got all my equipment, and I'm an expert at climbing. And now I'm ascending a brand-new mountain I've never climbed before, which is like living life in prosocial terms, and I'm going up the face, and even though I'm belted in and I've got all my hooks, and I've got my spikes on my shoes—I slip!

"'If I slip, what are my choices? Should I let go of the rope now, and just go splat at the bottom, or is there the possibility that when I slip a little bit, I regrip, I grab the rope a little tighter, I get my footing back, and I go up another route so I won't slip again?'

"And that's what we believe happens with substance abusers.

"We don't necessarily tell our clients that we expect them to use again, but if they do, we teach them how to deal with it when they get there. Or maybe they'll pick a different route now. Whatever. Whatever it takes."

He changes tacks: "As great as all of us in this room believe the Twelve Step program is, and AA is just a wonderful thing, with this population we look at the part about being powerless a little differently.

"When we challenge values, attitudes, and beliefs, that's one of the areas we challenge. Because you know what, you are not powerless. Step One—We admit that we are powerless over our chemicals, and our lives have become unmanageable. We tell them, '*Wrong.* You are totally powerful; you knew what you were doing the entire time. It's your decision making we need to work on. It's not about your being powerless.'

"You try to tell a group of men who are antisocial that they're powerless, and they'll prove to you a different story. So we tell them, 'No, you are totally powerful. But let's talk about what you're powerful *in.* Maybe you were powerful in indulgence. Maybe you were powerful in being impulsive. Maybe you were powerful in being a party animal. Whatever. *That* was your power. Huh! Did that power serve you?'

"The clients, so far, have proved us right. They're out in the world, and they report back about what they're doing, and they're using our terms. They tell us, 'I use a Thought-Report when I'm at work and I get really mad.' Or, 'I use a Franklin Reality Model when I think something's not the way it should be.'"

Now Rice grins. "When's the last time you heard someone say, 'I'm using something I got out of treatment—and I'm using it every day?'"

CHAPTER TWELVE

Turning a Sheriff's Vision into Reality

Sheriff Mike Carona

On March 14, 1997, I announced my candidacy for the office of sheriff of Orange County, California. I campaigned on a somewhat controversial ten-point plan. My commitment to the citizens of Orange County was, if elected, to improve public safety and enhance the quality of life for all my constituents.

The first of my ten points was to solve the problem of over-crowded jails that has plagued our county for nearly twenty-five years. As I campaigned, I spoke about innovative ways to construct and operate our county jails; I expounded on ideas for stopping the influx of offenders; and I offered ways to reduce recidivism.

I also urged the citizens of Orange County, as I still do, to work with at-risk youth today to prevent their becoming the inmates of tomorrow.

To keep offenders from returning, I argued for increased in-jail educational and job training programs. Challenging conventional wisdom, I proposed a partnership within the healthcare community to lower the numbers of mentally ill offenders who make up some 15 percent of our county's jail population. And I proposed a separate lockdown facility for the drug and alcohol offenders who now comprise in excess of 20 percent of our inmate population. Again, the goal was to both reduce recidivism and stop creating victims.

That is how I met Maralys. She had heard about my candidacy and my views and wanted to tell me, from a mother's perspective, what needed to be done to stop more sons and daughters from cycling repeatedly through jails and prisons. We shared ideas on what could and should be done to attack the drug and alcohol problems affecting our country. From those meetings a friendship developed.

On June 6, 1998, the voters of Orange County elected me sheriff. On January 4, 1999, I was sworn in as the eleventh man to hold that office since our area became Orange County in 1889. In the intervening six-month period, I was able to define strategies for implementing my campaign promises.

Maralys, already an accomplished author, used the six-month time frame to outline a book that had been in her head and heart ever since she learned what our department was about to do for Orange County's addicted inmates. She perceived our local plan as having great promise, perhaps even becoming a model for other jails, and potentially a way of saving thousands of sons like hers who were in America's jails and prisons.

She had a story to tell. I had a jail-overcrowding problem to solve.

Unlike this book, the final chapter of what I'm doing is yet to be written. The all-important conclusion—whether or not our Orange County program is successful—is many years away. But today I can describe the history of our addicted inmate population and how it's grown, and reveal our newly crafted strategy to stop creating victims.

To understand the reasoning behind a lockdown treatment facility for addicted inmates, it is important to know more about the Sheriff's Department and its jail operations. The Orange County Sheriff's Department (OCSD) is the fifth largest in the United States. With more than 3,000 employees and a budget of nearly $400 million, the OCSD is not only one of America's biggest, but also one of the most diverse. The men and women who make up the OCSD are, simply, the finest law enforcement professionals with whom I've ever been associated.

While the men and women of the OCSD have been recognized nationally for outstanding contributions in criminal investigation, forensics, patrol, training, and hazardous device disposal, less well publicized are the department's jails.

The OCSD operates the sixth largest jail system in the United States, with more than 5,400 inmates in custody on any given day. But size isn't our only claim to fame; the Orange County jail system is also the most overcrowded in America, operating at 145 percent of capacity.

Because of problems caused by overcrowding, in 1978 the American Civil Liberties Union (ACLU) sued the county board of supervisors and the sheriff, citing inhumane treatment of prisoners. In 1985, a U.S. district court judge issued a ruling in that 1978 case, *Stewart vs. Gates,* that still binds the Sheriff's Department to this day. The ruling, among other things, caps the number of inmates the department can house in its jails, mandates that prisoners be given a bed within twenty-four hours, and threatens contempt of court for any violations.

Thanks to budget constraints and a historic municipal bankruptcy, since 1985 the county board of supervisors was able to add only 752 new jail beds. As a result, my predecessor had only two options to stay within the judge's orders: (1) cite and release any new prisoners who were not a significant risk to the community, or (2) release some prisoners early, making room for the newly booked.

The magnitude of this problem is seen in the following statistics: from 1986 to 1998, nearly 500,000 prisoners were released early because of a lack of beds. On average, roughly 10 percent of those offenders committed new crimes and were rearrested during the time they should have been in jail. And those are just the *known* crimes that we could have prevented had these individuals remained in custody. This doesn't account for crimes that were never reported or those where law enforcement couldn't find a suspect.

Orange County's jail overcrowding obviously needed more than one solution.

Part of the answer was creating additional jail capacity, and we are now constructing nearly a thousand new beds, with plans for another thousand over the next four years. Another answer was reducing recidivism among the mentally ill offenders who make up 15 percent of our jail population. The mental health community is helping us develop programs to identify, treat, and provide aftercare for the mentally ill in the jails, hoping to dramatically curb repeat offenders.

We are working aggressively to provide job training and educational opportunities to our inmates. Roughly 93 percent are released back into the community, yet if they go back with no new job or educational tools, they will not seek employment but rather return to the criminal life they already know. While still in the embryonic stages, our programs have been highly successful, with 89 percent of inmates who enter the GED program leaving with a high school equivalency diploma—one of the highest percentages in the nation. The average nationwide is 78 percent.

The largest and most controversial element in our campaign against jail overcrowding is our commitment to build a 500-bed lockdown drug and alcohol treatment facility.

On average, 20 percent of our inmates are there strictly for crimes relating to drug and/or alcohol abuse—offenders arrested for simply being under the influence or for personal possession of illegal drugs. These aren't the people who sell drugs or commit drug-induced crimes, like burglary.

When we analyze our entire jail population, however, we find that regardless of what crimes brought them there, 60 to 80 percent are chemically dependent. Chemical addictions are directly related to a variety of violent and property crimes that wreak havoc on individuals, families, and the community. Of those arrested, many are repeat offenders. We in the Sheriff's Department believe that by providing substance abuse treatment in jail, we will significantly reduce repeat offenses of all kinds.

To determine what type of facility we should design and what types of programs we should implement, I assembled a team of professionals from both the Sheriff's Department and the Orange County Health Care Agency. The team was comprised of experts versed in jail operations, jail construction, and inmate classifications, plus those who understood behavior modification and the treatment of chemical dependency, as well as others who could institute educational and job training programs. The objective for the team was simple: look at substance abuse programs throughout the United States, both custodial and noncustodial, identify the most effective methods being employed today, and decide which programs could best be incorporated locally.

Over a five-month period, the team reviewed programs and made on-site visits to operations considered by experts to be the most successful or the most innovative.

Based on this research, our department is prepared to move forward with a pilot program that will become the precursor to a 500-bed facility—the largest in-custody drug and alcohol treatment program operating at a county level anywhere in the United States.

On July 1, 2000, the OCSD plans to open its 64-bed pilot program at Theo Lacy Branch jail in Orange, with the 500-bed facility scheduled to be on line sometime after June 30, 2002. The OCSD and the Orange County Health Care Agency will partner with a private provider to offer a variety of in-custody and aftercare treatment programs.

The OCSD in-custody drug and alcohol treatment program will be comprehensive and consist of the following components:

1. Substance abuse evaluation and inmate assessment to determine which inmates should be included in the program.
2. A therapeutic community that separates inmates in the program from those in the general jail population, allowing for total immersion, decreased distractions, and the accurate monitoring of inmates' behavior.
3. A minimum of three months of in-custody treatment before release or referral to an aftercare component.
4. Random drug/alcohol testing on a daily basis.
5. Structured activities six and a half days a week for a minimum of eight hours each day.
6. As part of these structured activities, at least the following drug and alcohol treatment programs:
    a. AA and NA programs
    b. individual counseling
    c. social model recovery–focused group counseling
    d. process groups
    e. substance abuse education
    f. anger management

      g. relapse prevention

      h. criminal thinking

7. As part of these activities, at least the following educational components:

      a. GED training/community college classes

      b. computer training

      c. job preparation/vocational training

      d. resume development

      e. parenting classes

      f. life skills training

8. The management, monitoring, and evaluation of both in-custody and aftercare program goals to determine the effectiveness of the program in reducing recidivism.

∿

The aftercare component, like the program itself, will be comprehensive and consist of the following elements:

1. A minimum of six to twelve months of continued treatment after release from the OCSD, including drug and alcohol treatment programs based on each participant's unique, individual needs.

2. Transportation to an aftercare program upon release from the Orange County jail.

3. Aftercare services based on accepted principles of treatment and recovery from drug and/or alcohol addiction, including exposure to Alcoholics Anonymous and/or other Twelve Step programs.

4. Random drug testing of all participants.

5. Transitional housing assistance.

6. Employment development and placement services.

7. Short- and/or long-term residential recovery services.

∿

Before the OCSD's program has even begun to function, we have had our share of both criticism and praise.

Our critics have identified the following weaknesses:

The length of custodial time is too short to adequately modify an addicted individual's behavior:

Most experts in the field agree that short-term therapeutic community programs are not nearly as effective as those that are one to two years in length. We recognize this as an inherent weakness but had to concede that the maximum time an inmate can be in our facility is one year, given the fact that we operate a county jail and not a state prison. We opted to set a minimum time requirement for admittance to our program at ninety days and backstopped our relatively short residency time with a mandatory aftercare component that would either emulate or build upon the in-custody programs.

A 500-bed facility is too large to be effectively operated at a county level.

We acknowledge that our program will be the largest of its kind operating at a county level anywhere in the United States. However, given the fact that Orange County already runs such a large jail system, coupled with our knowledge that at least 20 percent of our offenders (approximately 1,000 prisoners per day) are being held for drug and/or alcohol charges, we believe it would be irresponsible not to try to impact this vast majority.

The fact that we are beginning slowly, with a 64-bed pilot project, means we can make continuous adjustments as we design and implement the 500-bed facility. It is our belief that the program will be as successful, if not more so, than similar programs operated at a state prison level.

However, we will closely monitor the program, and if we fail in our goals, the county can, with minor modifications, turn the 500-bed facility back into a conventional jail operation.

We believe that will never occur and are prepared to meet the challenge.

The use of private sector aftercare breaks the continuum of treatment and could diminish the quality of the recovery program.

Again, given our relatively short in-custody time frames, we considered private sector aftercare a necessity. Through research we learned that other states, such as Arizona (see chapter 11), have had great success with collaborative efforts between county and community aftercare givers.

Furthermore, with our collaborative partners, specifically the Orange County Health Care Agency, we believe we will have aftercare components that will closely resemble the treatment within the jail.

Because aftercare programs are essential to our participants' long success, there will be continuous monitoring of all external programs—for program contact, effectiveness, and compatibility with the in-custody program. The goal of our program is not simply to modify an individual's behavior while in jail, but to see him make lasting lifestyle changes.

Programs like ours simply coddle prisoners rather than punishing them.

We would agree with at least half that statement. Our program is not designed to punish prisoners, but rather prepare them to re-enter our community sober and with a set of life skills that will allow them to become productive human beings. Punishment as a way of curing addiction has not proved successful, while programs like those we propose have, in other jurisdictions, had moderate to high levels of success.

With respect to coddling prisoners, we would strongly disagree. Our program is an intensive therapeutic community, with the inmate's week virtually taken up with AA, NA, and other educational programs, as well as with significant "household duties" to maintain the facility. On top of all this, each inmate must relinquish his rights to external contacts for a lengthy period of time and realize that he will have no contact with other prisoners in our general jail population. Treatment prisoners will be subjected to random drug testing on a daily basis and will be intensely supervised by sheriff's personnel and healthcare employees.

The great irony is that this program is far more demanding than simply "doing the time." Other jurisdictions have discovered that a large percentage of addicted inmates would *rather* be left alone to sit out their sentences, with no demands made on them for personal change. Offenders have learned that being forced to examine their thinking and reorder their priorities is actually pretty tough, and participating in such a program is doing "hard time," rather than its opposite. Only as they come to the end of the program do most inmates acknowledge that being forced to change was positive for them in every way.

Unless a person is motivated, he will not succeed in this program.

My data, and the data gathered by Maralys as we researched this book, all contradict this long-held belief. As described in prior chapters, addicted offenders who don't want help *can* be helped, nevertheless. Offenders forced to obey the rules of drug courts, for instance, stay clean at first because the judge orders them to, but later because a new set of values becomes internalized—and also because their lives improve so radically. Resistant inmates at places like Indian Creek prison in Virginia, for instance—and in many other jail and prison settings—fight rehabilitation at first, but later embrace it, calling such programs "the best thing that ever happened to me." Furthermore, some individuals never really "hit bottom," and for some, "rock bottom" is death, as it was for my mother.

In our program, we literally have a captive audience, so the motivation to enter the program might be quite different than if the same individual were not in jail and had to choose to go voluntarily into a residential program.

In spite of the above criticisms, support for our program has been equally vocal, and supporters have identified the following strengths in Orange County's plans.

In-custody rehabilitation is a proven way to reduce recidivism among criminals convicted of drug and alcohol charges.

While our program, once fully operational, will be the largest of its kind in any county jail facility, it is not the first of its kind. As we have discussed throughout this book, programs currently operated in state prisons and jails around our nation by providers such as

Hazelden, Amity, Walden House, and Phoenix House have had great success. Recidivism rates drop from a high of 60 to 70 percent in the untreated population, to rates as low as 15 percent in certain in-custody programs.

Given the number of inmates in our jails who are there because of chemical dependency, even a 25 percent drop in recidivism would dramatically reduce overcrowding.

The program is an innovative approach to the "war on drugs."

When the war on drugs was declared in the mid-1980s, it was because so many people were concerned about the cocaine addiction then sweeping our country. Our leaders feared that if the problem was not swiftly dealt with, escalating drug use would prove disastrous for America. The various "generals" in this war appropriately identified the "enemy's" strategy for victory as a matter of supply and demand. There was, and continues to be, a valiant effort to eliminate the supply side through an aggressive drug interdiction program that unites local, state, and federal law enforcement to fight the drug cartels in our nation and internationally.

As discussed in an earlier chapter, the component that lacked support was eradication of the demand side. A number of years ago, programs like Drug Use is Life Abuse, DARE, CounterAct, and other school-based antidrug education programs tried to impact our nation's youth, getting them to commit to a drug-free lifestyle. While these programs have had, in varying degrees, some measure of success, little energy was focused on rehabilitating known drug addicts. Chemically dependent offenders coming through our criminal justice system are the *known* demand element in the supply and demand strategy. We believe that to truly win the war on drugs, we must fight the enemy on all fronts.

The program is a cost-effective alternative to building additional maximum-security jails.

One point that needs emphasis is that Orange County's program is a custodial program, which means all the individuals in the program are in *jail*. They are, however, receiving treatment, plus educational and vocational training within the facility instead of just being warehoused.

The cost effectiveness of the program comes from two distinct sources: First, to operate such a program does not require construction of maximum-security facilities, since the individuals in this facility are prescreened and classified as low-risk, nonviolent offenders. Their charges are for chemical dependency—not murder, rape, robbery, or other more serious crimes. Because they can safely be housed in a less-secure facility, the savings over maximum-security buildings would be 10 to 30 percent.

The second cost-efficiency comes from the reduction in repeat offenders. To understand this dynamic, it is helpful to review the trends in our nation's prisons and jails over the last decade.

Today in America there are more than 2,000,000 people incarcerated.[1] Given a U.S. population of 271,626,000 residents, this means that one out of every 150 Americans is in prison or jail, which, on a percentage basis, is more than any other industrialized nation in the world.

Since 1990, prison and jail populations have increased nearly 60 percent, with costs for building and operating these facilities nearly doubling. Twenty-four and a half billion dollars was spent nationwide in 1996 alone. In many states, the cost of correctional operations now exceeds the cost for education. On any given day, 1.96 million children have a parent or close relative in jail or prison, and 5 million more have parents who have been incarcerated in the past. The number of female inmates has nearly doubled since 1990, with the vast majority being single parents.[2]

According to the Bureau of Justice Statistics, there has been only a slight percentage change in the types of crimes that land individuals in jail. In 1990, violent crimes constituted 46 percent of the total, with property crimes at 25 percent, public-order crimes at 10 percent, and drug-related crimes at 21 percent.[3] Of all the categories identified, those having the greatest potential for rehabilitation (and thus the largest reduction in repeat offenses) are people who commit drug-related crimes. Even small percentage drops in numbers of inmates incarcerated for drug charges would significantly reduce correctional costs.

One could also argue that many of the inmates who make up the drug-related percentage could later become part of the group that commits violent and property crimes, as they recycle through our nation's jails and prisons.

Regardless of the long-term cost savings, there are clearly short-term cost efficiencies that can be had by the introduction of our program.

The program provides more than just treatment for chemical dependency.

With such a high percentage of inmates returning to the community, it seemed important to focus not only on drug issues, but also on educational and vocational skills. By helping inmates earn a GED, or improve their reading, writing, and communications skills, we increase the probability that they will be successful in the job market later. The probability goes higher when we concentrate on skills needed by Orange County employers.

While these became value-added components of our in-custody drug and alcohol abuse treatment program, they were already proven commodities, long since used by the Orange County Sheriff's Department to reduce recidivism. With both programs operating together, we expect to see geometric increases in the success rate.

～

As Douglas Lipton, a senior research fellow at the National Development and Research Institute, testified in September 1997: "The incarceration of persons found guilty of various crimes who are also chronic substance abusers presents a propitious opportunity for treatment—propitious because these persons would be unlikely to seek treatment on their own; without treatment they are extremely likely to continue their drug use and criminality after release, and we now have cost-effective technologies to effectively treat them while in custody, and thus alter their lifestyles.

"Research over the past five years has proven that intensive treatment programs now available are highly successful at reducing recidivism among drug-addicted felons—especially high-risk offenders— chronic heroin and cocaine users with long histories of predatory crime. Experts estimate these addicted offenders each commit *forty to sixty robberies a year, seventy to one hundred burglaries,* and more than *four thousand drug transactions"* [emphasis added].[4]

While Lipton is only one of many researchers studying chemically dependent offenders, his statistics and conclusions are consistent with findings by others around the nation. And while the statistics quoted are for offenders now incarcerated in state prisons, it should be noted that all these individuals began their criminal justice careers with a stint in county jail. While the severity and repetition of crimes committed by debutant offenders may not be as great or as often, they are still sizeable in number.

There are both tangible and intangible costs associated with all these robberies, burglaries, and drug transactions. The societal costs are staggering and are only compounded when the addicted offenders are ultimately caught and incarcerated. We then add to the existing losses the cost of processing the individuals through the court system, from arraignment to sentencing. Then we increase the bill geometrically by incarcerating them—at a price anywhere from a low of $20,000 per year to a high of $90,000.

In a report from the California legislative analyst's office, "Addressing the State's Long-Term Inmate Population Growth," the authors concur that expanding the state's in-prison drug-treatment programs could save taxpayers millions of dollars each year. The report suggests that increasing the inmate population served by custodial drug treatment programs to 5,000 inmates would save taxpayers approximately $40 million each year in prison operating costs alone and $100 million in prison construction costs. If this concept expands to serve an additional 10,000 inmates, the savings jump to $80 million in annual operating costs and $210 million in construction costs.[5]

It should be noted that these calculations only take into consideration the state of California's prison population; they do not include prisoners being held in county jails in each of the state's fifty-eight counties, which, as of the end of 1999, was 75,548 compared to the state prison population in March 2000 of 160,846.

And there are tremendous savings to be had long before a chemically addicted offender enters a prison setting. An economist who analyzed the Amity program at the R. J. Donovan state prison found that "in the year before the last incarceration, participants were on average responsible for $93,000 each in emergency room visits, jail costs, welfare payments for children, court expenses, and other costs. Calculated over a criminal career, unless reformed, these felons could be expected to cost society more than $1.5 million each.[6]

The cost associated with drug interdiction is another taxpayer expense not subsumed within the numbers quoted thus far. Barry Glassner, in his book *The Culture of Fear: Why Americans Are Afraid of the Wrong Things* gives us a pretty good snapshot about monies spent by the federal government on drug interdiction over the last four decades. Glassner states, "Federal drug enforcement, a $6 million expense in the 1960s, passed the $1 billion mark in the mid-1980s during Ronald Reagan's presidency, and more than $17 billion during Bill Clinton's."[7]

Remember, these numbers do not represent what is truly spent on drug interdiction. Glassner's portrayal was only for funds spent at the federal level and did not include similar investments made by states, counties, or cities.

Suffice it to say that when all the costs associated with chemically addicted offenders are totaled, the economic impact on our nation is in the hundreds of billions of dollars. When you factor in the social consequences for which it is impossible to calculate a dollar value—impacts such as emotional trauma for victims of rapes, robberies, or burglaries; the separation of parents from their children; the agony a parent endures as his child slips ever deeper into addiction; or the horror a child experiences through a parent's death when the addiction wins—you now have the complete picture of the devastating socioeconomic impact of America's drug addictions.

While these statistics, viewed by themselves, are rather depressing, there is quite a bit of good news about rehabilitation and subsequent reduced recidivism. The National Institute on Drug Abuse evaluated the Amity drug treatment program at California's R. J. Donovan state prison (described in chapter 9) and offered remarkable statistics. NIDA found that one year after release from Donovan prison, only 17 percent of those who completed both the in-prison program and the community-based aftercare component were re-incarcerated, compared to 66 percent of a control group who received no treatment. Among those who went through the in-prison program only, 35 percent were re-incarcerated.[8]

The numbers distilled from Donovan are consistent with similar programs throughout our nation. With drug treatment programs in place, custodial programs report recidivism drops precipitously, somewhere between 25 and 80 percent.

Think about the billions of dollars that would be saved across our nation if even a small percentage of chemically addicted offenders did not re-offend. Those numbers grow exponentially when individuals stop being financial burdens and become productive, contributing members of society.

∼

The fact of the matter is simply this: *Drug treatment works.*

Study after study has shown the effectiveness of these programs. It is imperative that such programs be incorporated into federal and state prisons, nationwide, as well as into county jails.

But for other jurisdictions to jump on the bandwagon, documented successes must be shown to the public policymakers who ultimately vote to fund programs. In Orange County, California, we have opted to take a leadership role in documentation, hoping that our successes will motivate others to follow suit.

We are excited about the future and our commitment to make our community safer.

∼

When asked the obvious quesion, What is the motivation behind writing this book? Maralys had a much more direct answer than I. As a mother, she had witnessed firsthand that locking up drug offenders and punishing them for their crimes was ineffective. She watched her son progress from a few days in county jail to several years in state prison because punishment didn't change his behavior. Once released, he returned to the streets with the same addiction that put him in jail, only now with a newfound knowledge of how to "beat the system"—Criminal Justice 101: How to Be a Good Criminal. Maralys wanted to change the system for her son and other children like hers who were constantly being recycled through our criminal justice system. Hers was a personal crusade.

When I was asked the same question, I didn't have a direct answer. In fact, I had to think about why I was involved in this book. I am not a writer; I am a peace officer. Yes, I have a vision about making a positive impact on my community—by trying an innovative approach to reducing recidivism among our local drug offenders. But that is my job—to keep my community safe—and our lockdown substance abuse program is designed to do just that: keep Orange County safe by turning criminal drug addicts into functioning members of society. As the sheriff of Orange County, I am committed to improving public safety and enhancing the quality of life for everyone who lives here. And while the Orange County Sheriff Department's in-custody drug and alcohol treatment program will not, by itself, accomplish that goal, it is one part of a multifaceted plan aimed at achieving that objective. But there other motivating factors too.

It is my deep desire, and Maralys's as well, that this book—and the development and expansion of the programs it describes—will give parents and children of chemically dependent offenders new hope for a positive future, for the possibility of reclaiming the lives of loved ones seemingly lost to addiction.

Hope is something they've had in desperately short supply, and it's time for that to change.

And perhaps along the way, this work will even the score in our lives, as well—by saving just one mother's son or one son's mother.

CHAPTER THIRTEEN

Coming Out—To What?
Bridging the Gap from Jail to Job

The manager of a small fast-food restaurant glances at the job applicant and without conscious analysis knows this isn't someone he wants. The applicant does not look confident: he doesn't smile readily, he doesn't stand straight, he doesn't seem forthcoming, he doesn't look the employer in the eye. Everything about him is hangdog and suggests he won't be much of an employee—a low-energy person at best, untrustworthy at worst.

The manager doesn't find it hard to tell the applicant the job has been filled.

Later, the employer glances at the job application. As he'd suspected, it's vague and unconvincing and he tosses it out. Who needs to hire an obvious bad bet?

$\sim$

In just such scenarios all over the country, ex-convicts find themselves defeated in the job market, as everywhere else—with predictable damage to their already shaky self-esteem. It doesn't take many repetitions of this kind of hasty rejection to convince the offender that the job market is stacked against him and he'll never be hired.

In truth, with the classic look of "prisoner" stamped all over him, such an offender could very well job-hunt for months—all in vain. He might not be wearing the telltale striped shirt, but the stripes on his personality are there just the same.

Of course the typical, untreated offender won't search for months. He hasn't the patience. He has no tolerance for stress. And he certainly can't endure endless rejection. He's had more than enough of that already.

In many ways, the beaten-down ex-offender is a child. As we pointed out in chapter 4, his maturation ended when his drug use began. Reconstructing a childish man or woman into a mature adult is a slow, painstaking process, requiring the same patient guidance and help from caring mentors that are required to turn an actual child into a functioning adult.

Even with an addict who has received months of intense substance abuse treatment, more is needed. It's one thing to cope in a protected environment—in a treatment program where *everyone* has problems. It's quite another to deal with an impersonal world where the hiring guy really doesn't give a damn—where you're competing with all the well-equipped, confident people who've never known rejection on this scale.

$\sim$

Of all the points made so far in this book, none is more important than this: *Every addicted offender needs help to reenter society.*

The long-term offender needs intense help. Call it hand-holding. Or coddling. Call it anything. But he must have someone beside him paving the way. That someone can be a probation officer, a member of the Continuum of Care Center, a representative from Virginia Cares—anyone. But the offender needs someone wise to make calls for him, to vouch for him, to guide and direct him.

Validation from a third party can make all the difference: *"If you give this man a chance, you won't be sorry. I know him, and he's making a genuine effort to turn his life around. He's had problems, true, but he's been honest about them. He's trying. Take my number and keep me posted about his progress."*

With that kind of help, a defeated man can get a job. An employer who's been forewarned, whose compassion has been aroused, will be a thousand times more receptive about taking a chance than the employer faced with a beaten-down stranger. Luckily, there are numbers of employers here and there who have hired parolees with good results and are willing to work with probation/parole officers in hiring more.

～

It has been a welcome discovery for both of us that treatment providers everywhere have a strong interest in aftercare. Though the concept is relatively new, counselors are paying close attention to outcome statistics. People in the field now recognize that you can't fix an abuser in one environment and expect him to stay fixed if he gets no help "fitting in" after he arrives home.

Finding a job is the biggest hurdle. But next on the list would be a place to live—and not with the "old crowd," either. Third would be a caring support group that offers encouragement and replaces old, destructive friends. Without help in these three areas, the ex-offender has scant chance of staying clean. With help, his chances soar.

Elliott Currie, in *Crime and Punishment in America*, comments on Delaware's Crest program, the aftercare plan used in conjunction with Key, which treats inmates within the prison system.[1] Currie cites the following figures: in a control group that received no care whatever, 70 percent of inmates were rearrested within eighteen months. Of those taking part in the prison program only, 52 percent came back within the year and a half. But of those who participated only in aftercare, a scant 35 percent returned. The best results, of course, came from inmates receiving both programs—a low 25 percent. Currie writes, "the after-care experience, though relatively short, may have had the most impact."

～

A list of aftercare programs attached to treatment programs mentioned earlier is revealing. Some are adjuncts to drug courts, some to prison programs, some to therapeutic communities. But all treatment programs seem to have them.

Indian Creek Correctional Center, Chesapeake, Virginia: Peer program, plus transition specialists.

Drug court, Norfolk, Virginia: Second Chances program, Judeo

Christian Outreach. Help and intervention from probation officers. Virginia Cares.

Probation department, Norfolk, Virginia: Peer support group.

Drug court, Richmond, Virginia: Day Reporting Center.

Men's Diversion Center, Chesterfield, Virginia: Jobs arranged before clients leave.

Drug court, Denver, Colorado: Continuum of Care Center.

Cenikor, Denver, Colorado: Mandatory job, housing, and peer support arrangements made before client leaves.

Phoenix, Arizona: Alumni association (for drug court graduates) and ongoing events for graduates of other programs that include participation as mentors.

New York City: Stay 'n Out program.

R. J. Donovan Prison, San Diego, California: The Farm.

Corcoran Prison, California: Six-month aftercare program.

North, South, West, and Central Court, Orange County, California: Aftercare programs that emphasize continuing treatment, relapse prevention, and social reintegration.

～

The most innovative idea on this subject comes from Judge William Meyer in Denver, who supports reentry drug courts. For those addicted inmates whose crimes make them ineligible for regular drug court, it has been proposed that they attend a kind of aftercare court, where, instead of being set free with limited, sporadic monitoring by a parole officer, the paroled inmate reports to a traditional drug court. In this setting he will get the same kind of intense supervision and accountability by a judge that he might have gotten on the front end, *in lieu* of prison. Surely the tough law and order advocates who object to drug court as a substitute for prison can have no objection to the same kind of close monitoring of the offender *after he gets out.*

Although it is our contention that ordinary prison is *almost always* a waste of resources and time for the nonviolent substance abuser, a reentry drug court would be a strong, second-best solution—and far better than simply turning the unprepared offender loose on society and expecting some kind of miraculous turnaround.

～

Judging from the many, diverse programs we've explored across the country, it appears that a one-size-fits-all approach doesn't work any better in drug treatment than it does in clothing.

One size definitely does not fit all.

Some people respond extraordinarily well to a paramilitary approach. Others would be shriveled by it.

Some people "grow up" inside the caring, protected environment of a therapeutic community. (Although some such communities are not particularly gentle.) Others need concentrated treatment in the communities where they live.

Beginning substance abusers may require education, counseling, and little else, whereas hard-core, longtime addicts need long-term programs—a month for every year of addiction.

Addicts who have a criminal mind-set and have resorted to nonviolent criminal acts will almost certainly need intense cognitive behavioral intervention.

Some abusers benefit from voluntary programs. Others need to be dragged into coercive treatment, kicking and cursing. Yet both groups are equally "fixable."

All of which suggests that one of the most important contributions Arizona has made to drug treatment everywhere is its development of a *detailed assessment plan*, which painstakingly matches offenders to treatment programs.

～

With all the workable aspects to be found in treatment programs everywhere, it appears that a couple of features are too often missing. We believe that most programs would benefit by adopting a holistic approach.

Almost nowhere, for instance, did we find any emphasis on exercise. Yet exercise can play a vital role in bringing calm, and even happiness, to the recovering addict. With vigorous exercise, endorphin levels rise, bringing a natural high that in some ways duplicates the artificial highs sought through drugs.

Pleasurable, vigorous exercise—by that we mean sports the client enjoys—should be added to substance abuse programs everywhere. Fitness is only one goal. By far the more important goal is a feeling of well-being and new energy, as well as a sense of accomplishment when the client begins to feel like an athlete. Nothing is more rewarding than having one's muscles respond to a challenge. If we expect substance abusers to give up all the chemicals that once made them happy, we need to substitute other satisfactions. And exercise is among the best.

Furthermore, as a practical matter, nobody can concentrate indefinitely on treatment issues without infusions of oxygen to the brain. Exercise provides oxygen and a great deal more.

Validation of our thoughts on exercise comes from Judge Wendy Lindley, drug court judge in Orange County's South Court. With humor and affability, Lindley mandates regular exercise for all her clients, even making the point at drug court graduation. But so far Judge Lindley is the only person we've found who emphasizes physical activity as an important adjunct to drug treatment.

～

Another mostly overlooked idea is the use of dress-up clothing and attractive hairstyles to enhance self-esteem. With this issue, we're working from the outside in.

It's a rare individual who doesn't feel better about himself when he knows he looks attractive. The old cliché "Clothes make the man" has a very real psychological basis. Not only does an individual's choice of clothing reflect how he already feels about himself, but it works the other way: force him to dress up, and his spirit and self-image improve.

It has long been our contention that schoolchildren, and particularly inner-city kids, need to be given nice-looking uniforms. Not only do they feel worthier when they're dressed up, but teachers and outsiders treat them better.

Here we offer four examples, both negative and positive, of the role that dress and grooming have traditionally played in self-esteem.

Example one: When the French government decided to punish

and humiliate the females who collaborated with the Nazis, they shaved their heads—knowing the sense of shame that would be inflicted on a woman with the loss of her hair. (Even some of today's therapeutic communities use severe haircuts as a last-resort punishment.)

Two: On the plus side, doctors look for renewed grooming as a sign of physical improvement: the hospital patient who shaves, combs his hair, and so on is definitely getting better.

Three: Disneyland, that most commercial of all institutions, long ago discovered the role of clothing in influencing a teenager's behavior: on grad night, nobody is allowed into the park unless he's wearing party clothes. Disneyland knows that graduates who are nicely dressed are far less rowdy than those who aren't. Party clothes became the easiest, most workable method of kid-control.

Four: Nothing could illustrate more clearly the role of dress as a symbol of altered self-esteem than the statement from the woman in Phoenix who managed to turn her life around (see chapter 11). When she declared proudly that her clothing had changed from ragged jeans with holes in them to slacks brand new off the rack, her clothing represented all the profound changes taking place in her life.

We suggest, therefore, that substance abuse programs include regular dress-up occasions as a means of restoring self-esteem.

If it seems far-fetched to suggest that outward appearance and behavior can seriously affect inner self-image, this is the time to reiterate an old addicts' admonition to other addicts: Fake it till you make it.

~

The last overlooked element of some treatment programs is diet—and particularly the pull of sugar as another addicting substance. Often, substance abusers who are trying to shake their addictions substitute huge doses of candy and other sweets for their drug of choice.

The Wills family saw that in Kirk. The last time he got out of prison, determined to stay clean, he asked for candy bars and Cokes. And not just a few. He said, "I'll need about twelve Cokes a day. And

three of those big almond chocolate bars." Even knowing all that
sugar and caffeine was a mistake, they didn't argue. Somehow it
seemed infinitely better than three six-packs of beer.

~

Many treatment counselors, however, do recognize that heavy infusions of caffeine and sugar are traps of a different kind. Better traps,
yes, but with their own consequences. Some counselors, in fact, believe sugar can be as addicting as any of the illegal drugs and that it
does no good to substitute one kind of addiction for another.

A Denver counselor talks at length about the addicting feature of
sugar, noting that some clients have admitted they never entirely
shook their cravings for drugs until they also gave up sweet foods
and caffeine. Which may explain why a number of inpatient treatment centers, such as Cenikor and Peer One, do not offer their
clients desserts after dinner or caffeinated drinks at any time.

~

Other dietary considerations come into play with longtime alcoholics. Dr. James R. Milam and Katherine Ketcham, authors of *Under
the Influence*, stress the need for close dietary attention to the alcoholic who is trying to resume normal living. "All alcoholics," they
write, "are undernourished to some extent because excessive alcohol intake interferes with the body's ability to absorb and use various
nutrients."[2] They conclude that without therapeutic doses of vita-
mins, minerals, proteins, amino acids, fats, and proteins, the alcoholic will never fully recover.

~

We conclude, then, that successful programs can become even more
successful when they take a holistic approach. The oft-undervalued
virtues of exercise, good grooming, and diet can be exploited to increase the client's feelings of well-being and enhance his self-esteem—
ultimately increasing his chances of success. Certainly each of these
issues is accorded major importance by people who are *not* recovering
from drugs.

~

As we summarize years of research, a few conclusions stand out: more is being done around the country to solve the addicted offender problem than the average person knows about. More is being done than at first *we* knew about. In terms of programs, the late 1990s were decidedly better than the early 1990s.

But it's not enough.

Society is only beginning to tackle the problem.

So far, mainstream society and orthodox justice systems largely ignore the answers we've uncovered. The solutions we've found are just the earliest manifestations of social evolution—the work of an underground of compassionate human beings forced to get creative within a system that largely doesn't care about the people it stuffs behind bars.

~

What America has done for its addicted felons so far qualifies as a good start. But that's all it is: a start. Small groups within the criminal justice system and elsewhere have made a courageous beginning, and it's better than nothing. But consider what is still needed.

Let's talk in terms of sheer numbers. Roughly 90 percent of prisoners in San Diego's R. J. Donovan Prison, for instance, are there for drug-related offenses, yet only 200 substance abusers are currently being treated (which may soon expand to 400). Since the total prison population at Donovan averages 4,700, treatment reaches only 10 percent of those who need it! What's happening to the other 3,600 inmates?

The women's prison in Goochland, Virginia, now treats 40 women. Their population is 460. What about the remaining 420 women whose core problem may be addiction?

If it's true, as most people concede, that 80 percent of incarcerated criminals have a drug and alcohol problem, and slightly more than 50 percent of all inmates are nonviolent, simple math indicates that approximately 80 percent of addicted, nonviolent inmates— people who could be helped—are getting no help whatever.

Multiply these percentages by the extraordinary number of people now locked up all over the country—a recently attained record of two million!—and it's easy to see that the solutions lag miserably behind the problem. The United States has so far taken only the tiniest steps toward a national solution.

San Diego Superior Court Judge Robert Coats echoes this theme in the Voices section of the *Los Angeles Times* on October 9, 1999. "These [drug programs] are gestures, and we need a commitment to expand the gestures to deal with the scale of the problem."[3]

∿

Even drug court, one of the most promising solutions of the day, has a hole so big that most addicted offenders drop right through. Except in a very few jurisdictions, drug court is not available to the addict who has either a long history of drug abuse or numerous felonies—even if those felonies are all drug-related and nonviolent.

Yet who, among all the drug offenders, is most apt to come back with new crimes?

The repeat offender.

Who needs help most?

The man who's proved he can't quit using.

Who is the biggest menace to society?

The person with a long history of prior offenses.

Yet who is the least likely to get help?

Well . . . you see where this is going.

∿

As Judge Jeffrey Tauber says in the *National Drug Court Institute Review*, "While Drug Courts clearly are having an extraordinary effect on the criminal justice system, it is a limited one . . . it is estimated that no more than three percent of [addicted offenders] participate in drug court programs."[4]

Tauber agrees that violent, predatory, or significant traffickers need prison. Yet, he asks, "What happens to offenders who are considered 'too serious' for drug court but nevertheless are going to live in our communities on probation? . . . What happens to those placed on probation who are unwilling, or seemingly unable, to stop using illegal drugs?"

Good questions.

What *does* happen to these people?

The answers can be found in court records everywhere: they offend again and again and get ever-longer prison sentences—and with each incarceration become poorer candidates for rehabilitation. And cost society more.

∼

So why *don't* we broaden our approach?

Part of the answer is money.

The rest is attitude.

Substance abuse programs, drug courts, judges, probation/parole officers, district attorneys, and counselors all require up-front financing. (So does building new prisons, of course, but prisons have traditionally had a kind of sexy, funds-appeal draw that less dramatic solutions lack.)

But hear what the Rand Corporation discovered in 1995: to get a *1 percent reduction* in cocaine use across the country, $34 million is needed for treatment. To achieve the same reduction through local law enforcement requires $246 million. Through interdiction programs at the borders, the price is $366 million. And through eradication programs in source countries the cost is $783 million.

None of this surprises Denver's Judge William Meyer, who provided these statistics. Cut the demand for drugs, he says, and you don't have to worry much about the supply.

It's obvious, then, where the available money should be spent.

∼

A final thought about drug treatment: *a half-hearted substance abuse program is worse than none at all.*

The most damaging scenario we can offer recovering substance abusers is a dispirited, poorly executed program. Not only is such an approach relatively useless for the offender, but it provides skeptics with ammunition to shoot down good programs. "You see," they say, "we tried treatment and it failed. Why spend the money? Why not just lock them up, like they deserve?"

I actually got into an intense argument with a skeptical lawyer friend. He said, "My kids didn't use drugs. I don't use drugs. Why should we waste resources on people who do this to themselves?"

It was hard not to get angry. I said, "The truth is, some people do use drugs. They become addicts. They're a fact of life. They don't just go away. So we have to deal with them. Which is better, treating them until they become normal, tax-paying citizens, or supporting them year after year while they rot in jail?"

And then I said, "If you don't care about the addicts, you must care about the money!" M. W.

Our final prescription for reform is simpler than we at first thought: we need to do a hundred times more of what we're already doing.

Statistics abound from the Supreme Court of Arizona and from the Drug Courts Program Office and the National Institute of Justice, both within the U.S. Department of Justice, that drug treatment programs *do work*. The rest is a matter of national will. Instituting treatment programs on a large scale means finding people who are passionate enough to demand them.

Everyone knows by now that the status quo is an abysmal failure. Every voter who's been asked to approve more prison bonds; every D.A., judge, or prosecutor who's seen the flood of addicted offenders pouring through the system; every mother or father who has an addicted child who isn't getting help knows that our current system is a flop.

So guess what, folks—*it's time we did something!*

$\sim$

Nothing will change, though, until more mothers and fathers form advocacy groups (such as the PATH group—Parents for Addiction Treatment and Healing—in San Diego), until parents appeal to their local judiciary and write their congressional representatives, and until all of us send spokespersons to Washington demanding that our addicted sons and daughters be given compassionate substance abuse treatment, either in or out of jail.

New approaches won't be tried on a large enough scale until law enforcement professionals point out the futility of rearresting the same people over and over.

Programs won't be funded until treatment professionals lobby their state legislatures for additional funds to expand their work.

And the scope will remain small until judges speak out eloquently, as only judges can do, insisting that expanded drug court programs include not just the low-risk offenders, but the whole range of nonviolent addicted inmates.

~

Even as we finished these pages, my son was in danger of falling victim to a punitive concept called Enhancement. Unknown to most of the California public, Enhancement means an offender's past crimes will always come back to haunt him. It's a geometric thing. With any new offense, additional prison years are tacked on for all prior sins.

Thus, because Kirk got frustrated and walked away from a mandated halfway house (technically an "escape"), he was facing not only another year of prison for that offense, but also one or two additional years for each year he'd already served.

A few moments of terrible judgment. Four to six more years of prison.

To accomplish what? Who would be served? Who would pay the hundred-thousand-dollar bill? After another six years of prison, what would be left of him?

Fortunately, this didn't happen. Thanks to attorney Rich Pfeiffer, who pleaded as eloquently for Kirk as he'd once done for himself, the judge sentenced Kirk instead to a year in Phoenix House. M. W.

~

It seem likely, with our plans currently coming to fruition, that I'll get the programs I promised the voters. Thanks to the input of dedicated substance abuse counselors and mental health experts, the Orange County jail system has the potential of making a positive impact on the lives of numerous substance abusers. How many, we'll know in a few years. And though my mom's name won't appear on any plaques, I believe she knows that in the long run her life did make a positive difference after all. M. C.

∼

It's possible that I, too, may get my greatest wish—that my son, finally forced into treatment, turns his life around.

I try to imagine the sequence of events. I see him leaving Phoenix House with a new, confident expression. I picture him finding a satisfying job and imagine him back on the tennis court playing the game he loves, deftly placing balls in spots no one can reach. I see the look of him as he wins a match—that understated aura of satisfaction that means he's added another notch to a growing string of successes.

In the evenings I envision him talking to other young men, inspiring them to pick themselves up and head off in better directions. "Believe me," he is saying, "if I can do it, you guys, anyone can." M. W.

Notes

Introduction: What This Book Is About—And What It Isn't

1. "U.S. Offenders at Record Numbers," *New York Times,* 23 August 1999.

Chapter 3: Why Jails and Prisons Make Addiction Worse

1. Elliott Currie, *Crime and Punishment in America* (New York: Henry Holt and Co., 1998), 23.

2. Ibid.

3. John Braithwaite, "A Future Where Punishment Is Marginalized: Realistic or Utopian?" *UCLA Law Review* 46, no. 6 (August 1999): 1727.

4. Currie, *Crime and Punishment in America,* 74.

5. Ibid.

6. National Criminal Justice Commission, Steven R. Donziger, ed., *The Real War on Crime* (New York: HarperCollins Publishers, Inc., 1996), 199.

7. Ibid., 201.

8. Ibid., 202.

9. Ibid., 204.

10. Mark Gladstone, "Paroled Lawmaker to Push Prison Reform," *Los Angeles Times,* 24 February 1998, A-3.

11. *The Real War on Crime,* 204.

Chapter 4: The Nature of Addiction

1. Stanton Peele, Ph.D., and Archie Brodsky, *The Truth about Addiction and Recovery* (New York: Simon and Schuster, 1992), cover, 10.

2. Ibid., 10.

3. Ibid., 94.

4. Robert Mathias, *NIDA Notes* (The National Institute on Drug Abuse) 13, no. 6: 5.

5. James R. Milam and Katherine Ketcham, *Under the Influence* (New York: Bantam Books, 1983).

6. Denise Grady, "Science" page, *The New York Times,* 27 October 1998, 9.

7. Ibid.

8. Alan I. Leshner, "Addiction Is a Brain Disease—And It Matters," *National Institute of Justice Journal,* October 1998: cover.

9. Ibid., 2.

10. Ibid., 6.

Chapter 6: Helping the Addict Who Wants Help

1. Alcoholics Anonymous World Services, *Alcoholics Anonymous* (New York: AA World Services, 1976), 13.

2. William L. White, *Slaying the Dragon* (Bloomington, Ill.: Chestnut Health Systems, 1998).

3. Ibid., 203.

4. Ibid., 203.

5. Ibid., 209.

6. Ibid., 211.

Chapter 8: Why Prisons May Fight Change

1. *Fifty Years: Public Safety, Public Service* (California Department of Corrections, 1994), 8.

2. Ibid., 12.

3. Ibid., 20.

4. Alan I. Leshner, "Addiction Is a Brain Disease—And It Matters," *National Institute of Justice Journal,* October 1998: 5.

5. Eric Schlosser, "The Prison-Industrial Complex," *Atlantic Monthly,* December 1998, 58.

Chapter 10: Drug Court: The New Kid on the Block

1. Steven Belenko, *National Drug Court Institute Review* 1, no. 1 (Summer 1998), 21.

2. Jeffrey Tauber, *National Drug Court Institute Review* 1, no. 1 (Summer 1998), 89–90.

3. Judith S. Kaye, "Making the Case for Hands-On Courts," *Newsweek,* 11 October 1999, 13.

Chapter 11: Arizona: The Great Social Experiment

1. Arizona Supreme Court, Administrative Office of the Courts, Adult Services Division, *Drug Treatment and Education Fund, Legislative Report, Fiscal Year 1997–1998:* 11.

Chapter 12: Turning a Sheriff's Vision into Reality

1. Jesse Katz, "A Nation of Too Many Prisoners?", *Los Angeles Times,* 15 February 2000: A1.

2. Allan J. Beck, Ph.D., and Christopher J. Mumola, *Bureau of Justice Statistics: Prisoners in 1998,* August 1998 (U.S. Dept. of Justice, Office of Justice Programs), 1–5.

3. Ibid., 11.

4. Douglas Lipton, Senior Research Fellow, National Development and Research Institute, in testimony to the Little Hoover Commission, September 25, 1997.

5. Legislative Analyst's Office, "Addressing the State's Long-Term Inmate Population Growth" (May 20, 1997).

6. Little Hoover Commission: "Beyond Bars: Correctional Reforms to Lower Prison Costs and Reduce Crime" (January 1998): 67.

7. Barry Glassner, *The Culture of Fear: Why Americans Are Afraid of the Wrong Things* (New York: Basic Books, 1999), 131.

8. Rod Mullen, Mark Schuettinger, Naya Arbiter, and David Conn, "Reducing Recidivism: Amity Foundation of California and the California Department of Corrections Demonstrate How to Do It," *Frontiers of Justice,* vol. 2 (n.p.: Biddle Publishing Company, 1997).

Chapter 13: Coming Out—To What?
Bridging the Gap from Jail to Job

1. Elliott Currie, *Crime and Punishment in America* (New York: Henry Holt and Co., 1998), 167.

2. James R. Milam and Katherine Ketcham, *Under the Influence* (New York: Bantam Books, 1983), 92.

3. Gretchen Bergman, "Voices," *Los Angeles Times,* 9 October 1999: B17.

4. Jeffrey Tauber, *National Drug Court Institute Review* 1, no. 1 (Summer 1998): 87.

Index

About the Authors

MARALYS WILLS is the author of nine books, including a techno-thriller, *Scatterpath*, and her family story about hang-gliding champions, *Higher Than Eagles*. She earned her B.A. at Stanford and UCLA. With her children now grown, she devotes her time to public speaking, writing books, and teaching novel writing at nearby colleges. She lives with her husband, Rob, in Santa Ana, California. Wills welcomes comments and inquiries sent in care of Hazelden, P.O. Box 176, Center City, Minnesota, 55012-0176.

MIKE CARONA was elected Sheriff of Orange County, California, in June 1998. During his twenty-five years in law enforcement, he worked twenty-three years in the Orange County Marshal's department, eleven of which he served as Marshal. He earned both a Bachelor of Arts and a Master of Arts degree from the University of Redlands, and holds a Master of Science degree in Management from Cal Poly, Pomona. He is a Command College graduate and a graduate of both the FBI's Leeds programs and the National Executive Institute. Carona is actively involved in numerous philanthropic organizations throughout Orange County, where he lives with his wife, Debbie, and son, Matthew.